Tugging on the Sleeve of Fame

By Gary Craig

Tugging on the Sleeve of Fame
Gary Craig
© 2018 Gary Craig. ALL RIGHTS RESERVED.
No part of this book may be reproduced in any form or by any means, electronic, mechanical, digital, photocopying, or recording, except for inclusion of a review, without permission in writing from the publisher or Author.

Published in the USA by:
BearManor Media
P O Box 71426
Albany, Georgia 31708
www.bearmanormedia.com

ISBN: 978-1-62933-350-2
BearManor Media, Albany, Georgia
Printed in the United States of America
Book design by Robbie Adkins, www.adkinsconsult.com

Table of Contents

Dedication iv
Acknowledgements v
Foreword vi
Introduction vii
Chapter 1 "Gary, It's Getting Late. Come in for Dinner" 1
Chapter 2 "You Listen to Me. You Get a Trade. 15
   You'll Be Alright"
Chapter 3 "Are You Kidding? I Could Ruin You Just 19
   By the Way I Cut the Meat"
Chapter 4 The Acting Light Went On In My Head 23
Chapter 5 Suburban Coming of Age 27
Chapter 6 Stick Man 29
Chapter 7 First Announcing Job 38
Chapter 8 Free Shit 40
Chapter 9 Completely Lost 43
Chapter 10 Florida and the World of Radio 46
Chapter 11 "Miami, hello!" 50
Chapter 12 Tucson? With the Horse Shit and Hitching Posts? . . 61
Chapter 13 The Crazyman tv Show 86
Chapter 14 Finally, Hartford 102
Chapter 15 Hair Gone Tomorrow, Here Today 134
Chapter 16 More Stars Than There are in Heaven 142
Chapter 17 The Diana Drug 157
Chapter 18 I Own You 166
Chapter 19 On the Beach 176
Chapter 20 Second Time is a Charm 192
Chapter 21 Berle, Caesar, and Bill 199
Chapter 22 The Funniest Jokes I Ever Heard 209
Chapter 23 That Nagging Feeling 221
Chapter 24 I'm Sick of Looking at It 227
Chapter 25 What the F**k's Wrong With You, Kid? 235
Chapter 26 WOR 243
Chapter 27 M & L Revisited 252
Epilogue, Or Time to Go? 257

Dedication

For Rachel, Aaron, Hannah, and my wife, Diana,
who always believed in me.

Acknowledgments

When people get around to writing their story, so many people *in* that story are no longer alive. I, on the other hand, am very lucky. Three friends I spent most of my life with me are still here. In writing this book, I was able to go back to Jeff Cahn, Tim Ingstad, and Steven C. Brown, to double check my memory and details of our times together. I thank them for their support, their direction, and the incredible journey.

Foreword

Gary asked me to write a Foreword. He gave me strict instructions that it had to be one page, double-spaced. Who the hell can write a Foreword double-spaced in one page? I can assure you it is most certainly not a Lemmon. We Lemmons do a half-hour on "hello", but it's for Gary, so I'll try.

Mensch (Yiddish: מענטש mentsh, cognate with the German word Mensch, meaning a "human being") means "a person of integrity and honor." The opposite of a "mensch" is an "unmensch," meaning an utterly unlikeable or unfriendly person.

Thank God Gary Craig falls into the first category, because he's grown to become one of my best friends. This despite the fact that he totally busted me the first day I moved to Glastonbury Connecticut (our mutual home town, and you have to read the book to find out how) and, after the fact, invited me on his show, where the first thing he said to me was that he "saw me straighten a wedgie as I got out of my car" (the guy actually sits there watching the parking lot?).

The one thing I've always noticed that he has in common with my father, actor Jack Lemmon, is his ability to be both funny and serious at the same time. That's the genius of all great comics and clowns, renowned actors, and even most of my best friends. I value his ability to find the silly in the somber, but I've also learned to check the sugar bowl to make sure he hasn't filled it with salt. You'll feel the same way after reading this, and you'll love him all the more for it.

Husband, father, friend, neighbor. Actor, artist, writer, raconteur. Shtarker: You try getting up at 3:30 a.m. every day to go be funny in Hartford. And most of all Mensch. This book will make you laugh out loud, at the same time as you take a very close look at a very big heart.

-Chris Lemmon, January 11, 2018

Introduction

I got naked. Completely naked. I climbed up on the console and pressed my dick and balls against the glass. I believe my purpose on the planet is to make people laugh, but in this case, it was just one person—my newsman. Alan Young. There's something inherently funny about someone cracking up on the air, and the audience is clueless as to what's happening. In my mind, my goal was to derail this newscast any way I could. I was playing a fart sound effect that only he could hear in his headphones. I also drew a giant penis on a long piece of teletype paper and slowly moved it across the glass. Running in his studio and setting his news copy on fire also made him lose concentration, as his newscast unravelled. Those stunts didn't faze him, so I raised the bar, took a dump on a paper plate, and slid it in front of him.

All the audience heard was Alan commenting, "I think I'm going to throw up," and then nothing ... just dead air.

Although my attempts produced distraction and a stumble, Alan hung in there and always finished his newscast, but now I was naked and pressed against the window that separated his studio from mine. He looked up for a split second and saw me, but without missing a beat, he stood, pulled the mic up, dropped his pants, and continued. At that moment, a staff member brought a group of Girl Scouts to stand outside the studio and peer in. They wanted to meet The Crazyman. That was 1974.

Writing the story of my life is a daunting task. I'm forced to be introduced to my former self, and travel back to times and places I don't necessarily want to visit again. Such is the nature of remembering so that people I love and who love me will know about the journey.

My life is my message.

98 percent of what you hear or see is bullshit, and I'm not afraid to say so. People are put off by me, because I've never played the political correctness game. I usually tell people what I think—with unfiltered words—and that's gotten me in a jam more than once.

Others suggested numerous times that I run for office. I would never be elected, because I would have to tell the voting public what was bullshit and what wasn't. Of course, Donald Trump got to the White House doing just that, but I don't play well with others, and I would have to make decisions solely based on the benefit to the people that voted me in, not how it would impact another politician's agenda. I've been telling my kids all their lives, "You can't control anybody else. You're only in charge of yourself."

I can tell you that I'm in charge of the pages you read here, warts and all.

Chapter 1

"Gary, It's Getting Late. Come in for Dinner"

Their voices floated up from the sidewalk and through my window at 1212 Newkirk Avenue in Brooklyn. Peering out, I could barely make out the shadowy figures under a lamp post. They were trying to harmonize "Why Do Fools Fall in Love?" a song that was originally a hit for Frankie Lymon & the Teenagers in January 1956. They sounded pretty good for neighborhood guys.

I was six years old. What an incredible time to be a kid.

My mother's maiden name was Bernice Anzelowitz, but she called herself "Bunny." She agreed to marry my father, Mel Gopen, in 1949.

My grandfather on my mother's side, Louis Anzelowitz, was a successful restaurateur and could afford to give my mother a grand wedding. There were about 350 guests, a live orchestra, and a man that walked around from table to table with a portable record cutting machine to interview guests and family members, sort of like an on the spot Larry King. My grandfather also hired a still photographer and a cinematographer to film the entire reception. The orchestra played, as people were served from carving stations amongst massive ice sculptures. The setting looked like a giant society dinner.

Clarinetist Artie Shaw, a friend of my grandfather's, played. The wedding cost my grandfather about $50,000, a big outlay in 1949 (the same wedding would run hundreds of thousands of dollars today).

A year later, I was born Arthur G. Gopen.

Two years later, my parents were divorced.

My grandfather was pissed off and tried to get my dad to reconsider. He even threatened to come after him.

My dad told him, "I was in World War Two and had soldiers shooting at me! You think I'm afraid of you?"

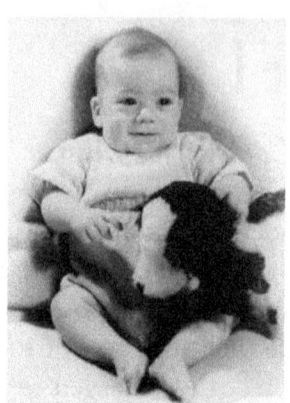

Gary as a baby.

Gary at 3 years old.

1212 Newkirk Ave, Brooklyn

Gary at 1212 Newkirk Ave. 1954 (4 years old.)

Mom and Dad, Mel and Bunny.

Mel Gopen, Dad, in Navy band.

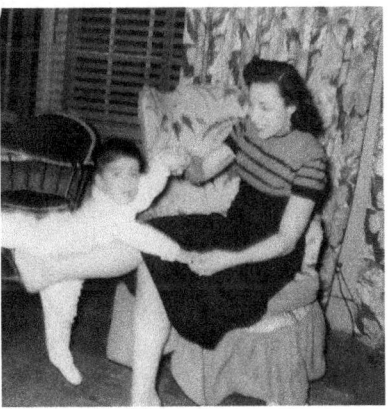

Mom, and me at age 4.

Stepdad, Al Covelman, from Bar Mitzvah.

My sister, Lauren.

Mom from Bar Mitzvah.

Public School 217, Brooklyn, New York

Gary at age 6 in the first grade.

Mel's second wife, Margo, with Rachel.

I don't remember actually ever living with my dad. That's understandable, because I was barely two when Mel and Bunny divorced.

A few years after the divorce, my mother married Albert Covelman, who became my stepdad, and both he and mother raised me, along with Mel. I look back at my life in Brooklyn with fondness, but to most people, the apartment building where we lived looked like a slum. Not to me. I loved the city sounds: the brakes from a distant bus, a fire truck screaming by, and honking of horns all lulled me to sleep. What's really strange is that I loved the smell of bus exhaust. My world consisted of about three blocks, Newkirk Avenue, Westminster road, and Coney Island Avenue.

I had everything I needed in Brooklyn. PS 217 was across the street. The grocery and the luncheonette was on the other side. I used to go into the grocer, shove my hand way down to the wooden pickle barrel bottom, and pull up the fattest, most sour pickle I could find. For some reason, we didn't give a crap about germs back then. There was no Purell® and no ebola. That pickle, along with fresh rye bread, was a meal. I sat on the apartment building's front stair stoop and ate.

Brooklyn was a melting pot of kids, Jews, Italians, Chinese, and Blacks. We were all friends and got along. (Years after I left Brooklyn,

I went back to see the old neighborhood. I was shocked to see how small everything appeared and how dingy and dirty the building and the surrounding area was. When you're a kid, you remember everything being bigger and better than it was.)

Walking to school every day meant that once in a while I saw a teacher out on the street. Seeing my teacher was very weird to me. I never expected to see them outside the school. My teacher and I made eye contact, but I never knew what to say, the same as if I bumped into my proctologist at dinner today and wouldn't shake hands. I was shocked to realize that teachers actually had a life out the classroom.

The 1950s neighborhood had its share of "greasers," hoods named as such because they used a thick hair gel glob to slick back their hair so it looked like a duck's ass. The tough greasers with their hair and their combs were later depicted perfectly by Henry Winkler as Fonzie on *Happy Days* (1974-1984).

Melvin Becker was a greaser the younger kids looked up to because he was tough, he left us alone, and he defended his turf, which was our turf. I'll never forget Melvin using the word "fuckin" in a phrase more than I ever heard anyone use it. I was just a jerky little kid. I walked up to him one day and asked, "Hi Melvin, what are you doing?"

He looked at me and said, "Hey kid, I just had a fuckin ice cream soda. Tree fuckin scoops. Fuckin chocolate, fuckin vanilla, fuckin strawberry. Biggest fuckin soda ya ever fuckin saw. Then I put a fuckin quarter on the fuckin counter and walked out of the fuckin place. Hey, the guy who owns it's a real fuck."

I laughed for three days.

My time was filled with school in the morning, but before school I heard the tv blaring Captain Kangaroo. There were only three tv channels back in then—all in black and white—and in the afternoon, I heard the collective chorus of tvs blaring Abbott and Costello, The Three Stooges, Mighty Mouse, Looney Tunes, Popeye, The Mickey Mouse Club, Officer Joe Bolton, *The Adventures of Superman*, Sharri Lewis, and Paul Winchell. Baby Boomers all shared this collective experience. Doesn't matter who you talk to, they all rattle off these shows and others like it's the gospel.

A gang of kids from our apartment and neighboring buildings hung out with us. When my mom became sick of me hanging around the apartment, she kicked me out onto the street, where I met up with the other kids whose mom's did the same.

My mother had a great sense of humor, and she didn't put up with any shit. One day, I was in the apartment whining, "I'm bored."

"You're bored? Go bang your head against the wall!"

My cue to get out.

We didn't have Nintendos, X boxes, Wii's, or Candy Crush Saga on cell phones, but we used our imaginations and made our own fun. There was Hide and Go Seek, Ring-aleevio 1-2-3, and a strange game called Skully. It was like shuffleboard with bottle caps. We took the caps, filled them with wax to give them weight, and then drew chalk boxes on the cement. The object was to flick the caps along the ground and get them into the high point boxes with the goal of knocking the other guy's bottle caps out. We spent hours playing this game, and we had great tournaments. Our bottle cap collections were sacred. One kid claimed that his Coke cap was weighted the best. Another claimed that his 7up cap was a champion.

I had nothing except a damned slinky, a box of crayons, Playdoh, Colorforms, Army men, and Operation!

When my mother wanted to get ahold of me, she opened a window and yelled, "Gary! It's getting late! Come in for dinner!" Every other kid's mother then screamed out the window at their kids. I was a little shit, always getting into trouble, like the time I saw one kids in his inflatable swimming pool. I decided to run my bicycle tire over it repeatedly until all the air was gone and water spilled into the street. The kid screamed bloody murder, but I just kept doing it with a wry smile on my face. Early on, you could see what my future was going to be—a wiseass always trying to go over the line.

Fascinated with cause and effect, I was always pushing the envelope. About five blocks away from the apartment was "The Plaza" with stores and subway trains. Watching the trains below coming into the station, I wondered, *What would happen if I put a penny on the tracks and the train runs over it?* I climbed all the way down to the tracks, which was no easy feat, since I wasn't supposed to be down there in the first place and there was no easy way to get down to the tracks. I placed a penny on the rail and waited. This was exciting. *Would the train derail?* I wondered. As the train came roaring in, I watched in amazement as the wheel flattened the penny, then hit by another wheel, flew off the track. I watched the train pull into the station, and then I ran over to the tracks to retrieve the penny that now looked like a mini pancake. The problem was, as I was watching the penny getting pulverized, a cop was watching me. He nabbed me, brought me upstairs, and began to read me the riot act.

"You know you're not supposed to be down there!" he yelled. "You're getting a J.D. card!"

As a kid, a Juvenile Delinquent card was the last thing you wanted. Visions of my parents being hauled in front of a judge or, worse yet, me being shipped off to a reformatory danced in my head. *Maybe he's going to take me home,* I thought, *and I'll have to explain myself as one of my parents screamed their head off.* The fact is, none of that happened, but the cop scared the shit out of me, and I ran home and never did that again, but . . . .

. . . I did other things. We stood on either side of a street and waited for cars to drive by. Then, we made believe we were picking up an imaginary rope and stretching it across the road. When drivers saw us doing this, they thought the rope was real and they stopped. We thought this was absolutely hilarious and laughed our asses off, as the drivers cursed us and drove away.

Sometimes, my pranks went too far. One day, in the apartment building's lobby, I decided to do the "Great Elevator Experiment." There was an actual door that opened to our elevator. Inside, there were brass rails that really served no purpose other than decoration. *What would happen,* I thought, *if I tied one end of a rope to the inside rail, tied the other end around the doorknob on the outside of the elevator, and sent it up to the 3rd floor?*

I got a rope from the apartment and carefully tied one end around the outside door knob and the other end to the inside brass rail. I hit the 3 button and closed the door. As the car went up, I watched the rope get tighter and tighter until the slack went completely out. When there was nowhere else the rope could go, it ripped the doorknob right off with a loud pop. Unfortunately for me, at this exact moment the superintendent walked into the lobby and witnessed the whole debacle.

God, was he pissed off, as he hauled me up to the apartment to inform my mom, "Look what your little asshole did now!"

I laugh about it now, but what was I thinking? Just a stupid kid with a big imagination.

One afternoon, a friend showed me a trick on his phone. "Look at this," he said. "If you dial this number and hang up, it makes the phone ring"

This was brilliant! It was a special number that the phone company guys used to test a new installation, but the special number wasn't for kids like us to use. For me, this was gold!

Saturday and time to put the code to the test. My stepdad, Al, was in the bathroom shaving, and I was in my room. The phone was all the way down the hallway. I waited until his face was all lathered up and quietly crept down to the hallway's end, picked up the receiver, dialed in the code, hung up, and ran like hell back to my room. The phone started ringing. Al walked down there, and I heard him pick up the receiver. "Hello? Hello?" He hung up and walked back to the bathroom.

I ran down and repeated the process. The ringing started again.

His face loaded with shave cream, he now *ran* down to the phone. "Hello? HELLO? Stop calling!" He stomped back to the bathroom.

I went back to the phone. It rang for the third time.

Now, he raced down there like a madman, shaving cream flinging off his face, and yelled, "HELLO? This isn't funny! Knock this shit off!" He heard me laughing and demanded, "Gary are you doing this?" He smiled and went back to shaving. He was such a gentle man, who rarely got mad at me. He had great patience.

My mom learned early on that it wasn't a good idea to leave me to my own devices. She had stepped out of the apartment to go to the grocery. I decided to turn the kitchen into a lab. I grabbed the big pasta pot and filled it halfway with water, and then I proceeded to put everything I could find into the pot: ketchup, liquid soap, milk, cheese, napkins, spoons, wooden chopsticks, and probably a dozen other ingredients. I turned the gas stove on high and just waited. By the time my mom came back, the entire kitchen was a disaster.

She walked in and screamed, "GARY! What did you do?"

All I could say to her was, "I was making glue."

My worst offense had to be the night she took me to the New York Philharmonic to attend a Leonard Bernstein "Young People's Concert," great classical or pop music programs geared towards kids. You couldn't blame her for trying to infuse some culture into me. The lobby was massive, ornate, and breathtaking. The adults engaged in their individual conversations while trying to keep their kids in check. All of a sudden, my mom ran into someone she knew and they started talking, which left me free to explore a giant winding staircase that went up what seemed to be three floors. I climbed to the top and peered down to a buzz of activity. The parents were engrossed in loud animated conversations and their kids fidgeted. Then, I noticed giant strands of glass beads dangling from the ceiling to the lobby floor. *What would happen,* I thought, *if I was able to hoist some of these beads up to where I was standing?* I grabbed as many strands as my arms could hold, and started pulling them up, inch by inch, higher and higher, until they were all bunched up at the top. Then, with one move, I let them go. They came down in a giant crash and swayed back and forth. The noise was so loud that everyone in the lobby stopped talking and looked up. Then, everyone heard one voice in the crowd screaming—my mother. "GARY!" She knew.

I'm not particularly proud of these incidents, but it did set the stage for me releasing six volumes of Phoney Phone Crank calls later in life. Cause and effect. I was a gregarious only child, and I was used to getting my way. I threw temper tantrums unless I got what I wanted.

One time, there was something I wanted to do, but the schedule or timing was off, so I dropped to the floor and in my best whiney voice, said, "But I want to go to the circus!"

My mom had enough. She also dropped to the floor and screamed, "But you *can't* go to the circus now!"

I was so shocked seeing her do that, I never did it again.

Life in Brooklyn was glorious. This is where I was totally happy inside and out. All I had to be was a kid. In the winter, I recall walking home in the dark, the snow crunching under my feet, and

Christmas lights everywhere with those big colored bulbs, not the little sissy strands we use today. A boy could walk home when it was dark and feel totally safe; there was no perceived danger and no fear. There were no terrorists. School in the winter was *rarely* cancelled because of snow. There would have to be five feet on the ground for them to close it. I remember many days when two feet of snow was the norm. School cancellations? No chance. "Get your little asses into class!"

We waited in anticipation for summer. Days were long, and we were free for months. There was the luncheonette across the street where my stepdad, Al, sent me to get a quart of hand-packed ice cream in a Chinese food box. I watched the man scoop it out of a large barrel and pack the container so that it was overflowing. There were Hostess cupcakes, Ringdings, Devildogs, Red Hots, Good & Plenty, Good & Fruity, licorice rope, CHERRY Phosphates, and Ebinger's blackout cake.

Summers were brutal without air conditioning. I don't remember my friends having it in their homes. All we had to cool our entire apartment was a box fan in a kitchen window. I had to keep windows open in my bedroom, hoping the box fan running on high would suck some air through the room and create a breeze. It didn't. I sweated my balls off, even before I realized what they were for. It was not unusual during the hot summer months to see people dragging small mattresses out on the fire escape to escape the heat inside.

When days were unbearably hot, the fire department came by and opened the fire hydrants so all the little neighborhood kids could run through them and cool off. Just bathing suits and bare feet running in the street.

In the middle of one summer, the building's water line broke and there was no water in the apartments. Huge problem. They opened the fire hydrant and people were bringing buckets down to the street to fill them. My mom had a better idea. She tied a rope to the bucket and lowered it out the 2nd floor window. I filled it, and she then hoisted it back up. I can't tell how many times I did this, but mom and I were hysterical the whole time. It was so stupid, but it did the job.

There were also summer's sights and sounds: old people sitting on folding chairs outside the apartment debating and solving the world' problems; baseball games blaring from transistor and car radios. We were too busy to pay attention. There was much to do. A few blocks away was the Leader Lanes bowling alley, and the Leader Theatre, where we could sit in the movie house and watch cartoons, Flash Gordon episodes, and other films all day on Saturday for 25¢. A few years later, admission jumped to 50¢.

We along hung out at the luncheonette across the street, sitting at the counter having a hamburger, fries, and a chocolate egg cream, which had no eggs or cream in it and was made with milk, chocolate syrup, and seltzer.

One of our pastimes was attaching baseball cards with clothespins to the rear spokes of our bikes. As we started peddling, the card made the bike sound like a motorcycle, but only lasted a few feet before the cards fell off. Then we found out that attaching a balloon to the rear wheel *really* recreated the sound, until it popped 50 feet down the street.

In the absence of cash, we were forced to be creative by building our own scooters. Back then, razor scooters did not exist. We found wooden crates from grocery stores that threw them out by the hundreds. Turning the crates upright, we nailed a long 2x4 to the bottom. Then, taking one side of our outgrown metal roller skates, we separated the front wheels from the back wheels and nailed each set to the bottom of the 2x4 on both ends of the wood. Two pieces of a sawed-off broom handle were nailed on each crate side for handles, and there you have it. The kids painted their crates, and then the competitive races began to see who had the fastest scooter. If nothing else, we were resourceful.

When I was 10, my sister, Lauren, arrived, an adorable, happy baby. Before she was 1, she was standing up in her crib. My mom had to run downstairs for a few minutes, and Lauren and I were in my room. I wasn't paying much attention to her, but before I knew it, she had reached into her full diaper and scooped out some organic art materials and proceeded to make a fabulous shit mural on the wall. When I looked up and discovered it, I didn't know what to do. I just sat there and started crying. My mom finally came back and discovered the crisis. I'm sure she had a good laugh.

As Lauren got a little older, we suspected that something about her wasn't exactly right. She was way behind learning some of the things a child her age should have mastered already. I remember Al and my mom going to see a doctor, and when they returned home, my mom was crying. She said, "Don't ever yell at Lauren. She has a learning disability."

It was more than that. Apparently, Lauren was a breach baby, born legs first. The story we were told was that in the time they took to turn her around, she lost oxygen, which contributed to her being mentally handicapped. Doctors made all kinds of predictions. She wouldn't learn how to talk, wouldn't ever be able to function on her own, wouldn't be able to hold down a job, and wouldn't ever function as an adult. I'm happy to say, for the most part, all of those predictions turned out to be wrong. Lauren lives in a group home on Long Island, New York. She's high functioning. She reads just fine, operates computers and cell phones, and has a job. So doctors—*wrong again*!

Lauren has endured a great deal—a severe operation to put rods in her back to correct curvature of the spine, and the loss of her father—but she's still standing.

Eventually, Lauren outgrew her crib and we moved her to a bed. My mom had taken the crib apart and the pieces were piled up in the corner of the room. I picked a long steel rod and was playing "Airplane" with the damn thing, flying it around in the air and making the engine sound . . . I jammed the rod into my right eye, scraping my cornea! My mom was out of the apartment at the time. She has always denied this, but in my memory, the next thing I knew, a neighbor ran with me in her arms to the doctor's office down the street. He treated me, and I had to wear an eye patch for some time. To this day, the vision in my right eye is still compromised.

I had mentioned all I had was a box of crayons. How I came to acquire those crayons served as a life lesson. I was coloring in my room, when my mother asked, "Where did you get the crayons?"

I stammered, but finally admitted, "I swiped them from the toy store."

She immediately collared me. "You're going to return those crayons and you're going to tell the man at the store what you did and apologize."

She took me right back to the store. It was scary and traumatic. *What would the man do? Yell at me? Call a policeman?* The man in the store gave me "the look"—that disappointed look of distain—while thanking me for my honesty. We returned the crayons and returned home. I spent the next few days moping around in my room embarrassed at what I had done.

My mom waked into the room one day and handed me a brown paper bag . . . with a brand new box of Crayolas, a big box of 64 crayons with more colors than I had ever seen. I never stole anything again.

Chapter 2

"You Listen to Me. You Get a Trade. You'll Be Alright"

My dad, Mel, whose nickname was "Manny," picked me up every Sunday for our time to be together. I cherished that day, because it was the one day I had him all to myself. We talked about how I was doing, saw a movie, and ended the visit with dinner out, usually either Chinese food or a great Italian restaurant named Vesuvius.

Sometimes, we went to his house in Mill Basin, Brooklyn. My dad had also remarried to a lovely lady named Margo, who treated me as one of her own. She had a daughter, Paulette, from a previous marriage, and a son, my half-brother, Jess. Whenever Jess and I were together, we laughed our heads off usually to the annoyance of our dad, who finally snapped and said, "Get outa here, the two of yas!"

My dad was a tough guy and very opinionated. When he told you something, you just accepted what he told you as gospel. Of course, when I got older, the things he told me over the years became life lessons of value. When he saw I was drifting along with no roadmap for my life, he said, "You listen to me. You get a trade. You'll be alright."

Mel owned a jewelry store on Avenue J and Coney Island Avenue called Melbun Jewelers, named after the first letters of "Mel" and my mom's name, "Bunny." After they divorced, he didn't bother changing the name, because, at least in that neighborhood, he had built it into a brand. Sometimes after school I took the Avenue J bus up to the store and hang out with him. I saw how he dealt with customers, always providing great service and joking around with everyone that came into the store. He had a tremendous sense of humor, and still does. He was the first jeweler to offer "ring sizing while you wait." He sized rings, and he repaired gold chains with a blow torch at his bench. When I turned 11, he got it into his head that maybe someday I would take over the business. He said,

"Look, you'll come in after school, and I'll teach how to do a few things. This way, when you get older, you'll have a trade."

Again, with the trade. He was always drumming it into my head that I needed a "trade." *What am I going to do with a trade? Did I want a trade? None of my friends had a trade.* The prospects of becoming a plumber, a carpenter, or a jeweler didn't really resonate with me. I wasn't totally sure that's what I wanted to do in life, but then again, I didn't have a backup plan. Maybe he saw I had no real plans on what to do with myself. Nevertheless, Mel pushed on, and encouraged me to begin to learn the nuts and bolts of becoming a jeweler. *Yeah, that's it, I'll get a trade.*

The first skill he thought might be helpful was being able to solder a gold chain that had broken. The proper way to fix a chain is laying one link on top of each other on both ends, and placing a small piece of gold on top of the links. Taking the blow torch, you go in very carefully until the solder melts, fusing the links together, thus restoring the circle. You have to know exactly when to pull the torch away so as not to melt the gold links themselves. My dad had me practice this over and over again, until he felt I mastered it. One day, as I was sitting at his bench practicing, and a customer walked in with a broken ankle bracelet. Mel walked it over to me, instructed me to fix it, and then walked back out to the counter. As I went in with the blowtorch, I heard a noise outside that distracted me for a second. I turned my head to see what it was. When I looked back, the bracelet had completely melted into a tiny gold ball. My dad threw me out of the store, and that was the end of my career as a jeweler.

Joseph Moskowitz.

Joseph Moskowitz.

Louis and Rose Anzelowitz.

Rose Anzelowitz, Grandma Rose.

Louis and Rose Anzelowitz anniversary.

Moskowitz and Lupowitz waiter outside.

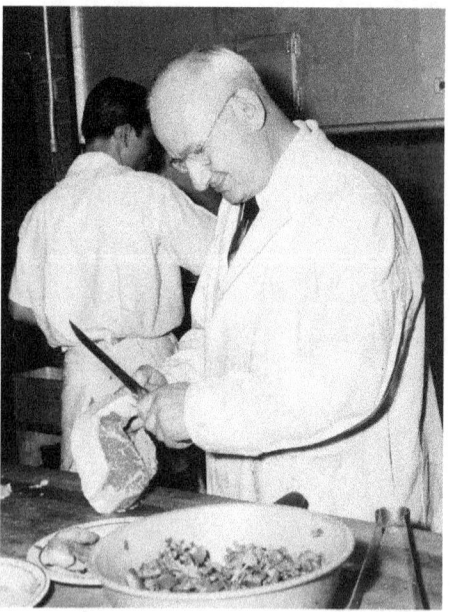

Louis Anzelowitz trimming steak in M & L Kitchen.

Chapter 3

"Are You Kidding? I Could Ruin You Just By the Way I Cut the Meat"

Born in Romania in 1879, Joseph Moskowitz, a child prodigy, mastered playing the cimbalom at age 11. By the time he arrived in America in 1908, he was performing in various eateries in the lower east side of New York in a district known as "Little Hungry." An enterprising entrepreneur, Joseph opened the first of several restaurants in 1913. He later teamed up with Sam Lupowitz and opened what was to become one of the most famous restaurants in the lower east side called "Moskowitz and Lupowitz," which instantly became a New York destination and celebrity hangout.

My grandfather, Louis Anzelowtiz, arrived in this country from Poland when he was in his teens. He met and married Rose Silverman, whose family originated from Romania. Rose's family were furniture makers. Louis had various jobs, but the one that would change his life was being a bus boy and butcher at Moskowitz and Lupowitz, also known as M & L. He quickly rose from bus boy to a waiter to a butcher in the kitchen.

One hot day, he took a break out in front and was wiping the sweat from his brow with a napkin. Joseph Moskowitz's wife caught him and dressed him down for using the restaurant's linen to wipe his sweat.

Louis said, "Are you kidding? I could ruin the place by cutting a piece of meat wrong, and you're giving me a hard time about a napkin?"

A huge fight ensued on the street. My grandfather quit on the spot, but not before vowing to come back one day and own the place. The story that was verified by several people in my family was that Joseph Moskowitz discovered that his wife was having an affair with Sam Lupowitz, and an illegitimate child was the result of that union. When he found out, he left his wife and the restaurant, choosing to relocate

Hy Anzel in Oklahoma.

to Washington, DC, where he lived until his death in 1954. Louis Anzelowitz, true to his word, bought out Moskowitz's share in the restaurant by assuming his debt in the business. At the time, I believe the amount was $500, but keep in mind, this was in the 1930s and $500 was quite a sum when an entire meal only cost 50¢. Eventually, Sam passed on, and my grandfather became the sole owner. Everyone in the family worked there, which included my mom, and my three uncles Max, Bob, and Hy. Hy shortened his name to Hy Anzell and became a working character actor, who worked on stage, in film, and on television.

The trip from Brooklyn into the city was an exciting treat. As a kid, I couldn't wait to emerge into the whirlwind of activity: the traffic, the flashing neon lights, and the awning at 2nd Avenue and 2nd Street, the location of my grandfather's restaurant. The second I walked into M & L, my senses were bombarded with cigarettes, laughter, loud happy conversations, and strolling violinists. Uniform waiters raced in and out of the kitchen with platters of skirt steaks, roasted chicken, and their famous chopped liver. As soon as a customer sat down, a plate of fresh bread, sour pickles, and tomatoes appeared. People arrived dressed to the nines, and they dined on white table cloths. Waiters added to the room sounds by barking orders to the bar as they walked by. "Bock? No, I said Dark beer."

My grandfather was the ultimate restaurateur, bowing at the waist to everyone that entered and anyone that was anybody walking through the door from the 1930s through the 1960s, and I have the photographs to prove it. Famous sports figures and entertainment giants from film, television, and the theatre frequently dined at M & L. The restaurant was often featured in gossip columns that wrote about who was recently seen there with whom, and what they were eating. James Cagney even had a scene in one of his movies where he's in a cab and says, "Let's go downtown to Moskowitz's for a steak." I'm certain, even though he didn't use the entire name, that he meant my grandfather's restaurant.

My grandfather always had photographer Sam Reiss on call to come over to snap photos of the stars. His studio was just a few blocks away. When he didn't make it, my uncle Bob, an amateur photographer, captured the image.

One night, Charlie Chaplin came in for dinner. Sam Reiss wasn't available, so it was up to my uncle Bob to capture Charlie on film. Bob has always contended that because Charlie knew so much about photography, that possibly as his own private joke, he lifted his glass in front of his face in such a way that it obscured the shot. I now own the picture. When you look at these glorious pictures, one common denominator is always present: customers used to dress up when they went to dinner, men in their finest suits, and their ladies in dinner dresses. It's a far cry from today, when a guy throws on a pair of Dockers and a golf shirt! When I was 5, my grandfather put me on the small stage in the main dining room, and I sang with the band. This event would have to qualify as my first public performance. I remember Grandpa Louie lifting me up and putting me on the stage, which seemed enormous to me, but in fact it more likely was a one- to two-foot riser. The pianist, who was most likely Nicholas Grabow, played "How Much is That Doggie in the Window?" I don't remember whether I screwed up the song or not, but I remember the thunderous applause and laughs. That was my first sip of the fame elixir.

Years later in the 1950s, my mom and I were at the restaurant during lunch hour, when James Garner walked in. I couldn't believe it. Here was "Maverick" in person in my grandfather's restaurant. My mom asked if I wanted to meet him, but I was so flustered by seeing someone in the flesh that I watched on tv that I ran and hid.

My mother got his autograph for me, and I had it for many years, but somewhere along the line it got lost. Wish I had it now.

I think coming into contact with all of those celebrities affected my grandfather. On one of his earliest matchbooks for the restaurant said, "Moskowitz and Lupowitz, DIRECTED by Louis Anzelowitz."

Chapter 4

The Acting Light Went On In My Head

My actor uncle, Hy Anzell, had a profound effect on me. He was hysterically funny. Whenever the family got together, they immediately launched into a jokefest, with my uncles and even my mom trying to outdo each other. Hy had them all beat, because not only did he know a million jokes but he was able to do the character voices and dialects perfectly. The first time I can remember understanding what he did for living occurred in the 1950s. We were all at my Grandma Rose's apartment at 187 E. 4th Street and Avenue A. Uncle Hy was going to be on one of those live black and white tv dramatic shows, and we were all sitting around waiting for his appearance. The Philco tv had a glowing green light that took a long time to warm up, followed by the 13-inch screen coming on, but we were ready for the show; the tv was already warmed up when the show began. Finally, the scene cut to Hy.

"There he is!" I said. *Shit, that's my uncle,* I thought. When my grandmother finally saw him, she started to make such loud, prideful, clucking noises that she drowned out what was probably a few lines of dialogue, and then he was gone. None of us even knew what he said, but the image of my uncle on television stayed with me. *This acting thing, could be something that I might want to do.*

My uncle, Max, married Janet Kaplan in 1950. They had two children, my cousins Lois and Steven. Max was a talented musician, a songwriter, and a gentle man that was quick with a joke and a smile. When I was six years old, Max had written a tune called "The Whistling Song." He wanted to record a demo, and he thought that I probably would be a good candidate to sing it. On a Friday, we went to a studio in New York. I was lifted up onto a chair in front of this big microphone. I listened to the music on headphones and sang into the mic.

Monday at school, it was "show and tell," and kids had to show something they'd done recently, or tell the class about something that happened in their life. So, I used the experience in the recording studio as my contribution. The next thing I knew, my teacher hauled my mom into school so she could talk to her in the principal's office.

"Your son, Gary," they said, "is making up stories in class. He fabricated this entire story about how he went into recording a song in New York, and how he recorded a song and made a record. You need to get him some help."

My mother said with a deadpan, "But, he *did* record a song."

I'm sure their chins were on the floor. That shut up the old battle axe pretty quick. But then, just to make things interesting, I started to bullshit about everything else! I'm sure before too long I told everyone that MGM put me under contract. *Hey why not? They would believe me now.*

I was extremely close to my grandmother, Rose Anzelowitz. In her eyes, I could do no wrong. When I visited her apartment in the city, she always had those tiny boxes of raisins that she knew I loved. I spent many happy hours with her, and she let me amuse myself any way I wanted. I used to line up kitchen plates on the living room in a giant train. She was all about the food, and no one could refuse her.

When I got older and arrived at Rose's apartment, she began, "Garala, you want something to eat?"

"No grandma, I'm fine"

"Well, you have to eat . . . eat a little something"

"Really, I'm not hungry grandma."

"You want some soup?"

She kept up with the food sales pitch until I finally caved in and succumbed to her home-made soup, her salad with the special dressing, or her famous potatonik. This was like a baked potato pie with outside crust that was golden brown and crisp, with spongy-soft potato inside. Many people in the family tried to replicate her recipe over the years, but nobody has been successful. She never wrote down the recipe for this or anything she made. When she died, the secrets went with her.

Rose was not a particularly sophisticated woman, and at times had trouble understanding the latest developments in the world. In 1964, I took her to see the New York World's Fair in Queens. One attraction presented by Walt Disney was the Hall of Presidents. Years later in 1971, they improved the animations and opened the attraction at Disneyland, but at the World's Fair, we sat in the audience, and one by one, each President stood and made a small speech about their presidency and the country. Grandma Rose sat transfixed through the whole performance.

When the show ended and the lights came up, she turned to me, clapped her hands, and said, "Oy, Garala, such wonderful actors!"

"No, grandma, those weren't actors, they were dummies."

"Of course they were actors! I know dummies. Those were actors!"

Gary at Bar Mitzvah age 13.

Gary at Bar Mirzvah age 13.

I was never able to convince her of the technology. She was a beautiful soul. I didn't realize at that time as a kid that people I loved didn't last forever. I'd give anything right now to just spend one more day with her.

In the Jewish faith, when a boy turns 13, they say, "You're considered a man." Studying for Bar Mitzvah is like getting your driver's license. You cram everything into your head, just to take the religion out for a spin. I had to go to Hebrew school in the afternoons after spending an entire day in regular school. I wasn't too thrilled with my afternoons being monopolized, but I had no choice. The classrooms were dark and depressing in the basement of a synagogue. The rabbi, who was all business, drummed everything in my head like a drill sergeant. I had to learn how to read, write, and understand Hebrew symbols, all of this leading up to the ceremony in the temple. The second the ceremony was over, I forgot everything I was taught. My mom and Al threw a giant reception for me. It was like a wedding. Tons of guests, live music, and lots of food. A professional photographer was hired, and my mom even had a portrait of me commissioned. I always thought that the party was more for the adults than it was for me. It went by in an eye blink. It must have cost thousands of dollars.

Gary in Junior High.

Chapter 5

Suburban Coming of Age

In 1962, my parents decided it was time to move out of Brooklyn and to the suburbs of Long Island. Everyone who could afford it was running out there. Perfect streets, quaint split-level houses, and finely manicured lawns. We moved to 1396 Holiday Park Drive in Wantagh, New York. My stepdad, Al, paid $23,000 for the house, and I finally had my own room, a big deal for any kid. Finally, some privacy! It was a place I could be alone with a playboy magazine and a box of Kleenex. Green lawns, no crime, and girls with big tits! I was coming of age.

A jingle blasted out of my Zenith transistor radio. I heard the jingle singers followed by the announcer, "Seventy Seven, W.A.B C. Hey cousins, this is your cousin Brucie, with a great one going out to my friends in Brooklyn, and a couple of love birds in Queens." Then, the opening bars of Frankie Valee's "Sherry" blared through the tiny speaker.

Soon, I assimilated into the neighborhood gang of kids: the Crain brothers, Steven and Mark, down the street; David Halpern, who lived directly across the street next to Amy Samuleson; Jeff Cahn, at the end of Holiday Park Drive, who became my best friend. I ran into him on the block with another friend, Mike Roth.

Roth was a wild kid. Out of all of us, he was the one that would have been referred to as a "hippie." He once told Jeff that he was going to take his life. Back then, when kids talked that way, we didn't pay much attention. These days, people take those comments seriously. Not too long after that, Mike committed suicide by jumping off a platform into an oncoming train.

I was enrolled at Wantagh High School, using the name Gary "Covelman," I guess because it was just easier, even though Al never legally adopted me. He was perfectly willing to do it, but I didn't want to change my name. After school, I often walked to Jeff's house and we hung out in his room, cracking each other up, and dreaming of becoming entertainers. Jeff and I had the same sense of humor. We constantly cracked each other up doing bits and voices. Of course, I've been doing voices since I was 7 or 8.

One day, I decided that I would be Ed Sullivan for the entire day in school, with friends, and even at home. I sat at the dinner table and, in Ed's voice, said, "Now right here on our really big dinner table, mother would you pass the really big salt?"

"Gary, stop being an idiot."

My mom would always react to those kinds of things like that, and, yes, those are the encouraging words that are responsible for making me who I am today.

Chapter 6

Stick Man

One day on my way down the block to visit Jeff at his house, an angry dog came out of nowhere and chased me, barking and with its teeth barred all the way. The next time I showed up, I was carrying a large stick.

Jeff's dad asked, "What's the stick for"

"I was chased down the block by a dog. I'm not going anywhere without it."

"Stick man!"

I was then forever referred to as "Stick Man."

Comedy about our parents was often the target of our amusement. Jeff's Dad, Willie, was a film editor. Jeff would eventually enter the same field and work in Hollywood on numerous feature films and tv shows, such as *The X Files, Las Vegas, One Tree Hill,* and *Orange Is The New Black.*

We started to whip up a plan on how we would become big stars. In our minds, we both had it all worked out. "We'll write some routines, do the comedy clubs, and get on the Ed Sullivan Show. We'll become stars, and get apartments in the city,"

"Let's form a comedy act!"

After all, there were great successful teams throughout history: Laurel and Hardy, Abbott and Costello, Martin and Lewis, Rowan and Martin, so why not Craig and Harris? Jeff had seen the name Craig Harris somewhere and thought it would work, so he gave me Craig, he took Harris, and we became the comedy team of Gary Craig and Jeff Harris. Years later, I just kept the name.

We started spending afternoons in Jeff's room writing routines and skits. I'm sure we laughed like idiots thinking we were writing award-winning material. We invented a couple of characters called Selma and Seymour, an old crabby married couple kind of like Edith and Archie bunker, but the truth is we weren't good. It's no wonder that I wound up in radio. At one point, we added one of Jeff's friend,

Craig and Harris.

Craig and Harris.

Ron Conti, a large lump of a kid, who had no obvious comedy chops and only served as the target of our fat and dumb jokes. We called that act, "The Mixed Nuts." I don't think we ever performed anywhere, and we dropped Conti.

Once again, without any money and using Jeff's camera, we had his dad take black and white head shots of us. Jeff had to lend me one of his jackets because I didn't own one. We developed the film and printed out a dozen. Two kids with no experience and a zero track record in show business had a zero chance of getting booked anywhere. Time was certainly a factor, with school every day, so launching a comedy career was difficult. I didn't know shit about show business

GARY CRAIG

Hotel light, where Craig and Harris performed.

Craig and Harris first press clipping.

Craig and Harris, Adam Dipetto press clipping.

or even how to get seen, never mind getting booked anywhere, but Jeff somehow knew a little about this stuff. I'm sure his father had some input that was helpful. Jeff got us an audition for The Clay Cole Show. Clay was a local tv personality, whose show was based out of New York, and reigned from 1959 to 1968. The show was similar to American Bandstand with music and dancers. Clay had an extra talent over Dick Clark: he could sing and dance. The Rolling Stones made their debut on Clay's show. Knowing all of this was a lot of pressure for two stupid kids with routines that weren't all that funny. We got up on stage to audition, and Jeff just froze. I fed him the lines, but instead of remember the script, all he could get out was, "Leave me alone." Opportunity killed.

Then one day, Jeff called me and said, "Get down to my house. I have something to tell you."

I grabbed my stick and headed down the block. When I got to his house, he informed me that we were booked for our first paying gig.

"The Hotel Light in New Jersey."

"Never heard of it." *How the hell did he get that booking,* I thought, *and why The Hotel Light?*

He had seen the hotel listed somewhere and just called and sold us over the phone.

We wanted to look our best, so we both went to hair stylists. We were paid about $75 for the gig, and the lady booking us wanted to know if we could bring a band. A band? For $75? That should have been the first clue that this was going to be a nightmare, but we were young and wanted a chance. After the haircuts and the train fare, I think we were left with about $10 each, but who the hell cared? We were in show business!

When we finally got to the hotel on Saturday, it was a real shit dump. An old dilapidated building with an aging sign out front that said Hotel Light, and an even older man on a rocking chair on the porch, who looks like he had oatmeal, or something else, caked on his chin. He sat comatose in the chair, staring straight ahead with no reaction as we walked by. Then, I realized he was stuffed. We went up to the front desk and announced ourselves to the concierge, a fat lady in a muumuu. "We're Craig and Harris. We're the comedy team."

"Okay," she said. "I'll show you were you're performing."

She took us into this little room that had twelve wooden bridge chairs, no lights, and no sound system. Our dressing room was a utility closet next to a platform they called a stage.

They showed us to our room—the attic—with a ceiling so dramatically slanted that we had to bend like a contortionist just to get into the damned thing. The one light source was a bulb dangling by a cord hanging in our face and swinging back and forth all night. Décor amounted to a big yellow stain on the wall from who knows what. We had plenty of time before our debut, and we were hungry, so went across the street to a small luncheonette to grab a bite. There was some old guy sitting at the counter wearing the most bizarre outfit I've even seen. We found out that he was some kind of performer and actually worked the famed Hotel Light. He started talking to us while eating a tuna fish sandwich, with little pieces of tuna flying out of his mouth and hitting us in the face! We couldn't escape! Right there on the spot, Jeff and I named him "Spit Face."

The guy started trying to sell us all kinds of shit. "I have a collapsible drum."

What the hell is that? we thought. He had all these bizarre song sheets from the 1920s, and an instruction book with primitive eye, mouth, throat, and stomach illustrations showing a reader how to sing. We felt sorry for Spit Face. He seems like an old Vaudevillian. I gave him $5 and bought the instructions called *Sing it Over*. I wanted to say, *Gotta go, Spit Face. Have our big show across the street. Our fans will be wheeling up any time now for autographs.*

Show time! We weren't the featured act; we were the *only* act. That should give you an idea of how bad this hotel was. While coming from the closet to make my entrance, I fought to keep a broom handle from going up my ass. The audience swelled to about 25 senior citizens.

We opened with "Together Wherever We Go" from *Gypsy*. I was always a natural singer, but Jeff had no timing, so as we were singing "Wherever we go, whatever we do, we're gonna go through it together," I had to tap him on the shoulder when it was his time to come in with the next lyric line. Terrible!

The jokes they could actually *hear* got laughs, but we bombed to no more than 25 people in the audience. Even though we thoroughly sucked, people still asked for our autographs after the show, thinking someday we'd be big stars.

When we were leaving the next morning, we went to the fabulous Hotel Light's front office to get paid. A lady resembling a beetle bug didn't want to pay us. We insisted on our check, and then she spent the next twenty minutes walking around muttering, "Fa-Cock-Ta check. I don't know where this Fa-Cock-Ta check is!" She finally produced it.

We had coffee in the little dining room, and were served by an old Black man named Raymond. All I said was, "Good Morning, Raymond, how are you today?"

He shot back with, "That ain't the issue!" and then spent the next hour going on and on about how Lincoln freed the slaves. We got out quick. With the haircuts, the *Sing It Over* book, outfits, and train fare, I think it wound up *costing us* $15 to play the fabulous Hotel Light.

Soon after our one and only paying gig, Jeff got us another audition. This time it was for *The Merv Griffin Show*. We went to the Little Theatre off Times Square. How Jeff got us in there for that was a mystery, because we had no track record whatsoever. This time, it was my turn to fuck it up. I totally froze on stage. Afterward, we went to get hot dogs, as I was totally oblivious that I just blew a major opportunity.

Even though we were probably the worst comedy act ever seen at a shit dump hotel in New Jersey, Jeff never stopped trying to get our names out there, and he pulled off a coup, the greatest thing that happened not just for our careers but something that helped us scam the New York Public School system. Jeff had called, and then sent a blurb about us to, Adam Di Petto, who wrote a column in the *Sunday Daily News*. The column was called "Strictly Youthsville." He took the bait, and put us in. The next thing I knew, Jeff was calling me one Sunday morning to tell me that we were in the column. Our picture was used to head the column, and he wrote, "Gary Craig and Jeff Harris of Wantagh, L.I., play local clubs and the Catskills resorts (bullshit) and believe they're the youngest comedy team around at 17 already. Their tickle: 'We heard of a billing clerk who went to a psychiatrist . . . kept hearing strange invoices.'"

That changed everything for us at Wantagh high School. Up to that point, all the teachers and the Principal hated my guts. Gary was, the class clown and wise ass that did sound effects in the back of the classroom and got roughed up by bullies. Now, we were instant stars, and the bullies loved us because we were cool. We used that bit of celebrity as an excuse to do whatever we wanted. We breezed into school late most days, showing up at the school office with a plethora of excuses relating to our new star status when lightly questioned for our tardiness.

"Oh, we were on the phone with our agents this morning. You know how that goes."

"Rehearsals. We're doing a guest shot on tv in New York."

They bought every bullshit excuse we could invent. The two biggest idiot losers at the school had become the two coolest idiots at the school.

Jeff and I were walking down the street one day. The Principal of Wantagh High, Mr. Kellerman, drove by us, slowed down, and hung out of his window smiling and shouting, "Hello boys!" He looked back at the road just in time to avoid crashing his car. The buying of B.S. went all the way to the top.

I was never a good student. It's not that I wasn't smart enough to get the grades, it's just I was always preoccupied with show business, always dreaming that someday I would make it. With Jeff and I skipping class and bullshitting the teachers, it's surprising that I graduated high school at all.

I was such a non-conformist. If everyone else were doing things like going to a school dance, football games, even graduation, I didn't. When the high school notified me that I was graduating, and asked what size cap and gown I needed, I told them, "Don't bother, I won't be going to the ceremony. In fact, just mail me my diploma." What a stupid ass. I regret doing that to this day. When Jeff and I graduated high school, we decided to take a trip down to Florida. We also decided to bring Ron Conti with us, with the thought that The Mixed Nuts could get booked somewhere. Fat chance. I showed up at the airport with Mike Roth, without ever telling Jeff he was tagging along. Roth, like I said, was a weird kid. He brought a suitcase with him, with one pair of underwear in it. The entire time he was with us, he had to borrow Jeff's clothes.

In the swinging 1960s on Miami Beach, many upscale hotels dotted Collins Avenue: Eden Rock, The Americana, The Castaways, and The Fountain Bleu, where Sinatra filmed Tony Rome (1967). We rented a room at a fleabag hotel on Collins Avenue called The Rendale Hotel. We made so much noise that we were thrown out at 3 o'clock in the morning. We walked down Collins Avenue in the middle of the night with nowhere to stay and wound up at The Atlantis. After it was clear that The Mixed Nuts was a dismal failure, Conti left.

All through high school, Jeff and I used to make fun of this one custodian. He had a strange, rough guttural voice. We named him Sam Shmogie and came up with this voice we used every time we saw him, and, of course, we cracked ourselves up. The next morning after we checked into The Atlantis, I got up and walked down to the lobby. I was at the top of the stairs looking down, when I saw Jeff . Using the voice we invented for the custodian, I shouted, "Mort Ziggy!" Don't ask me why I did that, where the name came from, or what the fuck it was supposed to mean, but from that point on to today, Jeff and I use that name addressing each other in person, and in emails. (Years later, I would use the Mort Ziggy voice for a character on the radio and television known as "The Crazyman."

After coming home, Jeff and I kept entertaining ourselves. One time, we dressed up as hillbillies and drove to a fast food place. After pulling into the parking lot, we spilled out with our teeth blackened out, overalls, and who knows what else, causing a racket. We thought it was the funniest thing and didn't care if we got a reaction from anyone. I'm sure we wondered why we weren't big stars.

When it was clear that my life plan was for me to just sit around the house like a lump, Al came into my bedroom and said, "If you're not going to go to college, you're going to have to get a job."

That was a sobering thought. I had no skills. My first job was at a fast food joint called "Bob's burgers." They put me at the front counter. I didn't know what the hell I was doing. A customer came in and ordered a hamburger. He got the burger and sat down to eat it. A few minutes later, he came back to the counter and said, "There's ink in my meat."

Ink in his meat? What the hell? I gave it to the cook.

He looked at it and nodded his head. What the customer was staring at was the USDA stamp that somehow made it onto that particular burger. The cook knew I was green. He called me over and said, "Get the customer's name and address and tell him we'll send him another one."

What did I do? "Uh, yes, sir, if you give me your name and address, we'd be more than happy to send you another burger."

He got so pissed off that he threw the burger at me. I ducked, and it just missed the cook's head. He was laughing his ass off.

My next job was in a factory. The pay was very good, but my job was monotonous as hell. Here's what I did for 8 hours a day. I took a piece of sheet metal, placed it on this machine, pulled a handle down, and it bent the metal into a 45-degree angle. I took the metal off the machine and stacked it with all the other pieces of metal I bent. Pretty soon, my mind drifted and I decided to start doing character voices as I was working. One day, I was Ed Sullivan for the entire shift. I stood at the machines and I started, "Now right here, on our really great metal bending machine, watch how this really big wedge comes down and bends this into a 45°angle. Next week, Topo Gigio will pull down the handle." I did this out loud. The next day, I was someone else, like Woody Woodpecker, or Humphrey Bogart. I had a captive audience. The factory workers loved me, which was my cue to keep going. It was a tedious fucking job, which ended one day after being called into the boss's office and fired. I was too much of a distraction. *What was wrong with these people? Don't they know they had the next "Jerry Lewis" right under their nose?* I should have charged *them* for the entertainment.

Chapter 7

First Announcing Job

The first job I held down as an announcer wasn't on the air; it was for TSS, Times Square Stores. Back in the 1960s, each TSS had their own "Store Announcer," a guy who sat upstairs in a booth that looked out over the store. Every 10 minutes or so, he would turn on the mic and announce a special or sale that a department sent up. I used to hear the announcements all the time and wondered, *Who is that and where was it coming from?* "Folks, here at Times Square Stores, we have a sensational sale going on right now in our photo department. Two rolls of Kodak film, just $1.99. That's in our photo department at the rear of the store." The guy had a great voice that could have easily doubled as the play by play announcer for a sports team. The next time I was in the store, I found out where the booth was and snaked my way upstairs. When I announced to an employee that I, too, wanted to be an announcer, I was brought into the booth and introduced to the man whose voice blared out of every speaker in the store.

"I'll tell you what," he said, "You come in for a couple of days and watch what I do and we'll see what happens."

School was out for the summer. I had all the time in the world. The next few days, I hung out in the booth, and department head after department head brought up the written copy for him to announce. There was a foot pedal on the floor. Once he stepped on it, he was live throughout the store. It was exciting to think about having that much power with just the pressing down of one foot. I shadowed him for two days and watched carefully how he executed the announcements.

Early morning on the third day, I got a phone call. They wanted me to come in and take over the announcing duties because he couldn't make it. What I didn't know was that he had a drinking problem and was shit-faced. In retrospect, if I had to sit there all day and announce dish sales, I'd be shit-faced, too. He probably was some kind of announcer back in the day, and now that was where he wound up.

I was nervous as hell, as I ascended the stairs to the booth. The second my ass hit the seat, cards with words starting arriving from the various departments. It took me a long time to make the first announcement, but I finally mustered enough nerve to hit the pedal. Of course, I started out every announcement with "Folks . . . ." because that's what the old man did. After a few, I felt more comfortable, but my inexperience shined through almost immediately. The seasonal department sent up some copy highlighting Bar-B-Q utensils. It was the first time I had ever seen the word "spatula," but that didn't stop me from opening the mic and saying, "Folks, it's Bar-B-Q time, and we have a great sale going on right now in our seasonal department on a terrific utensil set. You'll get a long fork, a serrated knife, and a terrific *SPAH-TOO-LAH*. I was so confident, that I repeated the announcement twice!

The regular announcer couldn't make it in the second day either. By then, I was feeling pretty confident, and I had the system down, but was still screwing up. I had an announcement that had to do with women's underthings, and I ended the copy with "See you in women's underwear." Then, getting bored, I started reading the copy in various voices. Ed Sullivan pushing sheets, Humphrey Bogart talking about silverware. That was my last day.

Chapter 8

Free Shit

We were always trying to score free stuff. One of the greatest scams happened at a place called "The Huntington Towne House," a giant venue on Long island that had multiple ballrooms and halls in one building. It wouldn't be unusual on any given Saturday for three weddings and a couple of Bar Mitzvah's going on at the same time. My friends and I put on suits and crashed these events. We just went from wedding to wedding eating until we were full. The food was spectacular, and we perfected the art of being an "unknown" relative at a wedding. We never got caught, but we were challenged. One time, I standing there stuffing my face, and this lady walked up, looked at me and asked, "Who are you?"

Most would have panicked. Not me. Without missing a beat, I said in an unbelieving voice, "Who am I? Come on! You know who I am."

She then asked, "Are you Joey's cousin?"

"Yes, of course." I kept eating.

Back in New York, I just hung around the house during the week, but on weekends I went into the city and used Grandma Rose's apartment as home base. Every weekend, I put on a paisley shirt and elephant bells pants and went into the village with the rest of the potheads, got high, and went to The Electric Circus, a giant music venue, where people far more brave than I dropped acid and listened to a DJ play psychedelic music. On some occasions, we listened to live bands. Everyone had long hair, and depending on what substance was surging through their body, they were transported to another place. Grandma never asked me what I was doing, she was just glad to see me.

Those weekend visits became permanent for a while after I got full-time jobs at department stores, such as B Altman and Company and Saks Fifth Avenue working in the stock room. When I stayed with Rose, she got up in the morning before I went to work and squeezed me fresh orange juice by hand. I used to play pranks on her, too. One night when she was asleep, I got hold of a syringe, filled it with water, and injected each orange in the fridge. The next morning, she got up to make me juice, and I heard her say, "Oy! Such juicy oranges! Oy Vey, I have to go back to the market and get more of these." The final job I had in the city was that of a Wall Street runner. I don't know how or why I had this job, but I worked for a company called Wexler and Krumholtz, a stock and securities company. I showed up in the morning, and they gave me a package filled with stocks, bonds, and securities. No fax machines back then, everything had to be delivered by hand. I then had to deliver them to another company on Wall Street. They only gave me a certain amount of time to deliver the packages. I clocked out when I left, and clocked in when I got to the other company. Thus, I had to be quick, and thus the term "wall street runner." They were absolutely crazy to trust some jerky kid with what must have been thousands of dollars of paper.

I hung out with another runner, a Black guy named Crazy Joe. He deserved the name. Joe was so fast that he was scamming three companies at the same time. Since Wall Street was a pretty compact area in New York, all the buildings were close together. Joe checked into the first company at 9 a.m. and picked up a package. Then, he checked into the second company at 9:20, and the third at 9:45. He raced down the street and delivered all three packages before lunch, checked back at all three companies, and took a quick lunch hour. Then, he started the second round of deliveries after lunch. None of the companies knew what he was up to, and to my knowledge they never found out.

It was spring and it was glorious. Pretzel and hot dog vendors everywhere. There was one particular morning when I was really running late to deliver a package. This time I was actually racing down the street, when all of a sudden this tall man walked down from an apartment onto the street and right in my path. My head was down, I didn't see him, and *bam*, I ran smack into him. What I *didn't* know was that he was part of an active film set. I heard the director—rather pissed off—yell, "CUT! CUUUT!"

I looked up and saw that I had had run right into Walter Mathau. He looked down at me smiling and asked, "Where's the fire kid?"

When I told this story to my friend, Chris Lemmon, actor, author, and son of Jack Lemmon, he said, "No! The director cut? You never cut until you're absolutely sure the scene is over. Walter is so good he could have ad-libbed the whole scene and they could have left it in."

Oh well, not my day to become a movie star and another opportunity vanished. This would become a familiar theme in my career. I was always tugging on the sleeve of fame. One morning as I finished making my delivery, I noticed some tv cameras shooting something on the street. I've never been able to nail down the show's name, but I think it was hosted by Gene Rayburn of *The Match Game* fame. I always had my harmonica with me those days. I was always very musical, and I used it to entertain myself during my down time. I sat down on the building's steps, pulled out my harmonica, and played as I watched the crew. All of a sudden, the host walked over and asked, "Would you like to be on the show?"

The camera rolled, as I told him, "I'm a runner."

He asked me about the harmonica, so I pulled it out and played "Oh Susannah." That was my first real foray into show business. It aired a few nights later on New York television, and they even used my harmonica playing over the credits. I couldn't believe it! I was on tv! Thrilling!

I lost that runner job, too.

I had to say goodbye to Grandma Rose. She begged me to stay. I really felt bad about leaving, but with no job and nothing to do, I returned to Long Island.

Chapter 9

Completely Lost

What the hell was I going to do with myself? I had no plan, and no apparent talent for anything, although if you took a look at my grade school autograph book, it told a different story. The autograph book was something that every kid got when they graduated. There, your friends and teachers wrote biting, witty, or inspiring things on the pages. Apparently, I made quite an impression on many of my teachers, because all their messages had the same theme running through them: "You have a great singing voice," one wrote. Another teacher scribbled, "I expect to see you on the stage someday."

Really? Did they know something I didn't?

By the time 1968 rolled around, Uncle Hy had been in many national tv commercials and feature films, including numerous Woody Allen pictures. Seeing him on the little or big screen still had an effect on me. I got it into my head that I wanted to become an actor. I was always cutting up, doing character voices and sound effects. *If Hy could do it,* I thought, *then I could.*

I needed to get some training. One of the most prestigious acting schools in the country was The American Academy of Dramatic Arts in New York. It's alum was a Who's Who of the acting world, with giants such as, Kirk Douglas, Spencer Tracy, Grace Kelly, Adrien Brody, and Robert Redford, just to name a few. In order to get into the school, I had to read, which meant audition. If they didn't see any glimmer of talent, I wouldn't get in. I was nervous as hell. I sat in the registrar's outer office. Someone came out and handed me a scene, the first time I saw it. "Take a look at this, and we'll bring you in shortly!"

Holy Crap! Everything was riding on this audition. I was sitting in the biggest acting institution in New York, and someone in that inner room was going to decide if I had any talent. They finally escorted me into this room, I read the scene for this man, and at the end all he said was, "Thanks for coming in, we'll let you know." (By the way, even to this day, when you go into an audition for a part, they say the same thing, "Thanks for coming in.") That's it! Nightmare.

About a week later, a letter arrived. "Congratulations, you've been chosen to be admitted into The American Academy of Dramatic Arts." I was over the moon, and a little scared at the same time. *If just getting in was nerve wracking, what would the classes be like?* I worried a lot when I was younger. I soon discovered that it was all about technique, but the exercises to bring me out of my shell were very strange. In one class, we were instructed to roll around on the floor making believe we were pieces of bacon sizzling in the pan. I flopped around making oil splattering sounds. Every day, there was another exercise just like that.

At the semester's end, the school put on their play. Family and friends were invited, along with agents scouting for talent. I don't recall what part I played, but I do remember that I started ad-libbing from the script. Why would I do such a thing? Who the hell knows, and who cared if the girl playing opposite me was getting pissed off as I went on with the improvisation? I was getting laughs!

I got bored quickly and left the school. I still thought I could be an actor, if only I could get a break. Uncle Hy arranged an audition for me for an off Broadway play, *Bang the Drum Slowly*. Back in the 1960s, you could get an audition for some pretty big projects even though you had never done anything. Hell, I didn't even have a resume. The audition instructions said I was to arrive with a piece of music to sing for the director. Well, I didn't know many Broadway-type songs, and I certainly didn't know any by heart. I went to the music store, and I can't imagine why I chose this one, but I settled on Peter Paul and Mary's "If I had a Hammer." What a wimpy choice!

I got to the theatre, and I was terrified. All of this was new to me, being in an actual theatre and surrounded by professionals. All my life, people had been telling me that I could sing, that I should be on stage, and that I was so talented. All that didn't matter, because I was a shriveled up little penis boy waiting for my turn.

I heard them call my name. I got up on stage for my big moment, trying to make believe I had confidence, that I'd done this before, that I'm the one they're looking for. I handed the music to the pianist. He started the intro, and I open my mouth to sing, "If I had a Hame—." I stopped. "Uh, sorry, wrong key. Let me try that again."

The music began again, and I sang "If I had a hammer, I'd a hammer in the—. Oh, that's not the key. Wait. I know which key it is. Let me—"

I was interrupted by the director. My face flushed red, as a disembodied voice from the back of the darkened theatre said, "Thank you, very nice, we'll be in touch."

That was it. I was destroyed. What I *should* have done was kept going. Every actor that has ever made it has stories of disastrous auditions. You have to have a cast iron stomach, and just chalk it up to experience and keep going.

Chapter 10

Florida and the World of Radio

During the Vietnam War, my draft number was 172, which meant that if I didn't get my ass into some kind of college and get a deferment, I might wind up in some ditch in Viet Nam eating beans out of a can. I don't remember my opinion of that war, but I'm sure fear and trepidation were attached to the possibility of being called up. That fact, coupled with being basically directionless, lit a fire under my ass to change course.

I applied to every college I thought might accept me. I wasn't a good student. I was more interested in cracking jokes, cutting up, and getting laughs. (In grade school, when we were studying World War Two, I used to sit in the back adding machine gun and bomb sound effects. I spent plenty of time in the principal's office.) Every college I applied to turned me down. The future looked bleak.

I still was listening to radio stations and was impressed by how the radio announcers sounded. Talking to millions of people and playing great music sounded like something I could do. *After all, writing bits and performing characters on the radio was a roundabout way of acting*, I thought. I researched where I could get some training, but there weren't really a lot of radio schools back then. I found out Miami Dade Junior college had a Radio and tv technology course, so I sent them an application. A week later, I was accepted. That gave me my deferment. By the time I had finished school, the Draft Board had stopped calling numbers. I missed the whole party.

Leaving home was a scary proposition. I'm sure every young adult leaving their parent's cushy home felt the same way. I didn't know a living soul in Florida. Miami Dade Junior College didn't have on-campus housing; the students to find a place to live. I didn't have or know any roommates yet, so I couldn't rent an apartment, but my stepdad, Al, had arranged for me to rent a room from an elderly couple near the school, Mr. and Mrs. Silverstein. I have no idea how the hell he found these people, but I didn't ask any questions.

After about two days into the arrangement, I thought I was living in a Nazi concentration camp. I wasn't allowed to use the kitchen. I had to stay in my room. I couldn't even play the radio! I was going to school to learn radio, but I couldn't play it in my room! Mrs. Silverstein was like Colonel Klink from *Hogan's Heroes*. If I watched tv in the living room by 8:00 p.m., she walked over and announced, "It's 8 o'clock, lights out!" and switched off the tv. One time, I begged her to let me use the kitchen to heat up a can of soup. I cut myself on her can opener.

"You're bleeding all over my floor!" she screamed.

She didn't give a shit about me being injured, just her floor. I didn't stay in that house long. Next, I found a roommate and we shared an apartment, which was owned by this Cuban guy. He was another kind of nut. He claimed that putting toilet paper actually in the toilet would ruin the septic system, so he insisted that after we wiped our asses we put the paper in a waste basket. I didn't stay there too long either.

I finally found a little efficiency owned by a lady that lived in her own house that was not attached to my living quarters. Everything *seemed* fine, and I got along with her, until I started coming home and found that she had been in my room and in my drawers rearranging my underwear and socks. *What the fuck?* I'm sure she meant well, but it was an invasion of my privacy. I voiced my objection to her, and for a while she respected my wishes, but she just couldn't help herself and went right back to rearranging my underwear.

One night, I was awakened by a strange itching sensation. I went into the bathroom, turned the light on, and looked in the mirror. My entire back had broken out in hives. It looked like one massive red itchy tumor. I took a shower with cool water and went back to bed. The problem didn't go away. Over the next seven days, it got worse. I was breaking out every day, and now my lips swelled up to three times their size. I finally got in to see an allergist, and he made a tic-tac-toe box on my back. In every little box, with a syringe, he injected me with various liquids.

"What are you doing exactly?" I asked.

"Well, these injections will tell me exactly what you're allergic to. Then, we can go from there."

25 injections and a few days later, the doctor called me in to give me the test results: I was allergic to everything under the sun: dogs, cats, birds, Mala-Luka Trees, grass, dirt, flowers, coconuts, cars, trucks, moons, asteroids, shit, whatever!

"Now what?" I asked.

"Well now, we'll re-inject you with just the material you reacted to, and—"

"Oh no you're not. I'm done!"

The next week, I moved out of that cottage, and magically, the hives went away and never came back. Maybe when the old lady was arranging my briefs, she added something that brought on the hive attack?

On the first day of Miami Dade Junior College, I met Jane. I saw her every day thereafter until we were divorced two years later.

I was very insecure about being alone and latched on to the first person I met. When I met Jane, I was basically a virgin. Oh, I suppose a case could be made about the time I met a girl that worked at B Altman in New York where I worked as a stock clerk at about 16, and she was a sales girl about 22. I persuaded her to move into a room with me, but I couldn't get it up. Let's not count that.

Jane and I were seeing each other when I had time. She lived in North Miami Beach. Her dad Harry owned a B.P. gas station and worked long hours. One night at her house, one thing led to another, and before I knew it, we were screwing each other on her kitchen floor. All of a sudden, we heard a key in the front door. Shit, it was her father! I think he knew something was up, because he took his sweet time about walking in, and the kitchen was only twenty feet from the front door. I never got dressed that fast in my life. At night back in my rented room, I chased loneliness away by listening to the radio. There was a guy on the air named Tom Adams, a funny guy, great communicator, and he told a lot of jokes and . . . he took phone calls. I started calling him, doing different characters and impressions.

I had studied people all of my life and built up a backlog of dialects and voices. Living in the east village of New York a few years back exposed me to all kinds of characters, and I was a quick study. I started calling Tom once a week, then once every couple of days, and then it got to the point that Tom would be airing my calls every day. I was funny. Hearing my bits on the air was thrilling. I couldn't imagine what it would actually be like to host my own show. It was a concept I couldn't wrap my head around.

Up to that point, Tom didn't know who I was, and I never identified myself, but one night I got enough nerve to call him and let the cat out of the bag. He was very kind. I told him I was majoring in radio and tv broadcasting, and wondering if I could come down and tour the station. To my surprise he said yes. *Wow! I'm going to see a real working radio station, I thought.*

It was one thing to be in a make believe studio at the college, but seeing one in action was the ultimate. WIOD, an AM 50,000-watt flame thrower on the 79th Street causeway in Miami. The second I stepped through the door, I could feel the excitement in the air. They had about ten studios with something going on in each one. A chief engineer sat in master control monitoring everything that was being recorded or going out on the air. I was mesmerized. I seized the moment.

"Let me hang out here," I begged Tom. "I'll do anything. I'll run for coffee. I'll scrub the floors. I'll answer the phones, just let me hang out and learn!"

Today, it's called an internship, but I don't think most kids want an internship. They're more interested in the instant payoff. Work for free? What? Well, I knew what I had there and I was ready to grab it. It was called work ethic, and I returned many days to help Tom and soak in the wonders of radio.

Then . . . I was introduced to Larry King.

Larry King at WIOD radio, Miami.

Chapter 11

"Miami, hello!"

Up until I met Larry King, I hadn't yet made my radio debut. The closest I had come was via the telephone bits on the Tom Adams show. Larry liked me right off the bat and invited me to come down to the station and help out with his show. Believe me, he didn't need my help. He was the King of Miami, at the time. He had his late night talk show from midnight to 5:00 a.m., he had a column in *The Miami Herald*, a weekend television show, and he was the color announcer for the Miami Dolphins, a heady time for him. I was thrilled to be part of it.

He was such a colorful and flamboyant character. To me, the wide-eyed broadcast student, he was bigger than life. With Larry, his thing was always the best money could buy—the best clothes, a new Caddy every year, the best restaurants, and the best-looking women. I saw early on that broadcasting could do all of this for me, and more. I wanted to be just like Larry.

At first, I answered the phones that would ring off the hook when he was on the air. Going from blinking light to another, I screened callers and lined them up. My duties also included meeting guests in the lobby and bringing them into the studio. I guess I was doing what would later be called a "producer." Today, every morning show worth its salt has a good producer.

One of my other unofficial jobs was running interference for Larry's girlfriends. He had so many it was hard to keep track. They stopped in and asked me, "What kind of mood is he in tonight? What is he thinking and feeling?"

"How the hell did I know? You're in bed with the guy. Ask him yourself."

I was just an intern trying to learn something, but I was close to him, so they tried to get close to me. Larry was a blunt, shoot from the hip person. One night, he came in about 4 minutes before he has to go on the air and breezed by me in the hallway. I greeted him as usual. "Hey, Larry, how are ya?"

"I've been fucking so much, I rubbed the skin off my dick. I have to go to the doctor and get some crème."

I think my jaw was still on the floor

Eventually, Larry used me on the air. I portrayed various crazy characters on his show, passed myself off as an actual guest, and the "Original Crazyman of the Radio" was born. One of my characters was Doctor Shvago. Larry allowed me to take calls and make asinine predictions. Today, they would call that the Psychic Hotline. Sometime during my stint at WIOD, Larry got himself into hot water and was arrested. The problem had something to do with taking money from Miami financier Lou Wolfson. Wolfson gave Larry $5,000 to give to Jim Garrison, who was involved in the Kennedy assassination investigation. Instead of forwarding the cash to its intended recipient, Larry allegedly spent the money paying his back taxes, and so he was arrested for grand larceny. Larry claimed it was a loan that he forgot to pay back. This big story splashed all over tv, radio, and newspapers. They took Larry off the air. I heard him pleading with the program director, "Biggie Nevins," to keep him on, but the company ruled. Then, it all fell like dominoes and he systematically lost all of his other jobs.

Larry took radio gigs on small stations in the market, and even left for a while. I saw his departure as a chance for me to make my mark. I asked management for a shot at the talk show, a chance to show my stuff. What stuff? I had no stuff. I didn't even know what stuff was. I knew nothing, had experienced nothing, I had been nowhere, and I hadn't talked to anyone. What the hell was I going to talk about? Hey, I was young and I had balls if nothing else. (Years later, I hosted a live, two-night audition on WOR in New York. I nearly shit my pants. They were auditioning people all week. The engineer told me that the girl who preceded me the night before sat down in front of the mic and, right before she went live, threw up. I killed myself for the two nights with prepared bits, interesting stories, and guests. When it came time to do a live read on a commercial, I nailed it. The sales manager at the time at WOR flipped and thought the station should have hired me on the spot, but the program director thought my presentation was too young for his audience and would alienate the upper demos of his listeners. In my opinion that was exactly what they needed to do. When your audience is dying off, it's time to bring in new blood. They didn't hire me.)

WIOD decided to give me a shot for one night. Failure! Talk is hard, especially sitting there by yourself without a cohost or anybody to relate to. There is no safety net and no song to go to if you run out of brain power. So even now, doing talk—pure talk—would be a challenge, and I've been in the business for over forty years, so what the hell was I thinking back in 1971?

WIOD had an FM sister station named WA1A. It was named, I'm sure, after the A1A interstate in Florida. WA1A's format was beautiful music. One day, I wandered into their studio, and there I found a funny-looking man wearing a fishing hat. His name was Charlie Baxter, a staff announcer. We struck up a conversation. Charlie was an easy-going guy with a great laugh.

"I'm starting a couple of local tv shows," he told me. "Interested in working on them? No pay, of course, but maybe we could get you some gas money."

Big operation, but who cared. I was young, and it was an undeniable adventure. The television station was WKID tv on channel 51. Back then, there was no cable. There were two bands on tv sets. The VHF band brought channels, 2, 3, 4, 6, 8, and all the way up to channel 13. *Wow!* Then there was the UHF band. You could get a splattering of rag tag tv stations, like WKID.

Charlie was going to do two shows every week, one on which he played a zany horror character, M. T. Graves, and another that was a children's show on which he was more like himself as "Captain Kidd." M. T. was a local cult hit. Charlie had been performing the bit for years on other tv stations in the

Charlie Baxter.

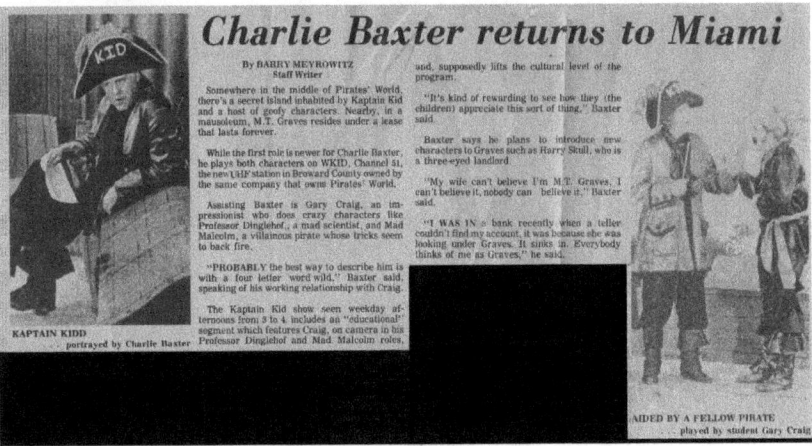

Captain KIDD article # 1.

Captain KIDD article # 2.

Captain KIDD with Mad Malcolm clipping.

Charlie Baxter as M. T. Graves.

1960s. When he made appearances, the local police were deployed to control the crowds. By 1971, he was performing the character again, maybe for the last time on this brand new cheap-ass television station that had $0 budget for anything. They didn't even have videotape machines, so all the shows had to be done live. I loved the rush of live television. *Shit, it's going out to tvs right now,* I thought. *You fuck up? Too bad. Everyone will see it.*

M. T. Graves came on during the breaks of a horror or sci fi film. The set took place in a dungeon that had a casket and a warden that wasn't seen but his voice was heard directing M. T. Graves through his routines. Charlie as M. T. was made up with green face paint, bizarre hair, ripped clothes, giant rubber feet, and terrible fake teeth.

I was M. T.'s Eyegore, and my makeup was murder. Charlie and I used a solution called "non-flexible collodion," which was used to make three-dimensional scars. It could only be removed with another solution called "acetone" that literally peeled away the skin from my face when removing the scar. My skin was red for days, but that was show business!

A few weeks after he launched M. T. Graves, he kicked off the second show, *The Captain Kidd Hour,* or it might have been called *Captain Kidd's Secret Island.* The show aired live every afternoon at 4:30. I played Mad Malcolm—a mean pirate, and Professor Dinglehof, a nut in a lab coat running around with a bad German accent. I ran out onto the set as Malcolm, did my bit, then during a 3-minute cartoon, raced back to the dressing room, took off the entire costume, put on the Professor's lab coat, doused my hair with white powder (to make me look older), then raced back out before the cartoon ended. I dumped such a shit load of powder in my hair that almost every movement I made on camera brought a cascade of powder down my face and lab coat. I'd give anything to have a copy of those shows. You've heard performers say a million times, "There's nothing like live television." There I was at 4:30 in the afternoon on the *Captain Kidd Hour* set. I use the term "set" loosely. It consisted of an old trunk that doubled as a treasure chest, and a boulder that Charlie sat on, while I stood by in my Mad Malcolm costume.

On one live broadcast, we were showing a cartoon and about to come out of it live in 45 seconds. Our bit was that I was to hide behind the boulder, and as soon as the Captain started to speak, I was to jump out in front of him, pull my sword out, hold it to his throat, and tell the kids about our new show.

The floor director said, "Places . . . coming out in 30 seconds."

I hopped behind the rock.

". . . and 5, 4, 3, 2, 1. You're on."

Charlie looked into the camera. "Hi boys and girls! I'm Captain Kidd, and we have a brand new show starting tomorrow (that was my cue) and—"

I jumped from behind the boulder, Charlie gasped, and I hopped in front of the camera. "Not so fast, Captain Kidd!" I shouted. "I'm Mad Malcolm, the mean pirate." I took my sword and pressed it to the Captain's neck. "I'm going to tell the kids about the show!" I continued, growling and acting mean, when suddenly the sword blade broke off and fell to the floor. I stood there like a moron just holding the handle. I looked up and saw the cameraman doubled over, convulsed with laughter. Charlie was trying to hold it together, but I started losing it. I continued with the promo, laughing out every single word while holding a menacing sword handle to the Captain's neck.

The promo ended and the director said, "Clear."

We all died laughing. From that day forward, Mad Malcolm was a little less mean.

It wasn't an easy time for me. Larry King had restored his career, and I was working with him from midnight until 5:00 a.m. Then, I rushed home to sleep for a few hours before getting up to go to classes. Once a week, I was at the tv station doing the live shows with Charlie.

To support myself, I got a job driving a cab on Collins Avenue in Miami Beach from 4:00 p.m. until 11:00 p.m. Driving a cab was a real experience and highly competitive. The silence was broken by the dispatcher's voice, "Do I have a cab in the area of 39th and Collins?" Then his voice would bellow in anger, "I said 39th and Collins!"

No answer.

"Do I have a cab out of the area?" he asked.

At that point, the nearest cab called in and got the job. I always stole jobs. I picked up my two-way and said, "Yeah, cab 18, I'm at 37th and Collins." It was bullshit; I was at 60th and Collins. Hey, I was a student. I never took a dime from my parents, and I had to eat.

"Ok, cab 18, go to the Eden Roc and pick up in the front," said the dispatcher.

I raced down Collins Avenue, and drove by a line of cabs that were way closer than I was. I got very good at reading lips, as some of them would mouth, "Fuckin son of a bitch." (Today, if I drove for Uber, I wouldn't be able to pull that off. Everything is built into an app.)

One time, I had four Japanese guys in the cab going to the airport. They didn't understand how the meter worked. If the meter said $8, someone in the cab paid the $8—once—but when we got to the airport, they all paid me $8 again.

One night, this guy got in and said, "You see that car pulling away from the curb? Follow it."

We spend the next two hours following the car around until we arrived at this fancy high rise. The cab was parked at the curb, waiting. About 15 minutes later, the guy looked up at a window on the 5th floor and saw the shadow of a woman in the clutches with some guy. "Son of a bitch!" the man said. "I knew it!" Turned out that the woman was the guy's wife and he caught her in the act. "Take me back," he said sheepishly. (This exact scenario was represented in a scene in *Taxi Driver* (1976) with Martin Scorsese playing the suspicious husband.) There was $120 on the meter, and he threw in a $50 tip. *That* was a big night for me.

There were other ways, of course, to add to a night's tips. Guys that got into the cab looking for some action—mainly women—were taken to this strip club named The Place Pigale. When I brought a man there, the doorman threw me $15-$20, and believe me, they got it back and then some. Guys like me that drove a cab were part of a kind of brotherhood. We were all made up of every kind of walk of life you could think of: losers, deadbeats, loners, and divorcees, guys who couldn't get a job anywhere else, and degenerate gamblers that had lost it all and now were driving through the night to fight off loneliness. We were all part of this dysfunctional club where meetings were held every night. When a dispatcher's calls slowed down, we picked a hotel on the strip and pulled into the cab stand, taking our rightful place in line. Then, like family arriving for the holidays, we piled out of our cars and bullshit for the next hour, or however long it was, until getting a fare. The stories would go on and on. "I got a $40 fare from this broad just last night. She had tremendous tits, and if I didn't have another call, I would have done her in the back seat," one might say.

"Yeah, well I got stiffed at the airport by these two chinks," another might lament.

I got tired of hearing about their wives or ex-wives and who did what to whom. For me, it was just a way to keep myself afloat.

Late one evening, as I was bringing the cab in for the night, a strange sensation came over me. My heart started to pound, then palpitate, which bought on hyperventilating. I didn't know what the hell was happening. I thought I was having a heart attack. It finally subsided, but continued for nearly a week. I finally went to see a doctor, who dismissed it as "stress" and prescribed valium. Then, without seeing me ever again, kept renewing the prescription for years. It appeared, from that point on, I was hooked.

I was busting my ass, wondering where it was all going to lead. The desire was there to make something of myself, but everything was so uncertain. *What if none of this worked?*

I was lucky enough to land an on air weekend shift at WGBS, another Miami AM powerhouse. I'm sure that the suck factor on my sound and presentation was high.

WFUN logo with Jefferson Stone.

There was also this little radio station, WHMS-FM, that operated out of a warehouse that sold their time for people who wanted to get on the air. I *paid them* about $20 every Saturday night for the privilege of having a place to suck for three hours. My friend, Jeff Cahn, found out about it and called in one night to be on the show with me. He taped it and sent me the cassette. I have it somewhere, but I'm afraid to listen to it. Trust me. It's bad.

One night while driving home and scanning around the radio dial in the car, I happened to hear the most unusual personality, Jefferson Stone, on WFUN. Of course, it wasn't his *real* name. Very few DJs used their own names on the air. They traveled like nomads going from station to station, state to state, and changed their on air names at the next gig. Harry Chapin's hit, "WOLD," is true to life. Jefferson Stone's voice was bizarre but commanding. From the sound of his voice, I thought he was a big Black guy. I started listening to his show every night, marveling how he broke the typical formula most jocks used. Stone didn't do the typical "Time and Temperature," rather peppering his show with crazy bits, sweat hog jokes (aimed at fat women), and total irreverence. I started calling him doing my own voices. There was Bruce, the hairdresser (who later became Rusty Hinge, the doorman), Harvey, the truck driver, Old Jewish guys, Jack Benny, Ed Sullivan, and the list went on. Stone seemed to have the same sense of humor that I had, loved the voices, and put them right on the air. This continued for weeks. Here's a typical call:

JS: It has been called to my attention that I have not answered the telephone tonight. Do that right now. Good evening. WFUN radio, may I help you?

Bruce the Hairdresser: Oh, is this—is this—oh, I don't believe I have you. Is it? Oh Oh, Mary, I have him. Is this Jefferson Stone?

JS: Yes it is.

Bruce: It's Bruce the Hairdresser.

JS: Bruce?

Bruce: How are you? I listen to your show every night, and you are—you have such—oh, is such a masculine show.

JS: (laughing) Thank you.

Bruce: Oh, it's everything. It's definite—if anything compared—oh, it's masculine!

JS: Oh, you say the nicest things.

One night, I suggested to Stone that we meet. After he got off the air around 10:00 p.m., I met him at Wolfie's 21 on 21st street and Collins. Wolfie's was a great joint. It was open 24 hours a day, and had the best coffee you ever tasted. As soon as your ass hit the stool, no matter what you ordered, they put a basket of fresh rolls in front of you. I could spend 30¢ on a cup of coffee and, with the free refills and the rolls, it was a meal. There were many lean nights when that was all I could afford. I waited outside for this Stone guy to show up. I had no idea what to expect. He showed up wearing a very bizarre full rubber mask of a bald guy with a giant scar running across the top of his head. The mask was modeled by Don Post of Hollywood after the B movie actor, Tor Johnson. Tor Johnson was portrayed in Johnny Depp's film, *Ed Wood* (1994). Sometime later, this mask would serve me well on television. Stone took the mask off, and I saw that he was this big, heavily tanned White guy with the wildest hair I've ever seen. I found out his real name was Tim Ingstad. I also found out that his brother was a famous Los Angeles radio personality named Shadoe Stevens, who went on to *Hollywood Squares* and *Dave's World*. Tim and I hit it off, and spent what seemed like hours talking in the restaurant. He kept telling me how great I was, how funny the voices were, and that I should have my own radio show. It was a revelation that someone was actually telling me that I had talent, because up to that point, nobody ever did.

"If I ever get into a position where I'm a program director at a radio station, I'm going to hire you," he said.

Sure, sure, when is that going to be? I thought. I wasn't going to hold my breath. I continued to do voices for his show, even going up to the station to perform stuff live. (Some years ago, I found tapes of those bits and listened to them. Some were still funny. Comedy has a tendency to lose punch over the years. What we thought was hysterical thirty years ago might not hold true today.)

KIKX album cover.

Chapter 12

Tucson? With the Horse Shit and Hitching Posts?

Shortly after I met Tim Ingstad aka Jefferson Stone, he got fired and left that radio market.

Well, that's the end of that. I thought. *Probably never hear from him again.*

Yet, in about five months, sure enough, I got a phone call from him. He was now the program director of a radio station and wanted me to come in and do the morning show.

THE MORNING SHOW? MY OWN SHOW? "Wow, uh yeah, where are you? Chicago? Los Angeles? New York?

"No, Tucson Arizona."

KIKX album inside.

Update
By Jonathan Hall
FCC Denies KIKX In Continuing "Kidnap" Case

It's been almost five years since KIKX/Tuscon staged a kidnapping hoax involving the mysterious disappearance of jock Arthur "Crazy Man" Gopen. Apparently the station had created the promotion/contest to cover several days that Gopen, a highly rated morning man, would be away from the station. It was so convincing, however, that it aroused the interest of the local police and had be be called off.

In an initial decision, an FCC judge said the station's owner, John Walton of El Paso, should forfeit the license because of his abdication of responsibility. The judge also noted Walton's failure to make sure that his EEO policy had been implemented prior to including it in his renewal application in 1974.

KIKX kidnapping, Washington Report.

"Tucson Arizona? What, are you kidding?" All I could picture about Tucson was a bunch of shit kickers, a horse tied to a post, and a saloon with two swinging doors. I told him, "Thanks, but no thanks."

Tim was persuasive. "Just come out here and check it out. If you don't like what you see, don't take the job, and I'll pay for everything."

I thought, *Hell what do I have to lose? It's a free trip to shit kicker USA, why not?*

Well, I must say, I was pleasantly surprised. It wasn't the backward town I thought it would be. It was modern, quaint, and the weather was great, sunny, and warm most of the year.

I took the job at KIKX radio and went on the air immediately. The studios consisted of two mobile homes situated on the top of a small mountain. Two trailers! One was used for the studios, the other was used as the sales office. A total shit dump, but who cared? I was young, and I was told to do whatever I wanted on the air. I had free reins—no rules! Back then, when they called us a DJ (disc jockey) there was a reason for it. We had to cue up a 45 rpm record disc on the turntable, and then get another one ready on the other turntable. (Today, it's done with CDs, MP3s, and computer files.)

I decided to go on the air as the single personality called "The Original Crazyman of The Radio." (I use that voice and character to this day.) It was the same voice I used for Sam Shmogie, Mort Ziggy, and Mad Malcolm the mean pirate years before. The Crazyman was the wildest, most bizarre, out of control personality anyone ever heard. I was "on" all the time. When I say I was "on", I mean every time I opened the mic, insanity flowed out. With the good came the bad, as well, all blended together like an amazing stew that people chewed on every morning. A million sound effects, a million bits, and no respect for the rules. I would go from The Crazyman voice to a dozen other voices with no rhyme or reason. I once played the same song—all morning long—just to bust people's balls. When listeners called in and made multiple requests, I routinely broke the records on the air if I didn't like the artist, or I just did that to stir controversy. The two songs I made the most fun of at the time were "Seasons in the Sun" (1974) by Terry Jacks and "Billy Don't be a Hero" (1975) by Bo Donaldson and the Heywoods. One day, both songs were requested, so, in the interest of time, I played them at the same time all the way till the end. People loved it, plus The Crazyman voice was so bizarre, nobody could figure out what I looked like. We ran a contest once to draw what listeners thought The Crazyman looked like, then took one of the listener's sketches and used it on all of our bumper stickers and T-shirts.

In the first three months, the morning show was a smash. Tim and I took an insignificant crap dump AM radio station with no ratings and very few listeners to #1 virtually overnight. I don't know if I was any good on the air, or maybe I was just so damned bizarre on the air, that people couldn't help but to listen, in the same way you slow down to see a car crash on the road.

Some years ago, I found a tape of me on KIKX and, against my better judgment, I listened to it. I thought it was awful and never listened to it again. Tim assured me that I was brilliant. We took over the town. Every kid and their parents suddenly made KIKX a household name. I was the ringleader with absolutely no restrictions. How could I have? My boss was also my best friend. He was also as crazy as I was, where every insane idea was immediately implemented.

KIKX was a heady time for me, my first taste of fame, and I drank it all in. I'm not particularly proud of some things I did, but with youth, there's plenty of stupidity to go around.

I terrorized the entire staff. There was this guy in sales who we called "Big Red," a real Dumbo with flaming red hair, who used to come into work wearing skin-tight pants revealing every fat roll. He walked into the sales trailer every day swinging a chain around and whistling. Nobody really liked him because he was always full of himself and gave everybody a hard time. In reality, he probably was deeply insecure.

One morning, before Big Red came in, I had a long break on the air. I also had to go to the bathroom. I ran into the sales trailer, found his desk, opened a drawer, took a dump in it, and closed it.

Later on that morning, he arrived and discovered the gift. He ran screaming into the other trailer to see Tim. "Somebody, took a shit in my desk! I want to know who it was!"

Tim listened patiently and vowed to get to the bottom of it, but he *knew* it was me. Who else would do such a thing but The Crazyman. Nothing I could do got me in trouble. Every new stunt I pulled just got a laugh and approval from Tim. On the show, my goal was to wait until my newsman was on the air, then do things to make him lose concentration or crack up, as I did repeatedly with Alan Young. Alan was an easygoing man, who liked a good laugh, but didn't know what he was getting into. From the moment he started on the air, my attempts to derail him began. I figured out a way to send sound effects only to his headphones and punctuated the end of his stories with farts, air horns, and pig grunts, hoping he would crack up before he started the next item. I went into his studio while he was on the air and lit his copy on fire. Alan tried to be composed, continuing the story as he frantically attempted to put out the fire. The news came over the teletype machine, punched out like a typewriter on long rolls of attached paper. I broke off what must have been an 8-foot piece of paper that had folds in it every foot. I spread it out in my studio and drew a giant 8-foot cock on it and then waited until Alan started his broadcast. I brought the giant dick into his studio and slowly moved each 1-foot piece in front of him on his desk until he saw that it was a giant penis. He lost it, laughing all the while trying to get through the copy.

After a while, Alan built up a tolerance to my stunts and was able to keep a straight face while on the air. I tried everything, but nothing worked. I had to resort to the ultimate. I waited until he was on the air and, once again, I took a paper plate, dropped a deuce on it, went into his studio, and slid it in front of him. Tim, who wasn't at the station at the time, told me that he was listening to his newscast when all of a sudden Alan paused and said, "I think I'm going to throw up," and then there was nothing but dead air.

All this newfound fame brought women. There was at least one giant sex party that I knew of, and the station saw a parade of groupies constantly coming through the front door. Very few people knew what I looked like. We deliberately kept my identity under wraps. We thought it added to The Crazyman's mystique if nobody actually knew what he looked like, but the women I allowed into my inner circle knew me intimately. People came into the air trailer's small lobby when I was on the couch under a blanket screwing some girl. Nobody thought anything of it, and just smirked and walk by.

Everyone was so intoxicated with the station's giant ratings that nobody said a word about any of the other stuff going on. We were completely out of control, and on the air, we just sounded like a giant party.

Tim not only was the Program Director but also did the afternoon drive show. One time, he was talking to some groupie on the phone when, unbeknownst to him, the call went out over the air. Thousands of people heard him ask, "What's the matter with you,

you cunt?" The phones lit up with irate listeners, and Tim called me into the office to tell me what happened and that management wanted to hear the tape. Back in those days, a documenter was always running. This was a special tape machine that recorded what went out over the air 24 hours day.

I told Tim, "Don't worry. I'll fix it."

"How the hell you going to fix it?"

"Simple. I'll get the tape, and I'll edit out the bad word you said and insert one that's allowed."

In my own voice, I replaced "You cunt" with "You runt." The only problem was, Tim had this very deep ballsey voice. Mine was four octaves higher. It didn't really work, but management let it slide.

The rest of the air staff were as quirky as I was. We had Nasty Norman, and The Benevolent Bill Freeman, who spend his entire shift farting in the studio, and Randy Lane and Chuck Jackson. I was having the time of my life, and making $250 a week. The problem was, I was still married to Jane, and she was back in Florida waiting for me to come back and help move all of our things to Arizona. So, all of us at the station had a meeting, and agreed that, because of the show's success, I couldn't just open the mic and tell listeners that I had to go back to Miami to get my wife and my dresser. Too boring, especially for The Crazyman. No! We had to come up with some kind of bit, some promotion, something to keep the listeners tuned in. What we came up with was so wrong, so illegal, so . . . well let's just say that the FBI was called in to investigate.

It seemed like overnight that KIKX jumped a million rating points in the first rating period. *How the hell could I leave the air now?* I had no choice, had to get my affairs in order, and Jane was still back in Florida. We all sat down and cooked up what we thought was a great scheme to retain the listener's interest while I was away. I was going to do a remote broadcast from a local stereo shop, my first appearance in public since I started. Coupled with the morning show's enormous popularity, you could imagine, from the listener's viewpoint, there was a great interest as to what the hell I looked like, but I thought keeping my identity a secret was the better way to go. It's the mystery that makes life interesting. I asked

Tim if he had another one of those bizarre rubber masks he was wearing when he met me in Miami Beach. He did, and I borrowed the mask. I bought a black turtleneck shirt, and I bought an old beat up trench coat from the Salvation Army. One problem existed: I had to speak on the air, and the mask covered my entire head including the mouth. I cut the mouth out, and now I could talk using my real mouth! The Crazyman, at least visually, took form! The plan was simple and, in theory, clever. I was to do the remote, get finished, and quietly go to the airport to fly back to Florida. Meanwhile, the station was going to say that I disappeared. I was going to call into the station the next morning to tell everyone that I was alright, that I woke up on a beach somewhere, that I didn't know how I got there, and that I was driving back to Tucson. I would stop in every little town along the way, and call in from that town. Then, the first listener who could list all the towns I called in from, and in the right order, would win a big prize. Great promotion in theory, right?

Unfortunately, when I finished the remote broadcast, I missed my plane. I also couldn't get out the next day because there was an issue with my credit card and I couldn't pay for the ticket. By then we had a real problem on our hands. The radio station went overboard trying to make my disappearance too real. First, they started doing news bulletins every half hour and embellishing on the facts. "The Original Crazyman was abducted against his will, and disappeared from the location of his radio remote." They went on with, "He was seen being thrown into a yellow van with California license plates. If anyone has any information as to his whereabouts, please contact the station immediately."

That's a *huge* mistake, taking an actual newscast and filling it with a bogus story. The phones started ringing off the hook. Tim and I got totally caught up in it, not realizing the can of worms we were opening. The station's General Manager was a wimp, off at a golf course somewhere, and couldn't give two shits about what was happening at the station. We started all of those announcements as soon as the remote was over, and continued to hammer away for two days!

The reaction was overwhelming. "Call the station if you have any info" turned into "Call the police if you have any info." What the hell were we thinking? We weren't. Eventually, we realized we went too far, but it was too late. All the phones at the police department were jammed with callers claiming to have seen that yellow van with The Crazyman inside. The police also fielded calls from hysterical listeners wanting to know what they were going to do about the situation. Their beloved Crazyman was kidnapped.

The police launched an investigation, and the FBI, I was told, was bought in to investigate. The FCC was also notified. Holy shit, what a mess. If this happened today, it would be all over CNN, and I most assuredly would be arrested. President Donald Trump often talked about "fake news," but we invented it. I finally *did* get out and flew to Miami. We forgot about the promotion, I gathered my things, my wife, and I came back. By the time the shit hit the fan, all media was focused on us, the local paper, tv, and national news. It was a fucking circus, but I kept doing the morning show for a while. The wheels of investigation move slowly. I was still the #1 radio personality in the market, and even back then, controversy enhanced the success.

Jane and I moved into a crumby apartment complex called Richie Gardens, but it had a pool. We lived right next door to Tim and his wife at the time, Maggie. For a while, life was good. The show was still wildly popular. I broadcast in the morning and lay out by the pool in the afternoon. We knew the boom was going to be lowered for our little stunt, but when? Tim was the program director, so he wasn't going to fire me, but he was in the same boat waiting for his fate, as well.

Meanwhile, the debauchery at the station continued. There was a bomb shelter that was buried underground with a staircase that lead off from one trailer. Routinely, the radio jocks had wild sex sessions with groupies. Nobody knew about sexually transmitted diseases back then; it wasn't an issue in 1973.

Chuck Jackson, one of our jocks, lived way out of town in a trailer in the middle of nowhere. One weekend, there was a party at his place, a gang bang with two groupies. There were no controls on any of us. My newsman, Alan Young, finally had enough and left the station.

His replacement was a peculiar little man named Paul Lotsof, a small man with glasses, who could never look anyone in the eye when shaking their hand. Paul had a great broadcast voice and was a complete pro, but he was a little weird. I always thought he could have easily landed a job at a network, he was that good.

No matter what I did, Paul never cracked up, and I tried everything in my prank kit. In town, there was a joke shop that carried this stuff called "Morning Breeze," a little bottle with 2 ounces of terrible-smelling liquid. If I just put one drop of this stuff in a room, the smell of rotten eggs was overwhelming and people had to clear out—one drop! I brought the bottle to the studio the next day.

Lotsof was doing his newscast, and he took a 2-minute commercial break, which he used to go into the little bathroom off the news studio. I ran around to his studio, opened the bottle of Morning Breeze and emptied the entire bottle into the room! Then, I ran back to my studio as if nothing has happened . . . and just waited.

Paul came back into his studio. I checked the expression on his face—nothing! *How could that be? A whole bottle of the shit? Any other human being would be gasping for air.* Lotsof did the rest of his newscast perfectly, got finished, said nothing to me or anyone else, walked from the studio and the trailer, got in his car, and drove down the hill into the sunset. We didn't hear from him for days.

Years later, I finally talked to Paul again. By then, he owned and ran a radio station in Benson Arizona. He told me, "KIKX was a mess in many ways. You'll recall that I arrived several months after the notorious kidnapping affair. I lasted maybe two weeks before I got canned. I still have the letter from "Jeff Stone" telling me that I was fired for having an unprofessional attitude. KIKX was a classic example of a company with an absentee owner, who didn't have a clue about what was going on. I don't recall who the manager was, and am not sure if I ever met him. Clearly, he was trusted, but shouldn't have been. Perhaps more amazing is that the two of you weren't fired on the spot."

I had to laugh over the irony of Tim, one of the two people responsible for the kidnapping snafu, firing Lotsof for being unprofessional!

The first celebrity interview I ever did was on Jack Benny. He was also one of the first impressions I ever did, and I'm sure I was convinced it was the best thing anyone ever heard. If truth be known, I most probably was doing my version of Rich Little's impersonation. I took a shot.

I tracked down Jack's personal manager, Irving Fein. Irving also managed the career of George Burns. I called him and left a message that I was Gary Craig and loved Jack, and that I would love to interview him. I didn't hear a word, and wrote it off. About a week later, I got a call.

"Gary? This is Irving Fein. If you call back in five minutes, Jack Benny will be at my house, and you'll be able to talk to him."

You could have scooped me up from the floor! I raced into the studio, found a tape, and spooled it onto the machine. I called back five minutes on the nose.

Irving said, "Gary, here's Jack."

I couldn't believe it. I was talking to a legend. During the interview, I informed Jack that I did an impression of him and went ahead with it, peppering my bit in his voice with the words "You see" and "You Know" after each sentence.

Jack said, "I notice you keep saying 'You see, and you know.' I don't ever say, 'You know' when I speak . . . you see?"

I played it on the air the next morning, and then stored the tape away in a box. I still have it. I am absolutely sure that the impression was bad, and that's why I haven't listened to it since the day I talked to him.

Tim and I had one thing in common: we were constantly scheming with our pie-in-the-sky ideas. We knew it was just a matter of time before our radio jobs were going to come to an end. There was a guy named Barry, who advertised on my morning show. He owned and operated clothing stores called The Joint Discount Boutiques. His ads were unconventional, because Barry was the spokesman and he talked in what sounded like a hippy in a drug-induced stupor. He was a big fat slob, but his prices were rock bottom, and he was making a fortune. Then all of a sudden out of the blue, he went out of business. Tim and I thought we could take his concept and do it even better. We decided to go into business for ourselves, but we had no idea how, where we were going to get the money, or what to do once we opened the doors.

We didn't know what the hell we were doing, but we had good ideas, and a "Fuck it, go for broke" attitude. Neither of us had two nickels to rub together. I cashed in my MasterCard and got about $1,200, and so did Tim. $2,400 to open a business! You could do it back then.

Crazyhouse discount boutique exterior.

Crazyhouse discount boutique interior.

Crazyhouse Broadway store exterior.

Crazyhouse window Congress St. store.

Tim working in Crazyhouse.

Gary and Tim working in Crazyhouse.

Crazyhouse Broadway store interior.

We rented a space on 6th Street right near the University of Arizona. The store called The Crazyhouse Discount Boutique. We rationalized, "Hey, as soon as the kids discover us, we'll be packed." The store was long and narrow. We painted every wall green. We swiped hundreds of free "Budman" stickers from a local bar and pasted them all over the walls. Then, we went to flooring stores all over town collecting carpet scraps, which we got for nothing. Getting on or hands and knees, we glued them to the floor, like a giant patchwork quilt. It was hideous, but for the time, looked pretty funky. Because the store had so much space, and we had nothing to fill it, we built this giant counter that went on forever. You were barely able to see my head above the counter. There was a pizza place right next door, so I walked over there and bought a slice, came back and glued it to the countertop. Then, we poured casting resin over it until the whole thing was encased. We had seen this technique used on tables in restaurants and bars, only those people knew what the hell they were doing. We didn't. Eventually, the slice rotted and we had to get rid of it.

Any discarded piece of junk that was still functional somehow made it into the shop's décor. Electric companies left these giant wooden spools around construction sites, so some wound up serving as racks to hang clothes. We also made racks with railroad ties.

After we rented the store, got the electricity on, and made all the shelves and dressing rooms, we didn't have a lot of money left for stock. I went down to the Lucky Supermarket—that's what it was called—they had these disgusting Hawaiian shirts they were selling for $3.99. I bought all they had, brought them back to The Crazyhouse, and re-sold them for $7.99.

Tim opened the store in the morning while I was on the air, then I got off and worked the store until early evening. What a life! What a star!

Because we were still working for the station, it was easy for us to buy commercial time to promote the new business. I remember doing live spots for the store in the morning show, touting, "Hundreds of jeans $5.99, $6.99 and $7.99. Dozens of shirts in every size!" We actually had five shirts, no pants, and a rotting slice of pizza under plastic on the counter. People walked in and said to Tim,

"Hey, where are all the jeans and shirts you advertised on the radio?" Customers said the same thing to me in the afternoon. Our stock answer was, "Oh we had a huge run, and sold nearly everything!"

What we did have was enough bullshit to go around. Eventually, we made enough money to take a buying trip to the fashion center in Los Angeles, where you walk from room to room as clothing manufactures show you their entire lines, and you buy what you think will sell. Again, we had no idea what we were doing, but seemed to always know what would sell well. One morning back at the station, I was called into Tim's office. There was some guy there I had never seen before, Chuck Dunaway, a big-time hired gun they brought in to clean up the station to show the FCC that they were taking steps to correct the obvious problems plaguing the station. They had let Tim go, and at least for the time being, Dunaway was the new Program Director. He was also a head case with his green teeth and trigger temper, just the wrong kind of guy to be in radio. He once pulled an air shift, and I observed him at least five times during his shift getting pissed off, yelling, and flinging records, cartridges, and everything against the wall.

They kept me on the air for a short time longer. Maybe they thought I wasn't really responsible for the kidnapping stunt, but whatever they were thinking, shortly after that, we all got blown out or quit. Tim and I were out of the radio business, at least for the time being. We didn't give a shit. We thought, *Hey, great, now we can concentrate on The Crazyhouse full time.*

Even though the two of us were fired from KIKX, it didn't stop me from still screwing with the radio station. KIKX had a call-in talk show on Sunday night. These days, it is standard for broadcasters to have a 7- to 10-second delay, so that in case someone says something on the air that's not acceptable, they can dump out of it before the audience hears it. I knew KIKX didn't have one. So, I call in, with a voice a little milder than my "Bruce the Hairdresser" character.

"I'd like to make a comment on your topic." I said over the phone. I started out sounding serious and sincere, but then I went into a crazy swearing rant using "mother fucker, shit, piss, fuck, cunt, cock suck, and tits."

The guy on the air did nothing to cut me off, because he was in complete shock.

When I finished and hung up, he calmly said, "That was nice."

I really miss those days of radio! (Recently, I fell down the rabbit hole on YouTube, and decided to search for KIKX. I found a news piece that was done when the station finally went dark and stopped broadcasting. By then in 1982 it was a Country station. They interviewed the jocks, who were whining about losing the station, but yet I found it curious that they never mentioned who was responsible for its demise. "Yeah, you guys can go out and cover this story, but whatever you do, don't mention that asshole Gary Craig!") We were getting a reputation around town for being brash young renegades that were willing to try anything. The business was taking off. We started having $200 days, then $300, then $500, then $600—in one day—making our heads spin. Keep in mind that I had to work all week on the radio to make $250.

Then one day, we did $1,000.00. I couldn't believe it. Tim and I ran every kind of crazy sale you could think of, and more money came in. The customers were the pawns in our little insanity play, and were subject to any crazy idea I came up with. In The Crazyman costume, I came out in a crowded store with a ladder. I climbed up to the top rung with a megaphone and announced a clothing auction. I grabbed a few shirts and auctioned them off in reverse. I auctioned the shirts off coming down in price until they went for a buck a piece. People thought I was out of my mind, but I guarantee you they told their friends.

We bought time at the local tv station and produced our own commercials. I took out a print ad that urged people to be at the store on a certain day and time and "get on tv" in one of our commercials. The entire store was packed. I always appeared in the commercials in The Crazyman mask and trench coat. The spots were wild and the talk of the town.

We were still stupid inexperienced kids, who made bad business decisions, like buying a closeout of the ugliest-looking jeans just because we could get them for a buck apiece! In the store, there was "Crazy's Tub," an old bathtub with legs on it. We filled the tub with all the reject clothing we wanted to get rid of. Years later, those idiotic jeans we paid a buck for were still on the tub's bottom collecting dust.

Tim and I, the big dreamers, were really onto something, but we had no idea on how to direct all the success we were creating. The clothes were dirt cheap because we bought them that way. Back then, when a jeans manufacturer found some of their product had a misplaced stitch or a little imperfection, they pulled those jeans off their line and called them "select irregulars" or "seconds." They then sold those to us for $2.99 a pair, and we turned around and sold them for $5.99 or $6.99 a pair. It was the same pair that was selling in all the other stores for $12.99. Students, looking for a good deal, flocked to the store to save money. (Today, you'll pay elsewhere $60.00 for a pair that is filled with imperfections.)

In the store, we had a novelty joke counter. We sold rubber vomit, fake doggy doo, shock books, booger nose, innocent-looking white soap that turned your hands black, itching powder, dribble glasses, exploding cigars, snap gum, cigarette loads, black eye telescope, and stink bombs. Stink bombs came in this little glass tube. When broken, the smell was unbearable. You could clear out a room. They sold like hotcakes, and for a good reason: people were setting them off on busses and in movie theaters. It got so bad that the city passed an ordinance to force us to stop selling stink bombs! Now what the hell did all these novelties have to do with jeans and tops? Zero. Things were going so well that we found a second location uptown near a shopping center. Bad idea. This was the beginning of the decline, in my opinion. We had big heads that were swelled with some early success, and we should have waited until we were more solvent before we grew. Our Broadway store was more professional-looking. This time, we had a counter built. The shelves were better, more railroad ties for shirt racks, and our patchwork carpet skills had improved ... but it was still schlock, and people didn't care. All they knew was they were getting a great deal on clothes. What we promised them in our ads, we delivered.

One day, we discovered a company right in town wholesaling jeans and tops. It was run by an Arab guy named Sharif. *Oh great, the Jew was now buying from the Arab!* Who cared? We were getting great deals buying jeans by the case, but there was a shit factor in that case.

5 pairs of jeans out of 80 were screwed up. One pant leg might be longer than the other, or have only half a zipper, or no pockets.

One day, Tim and I were in the store, and this guy came out of the dressing room with one of these reject pants on. I took a look at him and saw that one leg was completely too long with the material dragging on the floor, and the other leg was too short, the material falling right below his knee.

He said, "Hey man, what the hell is this shit? What kind of crap you guys selling?"

Sweat beaded on my forehead. *Shit, what am I going to tell this guy?* I thought.

Tim spoke up. "Aha! You found it!"

The guy answered, "Found it? Found what?"

"Our *gag pair* of pants! Now, you can have anything in the store half off."

The guy smiled and wound up buying a ton of clothes.

Tim and I always attracted the biggest bunch of deadbeats and losers, and we hired them. Our stores were staffed by a circus of the weird. One guy, Tim discovered sleeping on a sheet of plastic under the highway . . . we hired him. His name was Chris. Every day, he came in reeking of body odor and old clothing because he had no place to shower. Eventually, he made enough money to rent an efficiency apartment and actually bathed.

Then, there was Fat Tony, who came to work with about 2 pounds of grease in his hair. He was a gem. Anytime Tim and I bought something for ourselves, Fat Tony got pissed that we didn't buy him the same thing. Psycho.

There was also Ida and Rosie, the twin sisters with the huge tits. They didn't last long. They were doing alright until the day they baked Tim and I some brownies but failed to tell me that ingredient's included hashish! I was stoned for two days, and I made Tim fire them.

One day in May 1975, I was in the Broadway store, and in walked this knockout in a tiny little tank top, long brown hair, tight pants, and a great tan. She was looking for a job. Any experience? Nope. Did I care? Nope. Tim and I hired her on the spot. Her name was

Stephanie, and not too long after she started working for us, she became my second wife.

We were in a position of power. Everyone knew us. We indulged in whatever came our way. All the radio stations dealt with us even though we were off the air. Radio salesman came around trying to sell us advertising, but we couldn't be snowed, because we knew all the tricks.

Tim had a girlfriend named Maggie, a knockout blonde. After a while, Stephanie and I became more than boss and employee, and the four of us hung out together. I dated Steph for over three months before she found out that I was still married to Jane. That marriage was all but over, and I was looking for any kind of a way out.

Meanwhile, we were workaholics. We wanted to be so successful that we devoted our lives to it, at the cost of anyone else in our lives, at the time.

One day, I walked into the store and Tim said, "Look at these, they're great!"

"What are they?" I asked.

"They're giant weather balloons,"

"Yeah, so?"

"We'll get 'em, we'll fill them up with helium, and fly them over the store to attract customers."

"That's a stupid idea," I said

"No, this could be nuts." Tim continued, "Could you imagine a giant black balloon about 30 feet in diameter floating above the store? People will be driving and point and say, 'Geez, what the hell is that? Pull over!"

"So, you think people are going to come into the store because we have a couple of stupid fucking balloons flying above the roof?" I countered.

"You don't know what you're talking about. I'm telling you, this is great."

In the ensuing days, he didn't give up on his quest to convince me that it was a brilliant promotional idea. After days of hammering away at me, I finally relented and agreed, but I said, "We can't afford renting helium tanks."

Tim answered, "That's okay. We'll go down to the helium place and inflate them there. That way, we're only going to be charged for the exact amount of helium we use. It will only coast us a fraction!"

I was still skeptical. "Really? And how the hell will we get the balloons back to the store?"

"No problem. We'll just tie them to the bumpers of our cars with rope, and drive back."

At the time, we had the limo and a Luv Truck. Again, two idiots. What the hell were we thinking? This could only end badly. So, we got down to the helium supply place and had them blow them up. They were GIANT. Tim tied his balloon to the limo's back, while I stood there and watched him drive away. I decided I wanted to have more control of it, so I got into the truck, rolled down my driver's window, pulled inside the cab all the rope tied to the balloon, pulled the balloon tightly up against the door, and then started to drive away. Of course, we were driving about 7 miles an hour, because we didn't want anything to happen to the balloons. Tim was in front of me in the limo. His balloon started moving back and forth, more and more, faster and faster, until eventually it started to hit the road on either side like a clock pendulum! I was right behind him in the Luv Truck desperately holding on to my balloon through the driver's window, like a giant growth from the truck. Our cars at one point were driving through the poor part of town and people were coming out of their houses to watch us go by. They thought it was some kind of parade. With each hit of the balloon off Tim's bumper, I could just feel the thing about to explode any minute. Eventually, I slowed way down, and Tim went ahead of me. In route, a motorcycle rider came up alongside me, and I don't know exactly what happened, but the giant weather balloon filled with helium exploded and knocked the cyclist off the road. I stopped. He wasn't hurt, just shaken up.

I got back to the store, and there was Tim, grinning like an idiot. I asked, "Where's the balloon?"

"Exploded."

"You asshole! We spent all that money or those damn things . . . we just should have rented the fucking tanks!"

We were doing pretty good, making more money than we ever dreamed about, but we had no business savvy at all. The "Ah, what the hell, let's go for broke" theory got us pretty far up to the point where we wanted to add another store in addition to the one near the University of Arizona and the one uptown. We chose Sierra Vista, a little one-horse nightmare about an hour's drive away. That was a mistake.

Tim walked in one day and informed me he had found our next location.

"Next location? Wait a minute who needs another location? We're doing fine right now, so why change anything?"

"Hey, you want to be a chain? Then, ya gotta go for broke."

It was the going for broke part that worried me. We went downtown to look at this empty store. Downtown Tucson was a horrific shit hole. Old stores, hookers, and wino piss. The rent was really cheap because the giant cavernous space had sat there for a long time. It became store #4. Off we went with the patchwork crap carpet, Budman stickers, the railroad ties, and any other bizarre garbage we could nail to the walls. We filled the display windows with mannequins wearing horror masks, cigars in their mouths, and chains hanging around their necks. Yes, now there's a clothing store you'd really want to walk into! But oddly enough, the people came.

Our bookkeeping methods sucked. We had no accurate system to keep track of everything. The cash registers we used looked like they were from World War Two. We found an old retired accountant, who could barely see, to do our books, and we kept rolling on. Every Friday, Tim and I took a draw, whatever we wanted, $700, $800, maybe $900 in cash, a lot of money back then. Every morning, we were at the bank depositing the cash from the day before. We walked in, sat down at a table, and started counting and stacking up the cash. I know people were looking at us and thinking, *Who the hell are these young assholes?* We dressed like slobs and laughed at everyone else. The money kept rolling in. The bank was completely enamored with us. We were the golden boys, performing all of our financial wizardry every day, except we didn't know which end was up. We operated strictly on our gut. If only we had someone who could have guided us, advised us, and given us some business sense, there's no doubt that I probably would have become a multi-millionaire.

One morning driving from one store to another, Tim and I passed a car lot, where two beautiful Lincoln Mark Vs were sitting out front, one white, the other silver. The price for the cars were $8,000 each. The next day at the bank, we told them we need $16,000 *cash*. By the afternoon, they called us to come in, sign, and pick up the money. That easy. No credit check, and very little paperwork. Amazing and scary that we had that kind of power, but we didn't have a clue what we were doing.

Two luxury cars, four stores, money coming in like crazy. Life was good. We were still shuttling customers in the limo to the stores if they promised to spend a certain amount. Even with all of this, we were always behind. Bad bookkeeping meant we were always understocked, and borrowing from Peter to pay Paul. Just as one store was getting well-stocked, we opened another location and took half the stock away to fill the new store. Spread too thin. On top of all that, we were spending money like it was going out of style.

Then there was pizza. We became friends with the owner and family of the pizza joint right next door to the Crazy House Boutique on 6th Street. When business was slow, we hung out with the owner's son "Chuckie." He was always ready with a joke or a story that he peppered with "Fuckin, Shit, AND Mutha F*@%!ER." hanging around a pizza place with the guy who's running it hardly made us an expert in the business, but that never stopped any of our other ventures.

There was a shopping plaza right outside the University of Arizona, just steps away from the school. One day, we noticed a space upstairs that seemed to have our name on it. We imagined that our crazy approach to business, and the way we promoted, would have customers lined up and down the stairs. So, we rented the space, used the giant wooden spools as tables, with plain wooden chairs around them. We hired some funky carpenter to build us a counter, and nailed all kinds of weird junk to the walls. It looked like a museum of crap. Every time we went to a garage sale or a swap meet, we found some artifact that wound up on the walls at

At New York City Pizza, artist Bruce Humphrey did all of our artwork.

Gary working in New York City Pizza.

New York City Pizza. Following the decorating of our walls with junkyard gems, we outfitted the kitchen with all used equipment.

Sitting in the space one day, scratching our heads trying to figure out how a Jew and a Viking were going to open a pizza restaurant, in walked Pete Straface, an imposing, grey-haired man, who looked like a character from *The Godfather* (1972). "I understand you guys are opening a pizza place, and wondered if you needed any help."

Are you kidding? we thought. *We don't know shit about making pizza or even running a restaurant.*

Mr. Straface guided us through every aspect of the operation. All the recipes, how to make the food, how to store it, menu selection, buying supplies, every possible detail. What were the chances that some guy that knew the business inside and out would walk thru the door to help two guys that were completely lost? But here's the strange part: Pete was there for two weeks, and he left before we could give him his paycheck. He walked out the door and disappeared. We tried to track him down, with no success. We finally contacted the Social Security Administration. Pete Straface did not exist. Tim still thinks he was some kind of "Pizza Angel" sent down to help us.

Crazyman tv show with beans on head.

Crazyman tv show on the set.

Crazyman on camera.

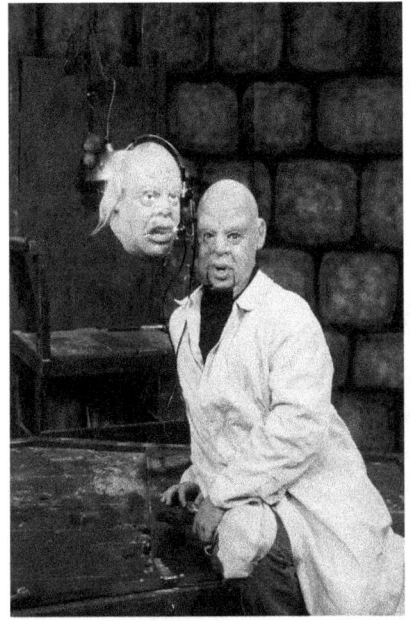
Crazyman with Streamline.

Crazyman with Streamline.

Crazyman tv show Streamline on dark set.

Crazyman telling war stories.

Chapter 13

The Crazyman tv Show

In 1974, always looking for a creative and unique way to promote the stores, we decided that The Crazyman needed his own television show. We approached KVOA tv, the NBC affiliate, and made a deal to buy airtime outright. Every Saturday night, *The Crazyman Show* would follow *Saturday Night Live*. What a lead in! The premise was that The Crazyman, because of his crimes against humanity, would be sentenced to spend the rest of his life in a dungeon with an electric chair, a coffin, an idiot door, an old radio, and a warden, who he didn't see but would talk to off camera.

I modeled the dungeon after what Charlie Baxter did with M.T. Graves. We needed stone walls, but we had very little money, so we made the set ourselves by stretching white sheets over wooden frames and spray painted the sheets to look like a stone wall. In fact, we built all the props on the set.

The tv station ran an old sci-fi movie or horror movie, and The Crazyman came on during the breaks. Since we paid for and owned all the air time, we just used the commercial breaks to advertise our stores. Special guests made appearances and were promptly fried in the electric chair.

On any given Saturday night, viewers saw live goats running around the set, the Mayor of Tucson showing up, or some sexy bombshell. The Crazyman got bulletins and news stories on the old radio.

KVOA never knew what the hell to expect out of me, but one week I really pissed them off. I was talking to the character known as the Warden, and every time I used a word that could also mean some kind of food, that food was dropped on my head. "Warden, I've got this honey of an idea...."

The Warden said, "Did you say, Honey?"

Tim, who was on a ladder out of camera frame, started drizzling honey on my head.

The Crazy Man looked up at the ceiling and said, "Warden! Are you trying to egg me on?"

Next, raw eggs were dumped on my head.

The Crazyman cried, "I've been a little depressed."

The Warden answered, "Did you say *bean*, Crazy?"

With that, Tim dumped a giant can of beans in sauce on my head. That entire disgusting mixture slid down my chest and got onto the lavaliere mic I was wearing, so we had to stop taping, clean it up, and try it again. On the second take, we just shit-canned the whole script because we knew it was going to get messy and might not have another chance to finish the segment.

I just starting doing a trivia contest, and as I was going through the paces, beans were dropped on my head, and then the empty can hit me in the head, then fresh eggs, and then he added bird seed, and to top it all off, a giant can of honey. This time, when all of that crap hit the mic, it ruined it. It actually muffled the sound! We got the take, but the station was ripped because the mic was ruined. They made us pay for it, and it wasn't cheap. (There is a video of this exact scene on YouTube.)

Stephanie's brother, Phillip, was an electronic genius. He could have emerged as one of the great inventors. I brought him an idea one day. "Phil, what if I gave you one of these masks, could you figure out a way we could make the mouth move while it's on the set?"

The result of his invention was genius. "Streamline," as the head would be called, came down on a set of invisible wires from the ceiling. Not only did the mouth move, but the eyes lit up and the head was able to smoke a cigarette! It was wild.

We put The Crazyman on camera doing some bit, and all of a sudden Streamline came down right next to his face and had a conversation with him, which was voiced live off camera by Phil. In fact, Phil operated the whole thing. Of course, Disney would become famous for doing exactly what Phil had done with their Animatronics in their theme parks.

Our show became a cult hit quickly. Based on the amount of mail that was coming in, I knew everyone was watching The Crazy Man on Saturday nights. We could have taken the concept nationally if we had the wherewithal.

Eventually, the show ran its course and we planned the final episode. The Warden called down at the show's beginning to tell The Crazyman that there might be a slim chance he would be released. We milked it all throughout the movie, until the last segment. As The Crazyman had all his belongings rolled up in a cloth at the end of a stick, he said goodbye to the dungeon that was his home all these years. The Beatles song, "The Long and Winding Road," started playing, as the camera pulled back slowly to show him walking out, then followed him through the production studio to an open garage door that led down a grassy path into the sun. The camera followed me until the song ended and I was out of sight. We were told later that tons of people at bars that Saturday night, who routinely watched the show, lifted a glass in a toast to The Crazyman. Years later, I was cleaning out my office and found some VHS tapes I had forgotten. Among them was a tape marked "KVOA." On it was lost footage of the original Crazyman show. I put up a few segments on YouTube, including the bean-egg-and honey episode. I started to get emails from fans wanting to know if the show was coming back. So, as a lark, I produced some new episodes for viewing on the Internet. They can be seen at www.crazymantv.com. So, far, I haven't been able to launch the concept nationally, but with a few changes, I'm hoping that I will. This time, The Crazyman is in a mental hospital, and the Warden is replaced by a head doctor that he talks to.

At this point, I'd been out of radio for some time, but radio was always a good catalyst for us to promote our businesses. Tim wasn't going anywhere, and at that time he wasn't interested in getting back on the air. I approached KHYT, an AM daytime radio station that signed off at sunset. The station was owned and operated by Bob Scholz, a piggish, obese man with yellow teeth that were a result of his chain-smoking every waking moment. I remember the first time I met him, everything about him was filthy, his teeth, his hair, and even the dirt on the rim of his pants pockets from his hands going in and out, but he liked to laugh and was enamored by people who could accomplish that.

KHYT was another crap dump radio station, but Bob was doing a morning show with a guy named Bill Adams, who owned a sign

THE ARIZONA DAILY STAR
A new era for 'Crazy Man'

By DAVID HATFIELD
The Arizona Daily Star

Get ready, Tucson radio listeners. Personalities are on their way at KHYT and Arthur G. Gopen is in the forefront.

Who is Arthur G. Gopen, you ask?

A few years ago he was known to listeners as Gary Craig or "The Crazy Man" when he was on KIKX and an earlier stint on KHYT.

But those days are past and Gopen says he'd just as soon forget them.

He doesn't like to talk about the January 1974 promotional stunt at KIKX where he was to pretend he was kidnaped, which has led to a raft of problems that station still is having with the Federal Communications Commission. Gopen leaves one with the impression that he feels he got a bum rap.

Saturday morning he begins what he hopes is a new era in his radio career on KHYT. His show will be on from 7 to 10 a.m. Saturdays and from 11 a.m. to 3 p.m. Sundays.

Part of the new Gopen radio personality is to use his real name.

"I feel the Crazy Man was a personality who was right for that time," Gopen said. "But here (at KHYT) the goal is to appeal to a more adult audience so there won't be any yelling and screaming."

He will continue doing impressions of famous voices and he says he has added people such as President Carter to his repertoire. Short comedy sketches will also still be a part of his radio show.

Bob Scholz, general manager of KHYT, says "People will probably think I'm crazy for putting him (Gopen) on

Gopen   Scott

the air but I think he has developed his personality to a point that he will now appeal to our listeners."

Gopen won't be the only change as KHYT seeks to further develop its personalities. The popular early morning show with Scholz and his partner Bill Adams will be expanded to three hours and begin an hour earlier at 6 a.m. beginning Monday.

Also added to the early morning show will be local newscasts by John C. Scott, who will continue to co-anchor the newscasts at KZAZ, Channel 11.

Scholz' announcement comes on the heels of word earlier this week that KHOS is dropping its country music format to become a personality station, but he said he had been working on the changes before learning of KHOS' plans.

Regardless, it's an exciting prospect to think that radio in Tucson is coming alive again. Too many stations have succumbed to formats in which all of the disc jockeys sound alike.

TUCSON CITIZEN
Controversial disc jockey returning to air on KHYT

By RICK PODGONSKI
Citizen TV-Radio Writer

Banished from the crazy quilt of Tucson radio for the past three years due to a kidnaping hoax broadcast on radio station KIKX, disc jockey Arthur G. Gopen, alias "Crazy Man" Gary Craig, returns to the airwaves this Saturday at 7 a.m. on radio station KHYT.

The hoax involved a KIKX promotion in which Gopen was reportedly kidnaped during a weekend visit to Miami, Fla. The FCC nearly cited the station for misrepresenting information to the public and, as a result of the hoax and subsequent reported broadcast violations, KIKX is still very much in danger of losing its broadcast license.

The most immediate result of the incident was the firing of Gopen and his subsequent inability to find work within the Tucson broadcast community. During the past three years, he has owned and closed four clothing stores and one pizza parlor. Currently, he drives a Yellow Cab, a job he will retain while jocking on KHYT.

Gopen is, in fact, an original and multi-talented radio personality whose program will be more variety show than straight disc jockey stint. In addition to playing the pop music that is KHYT's fare, Gopen will do impressionistic (Jack Benny to Jimmy Carter) character voices (a 98 pound weakling?), and features such as calls "Idiot Ladies," "The Arthur G. Gopen 98 Second Theatre," and the "Occasionally Accurate News."

Asked what he, of all Tucson broadcasters, hoped to get out of "Crazy Man" to justify giving him a second chance, KHYT's innovative and independent general manager Bob Scholz replied, "He's going to give us his talent. I think he basically has more raw talent than any person on the air."

Scholz added, "Now, a lot of people will think we're all crazy here. The fact is that, at a station that broadcasts only during the day, these personalities and special features give people a real reason to tune in to."

Gopen, whose show will be heard Monday through Friday from noon until 3 p.m. and on Saturday from 7 a.m. until 10 a.m., will be a guest on the "Dr. Leonard Lomax Show" on KHYT this Thursday evening to discuss the KIKX hoax and his earlier radio plans. Call-in questions from the listening audience will be entertained.

Reincarnated
Arthur G. Gopen

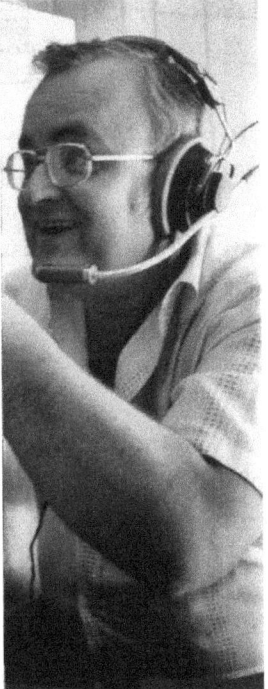

Bob Scholz owner of KHYT.

Steven C. Brown. Shortly after this picture, he started at KYHT.

company but had no experience in radio. Their morning show, *Adams and Scholz*, consisted of Bob being cracked up by Adams in-between the songs, news, and commercials, and I think they actually enjoyed some ratings success.

I saw Bob about doing the afternoon show. He agreed to have me on the air, but not as Gary Craig. I guess he was concerned with what negative attention the name would attract considering the KIKX debacle. So, I wound up using my real name, Arthur G. Gopen. What a terrible air name, but he insisted.

Michael Cassutt was a young 23-year-old Program Director at the time. "Gary was notorious before he joined KHYT, and owner Bob Scholz was convinced it was a race between ratings gain and destruction. But what the hell, we were a 500-watt daytime operation who would have done just about anything to put ourselves on the map, such as it was."

I worked at the store in the morning, and went off to do the radio show in the afternoon. One jock doing mid-days was Steven C Brown. We kicked off a friendship immediately and started a history of pranking each other. When Steve was on the air, he was behind the board looking out toward the lobby, but the panel on the board's other side was open, revealing all the wires and plugs. I stood by the open panel and started up some kind of inane bullshit conversation with him right before he was to go on. While he was distracted, I disconnected the mic cable and calmly walked into the next studio to listen to his show open. He hit the jingle, opened his mic to talk, and nothing came out. I was in the next studio doubled over laughing my ass off, as he ran around to the board's front and tried to reconnect the mic.

The next day, he got me back. I was getting ready to go on. I cued up a record on the turntable, which had three speeds, 78 rpm, 45 rpm, and 33⅓ rpm. I don't know how he managed this, but he placed the speed at 78 rpm. I did the top of the hour I.D., I hit a jingle, opened my mic, and hit the record. The song was now on live but sounding like Alvin and the Chipmunks. I actually had to shift it down to the right speed, which sounded even worse. I raced from the studio and chased him down the hall screaming, "You fuck! I'll kill you!"

I was always doing things to piss Bob Scholz off, and I don't think he ever really trusted me on the air, but I was so well-known that I think he resigned himself to just letting me just do my thing in exchange for some excitement on his station.

KHYT had to sign off at sundown, a directive from the Federal Communications Commission (FCC) that couldn't be monkeyed with, or they risked losing their license. Because Scholz didn't know what I would do at the broadcast day's end, he assigned a part-time DJ by the name of Michael Cornelius to baby sit me and actually be in charge of shutting the signal down. Cornelius was part Iroquois Indian, a fact that he readily shared with me. That was a mistake. After I found out, I was constantly busting his balls. I think I gave him an Indian headdress one day as a gift. Every day at sundown, there was Cornelius in the studio getting ready to play the announcement, "At this time KHYT 1330 is going off the air. Join us tomorrow morning at sunrise." He then hit the switch and that would be it. One day, during my air shift, I took an audio cart dubbed on it Paul Revere and the Raider's "Indian Reservation," then switched the cart labels with the sign-off announcement. Cornelius went to hit the sign-off, and the song started playing on the air. I just sat there smiling.

Scholz, who always listened for the sign-off, called the station yelling, "What the fuck is going on down there?"

Cornelius screamed, "Where's the cart? Where's the right cart?"

The next day, when I told Scholz what I'd one, he cracked up, then added, "Just don't do it again."

That wasn't the stunt that pissed him off the most. Now that I was on the station, I was able to buy radio time at bottom rates, which was nearly nothing. Tim and I were routinely in the production studio putting together Crazy House commercials. Late one night, trying to come up with an idea for a holiday commercial, I asked, "Why don't we take the tune, "Frosty the Snowman," and I'll rewrite the lyrics and have Crazyman sing it?"

"Great!" he said. "Let's do it."

I wrote a few lines and we started to record, but our innocent idea for a spot got out of hand. When sung to the tune of "Frosty the Snowman," this is how the commercial was going to sound:

Crazy House Boutique,
has jeans and tops galore,
and for every buck that you spend with us,
you'll be getting lots lots more.
We've lowered our prices,
so you won't feel the pinch,
Bank Americard and Master Charge
makes shopping here a cinch.

That was supposed to be it, and then Tim was going to tag the spot with the address, but as I was recording, the music, of course, continued, so I started to just ad lib lyrics that didn't rhyme and made no sense, and that went on for another 3 minutes. After I shut the mic, the two of us were hysterical. Since Scholz was doing the morning show, and the spot was scheduled to run the next day, we thought it would be a riot if we got the number, labeled the cart, and just put it in the rack for his lineup.

Next morning, Adams and Scholz was on, and they come to the appointed station break and started the commercial. Tim and I were in the store listening, as the commercial ran on and on and on.

After 30 seconds, Scholz turned off the mic and asked, "How long is this spot going to run?" Then, "What the fuck *is* this?" Then finally, "Fucking Gopen!"

I also took great relish in screwing with local, terrible DJs on other stations. One night, Steven C. Brown and I were hanging out listening to KTKT, which was a legendary Top 40 station. There was this guy on the air named Gibbens or Gibbons, who was just terrible. The two of us were sitting there laughing our heads off listening to him. I decided I had enough, and picked up the phone.

"KTKT," he answered.

I began, in a very deep voice, "Hi, this is Big Johnny Suitcase from KHJ in Los Angeles, I'm here in town and I'm listening to your show."

"Oh, HI!" Gibbons said, as if he had heard of this fictitious person.

"I gotta tell you man, you sound great," I continued. "You're hot man, you're on a roll ... killer show."

"Oh, wow!' Gibbons said. "Thank you so much. It's a great compliment coming from you."

Yeah, the Big Johnny Suitcase that didn't even exist.

"You have a break coming up?" I asked.

"Yes, I'm going to do one right now!" He excitedly opened the mic, and I could tell that he was all fired up. "KTKT, we've got another 30 minutes of commercial-free music ... yeah!"

He got back on the phone, and I said, "Killer, man I know when someone has the goods, and you've got em! Gibbons, I want you to work for KHJ ... that's right ... Los Angeles has to hear you. Here's what you do, pack your bags, tell your program director to go screw himself, and get on a plane. Be here on Monday."

"Are you kidding?"

"When you get to the studio in L.A., just ask for Big Johnny Suitcase, and we'll hammer out all the details." I hung up.

We laughed our asses off. I never heard another word about it, but I could only imagine the poor idiot showing up with a suitcase, and the receptionist greeting him, "Hi, may I help you?"

"Uh, yes, I'm Gibbens, I'm your new jock. I'm here to see Johnny Suitcase."

"Who?"

"You know, Big Johnny Suitcase, the guy that hired me."

"I'm sorry, there's nobody here by that name"

DOH!

Tim and I had bought a house, with the down payment coming out of the business. It was a small cracker box with awful walls, bad carpeting, old appliances, but a great in-ground pool. Yeah, screw the rest of the stuff, dammit, it has a pool!

We all lived there, Tim and Maggie in one room, Steph and I in another. The house was barely big enough for two people, never mind four, and the walls were so paper thin that you could hear everything. Our weekends were spent around the pool, which overlooked the highway. There was no privacy. In Arizona, a pool is not a luxury; it's a necessity with the temperatures soaring to 112° in the summer.

Every weekend, Tim found these poor Mexican kids, who had nowhere to go, and invited them over for swimming and bar-b-q parties. I have no idea how he found these kids, but every weekend, there they were, a backyard filled with Mexican kids, and Steph and Maggie sitting there pissed. What a Life!

Steph and I had planned to get married, and she wasted no time telling me that there would be no way we'd be sharing the house with Tim, Maggie, and the band of Mexicans. "Someone has to leave," she told me.

I approached Tim and told him, "You can have the house. We're leaving."

"Oh no you don't," he said. "You're not sticking me with *this* shit box. *We'll leave.*"

We argued back and forth for days, but finally came to an agreement. I would buy out Tim's interest in the shit dump for $1,000, and the house was ours.

We spent the next several years fixing it up, and in the end, I suppose it was a more nicely-decorated shit box. Our lives were bumping along pretty well. The clothing stores were doing well, and the pizza restaurant was humming along. We should have become millionaires, if it weren't for *one big mother of a mistake that sunk our ship!*

On University Boulevard, the same street where New York City Pizza was located, there was a shop called Franklin's Mens Store, a heritage men's clothing store that would compare to a Brooks Brothers today. They were always doing a tremendous business, and Tim and I were curious as to how they operated, so we scoped them out. The store was filled with preppy shirts, dress slacks, suits, and accessories, a far cry from crappy Hawaiian shirts, cowboy castoffs, and irregular jeans with one leg longer than the other that were found at The Crazyhouse. But something caught our eye: on the front counter, there was a sign that read, "We accept any major credit card." Not just MasterCard or American Express, but *any* card. *How the hell are they doing that?* we wondered.

We were told that the store wasn't running the charges, but a private company that allowed them to take any card a customer presented.

"What about a Shell gas card?" we asked.

"Yup," they answered.

"How about a Sears card?"

"Yup."

Tim and I rationalized that if it was good enough for Franklin's, it would be good enough for us, and that they weren't using the service right. They weren't promoting that credit card program to its upmost potential. What we didn't know, which we found out too late, was that they used that service *occasionally* and only for their best customers, the customers they knew well. That didn't matter to we two maverick business guys, who, with no business experience, and with a knee-jerk decision, went full speed ahead.

Christmas holidays were approaching, and to capitalize on the spending frenzy, Tim and I launched a major campaign to get people in. Our radio ads sounded like, "It's the holidays, and you say you need jeans and tops? You have a bunch of people to shop for, but you have no money? Well don't worry about it because here at The Crazy House Discount Boutiques, we take plastic . . . ANY KIND OF PLASTIC! That's right. You have a Gulf gas card? We take it! Sears card? Yup, take that too. If it's on plastic and has your name on it, come on in! And there's no limit on how much you can charge. Come on in to The Crazyhouse and get your Christmas jeans and tops!"

Were we out of our minds? Yes, but Franklins took them, and they had been in business forever. As you can imagine, the response was unprecedented. Our stores were mobbed. We were giddy. Money was flying in as fast as we could collect it.

We didn't know we were on *The Titanic's* deck getting ready to sink. In less than two weeks, we had literally sold off nearly every item in the stores, but 90% of sales were in credit card charges, but the company we used to accept all of that plastic went belly up along with our money. At the end of the holiday season, we had no cash, we couldn't get paid by the company let alone get them to answer the phone, our stock sold off during the mega sale, and our suppliers wouldn't ship anything else before we paid off what we owed! Three strikes, baby, you're out!

We limped along for a while, but soon that event put a strain on my relationship with Tim, and eventually we split our partnership, with Tim getting the clothing stores, and me taking New York City Pizza.

I erroneously believed that I would be safe having a business that at least was still doing business, but in the end, the failed clothing stores, like a black hole, sucked everything down with them, and Tim and I had to declare bankruptcy. That was a low time in my life. I had to sit in court and watch helplessly, as the remaining assets of anything that was left was auctioned off to the highest bidder. I was able to retain the house on 28th Street and my car. That's it. The court came and took everything else that wasn't nailed down, tvs, tools, and furniture. I don't know what they thought they were going to do with all of that, but they took it, nevertheless.

Stephanie and I were married on June 4, 1977. She was advised not to marry me *before* I declared bankruptcy. There I was, my career is in the dumps, no money, and I had just lost everything I had. I was some catch, but she married me anyway.

I went through a major struggle. To supplement the little amount I was making at KHYT, I went back to something I knew and started driving a cab at night. Steph worked at a Howard Johnsons, and between us, we scratched out a living.

There was no future for me at KHYT. I knew I had to get out, and I wanted to get away from Tucson. I started sending out tapes to radio stations around the country to try to find another job. Publications existed that came out weekly listing radio jobs in various markets. I sent tapes to every station that had an opening. I also targeted markets that I wanted to work in, and flooded every station in that city with my air checks.

One time, I purchased cassette players and sent a note to the program directors that said, "Just press play." I thought it was creative, but the gimmick never got me hired. Then, the female program director from KVOR in Colorado Springs, Colorado called. She heard the tape and wanted to hire me. *This is great!* I thought. *A new town, a new beginning.*

Steph and I packed up the car and drove there in one day. We set up at a local motel, and spent the rest of the day checking out the town. Everywhere we looked were unfriendly military people that seemed to be under a cloud of extreme structure. I was due to go on the air the next day, in the afternoon.

I showed up at the station, and the program director didn't even take the time to meet me. In the studio and on-air was a guy that looked like Lurch from *The Addams Family* tv series. He muttered a guttural hello and went back to what he was doing.

I said, "I'm Gary Craig. I'm the new afternoon guy."

He grunted.

"I've been listening to the station," I continued, "and I notice that you guys aren't playing any hit songs. In fact, what I'm hearing is very weird."

This was supposed to be a hit radio station, but I can't even describe to you what the format was. It was just a conglomeration of the worst music I ever heard.

Lurch answered, "Well, there's a box of records on the floor in the back of the studio, but if you put a song on that's too loud or too much rock, the owner will come down here and rip the record off the turntable."

Oh, that's just great. What the hell have I gotten myself into? The music sucked, the station sucked, their DJs sucked, the program director sucked, and the town sucked. I did that one shift, got off the air, drove back to the motel, and called the program director. "I won't be in tomorrow."

"Oh, are you not feeling well?" she asked.

"No, I won't be coming in ever."

That was it. The station gave me a hard time about paying me for the one shift, and reimbursing me for my expenses coming there. I had to get the Colorado labor board to crawl up their ass to get my check. Back in the car all the way back to Tucson. After KIKX, KHYT, and now the failure at KVOR, I was burned out. I didn't know what my future had in store for me. It was depressing. Steph wasn't thrilled to have to schlep all the way back to Tucson, but we had no choice. I decided that I need a break from hit radio.

I went over to KAIR and applied for a job. KAIR was an AM beautiful music station. Harry Reith was the program director, a really nice man, who knew who I was but was hesitant to take a chance. "You know this format is middle of the road, and beautiful music, right? There's no funny stuff."

I answered, "Yes, I know, and that's what I'm looking for. I need a break."

Harry then handed me a weather forecast and told me to go into the production studio and record it. I knew what to do and what he wanted to hear. It just so happened, the morning shift was going to become available, and a few days later, he called to tell me I had the job.

Any decent radio personality can switch gears and work in another format. It's like a director handing you a script and saying, "Now you're going to play this character." If you're a good actor, you can pull it off. In radio, "Now you're going to work on a Country station," or "Now you're going to do oldies," or specifically in my case, "Now you're going to be a comatose idiot who opens the mic every fifteen minutes just to do the weather." After fifteen minutes of brain-numbing music, I pushed a button, which triggered a tape machine to play what they called an "empathy," a tape that was filled with sickly sweet, syrupy announcements. A short piece of music then began, and an announcer was heard saying, "It's a beautiful sunrise, and you're comfortable with KAIR," or "The lizard is sunning himself on a rock, and you're comfortable with KAIR."

My first morning on the air, what I didn't know was that the all night guy was fired the night before—on the phone! He vowed to get his revenge. On the empathy tape were these two announcements, "You're slipping into freshly laundered sheets, and you're comfortable with KAIR" and "You're sitting next to your favorite girl, and you're comfortable with KAIR." The night before I started—after he was fired—he got that empathy tape, located those two announcements, edited them together, and put them back on the reel in such a way that they would come up in rotation on the morning show. There I was on a new job the first day, and the Montovani strings ended. I hit the button. The audience heard the music start and then, "You're slipping into your favorite girl, and you're comfortable with KAIR."

The phones lit up with complaints, but at least, I wasn't responsible, for a change.

After a while, the job really started getting to me. I am a creative person by nature, and sitting there doing time and temperature every fifteen minutes was just killing off any creative brain cells I had left. For me, working there was mental castration. I couldn't help it. I started adding some personality to my breaks, then a funny line or two, and I started opening up. Of course, this was not what I was hired to do, and pretty soon, Harry had to let me go. His eyes welled up and he said, "I'm sorry about this ... you're a terrific personality, and you need to be on a station that can use your talents." Harry was very nice about it, and I felt bad that he probably was forced to fire me against his own feelings. He was gracious enough to let me use the studios to put together any tapes I needed to send out.

Hope is a powerful thing. Every being on the planet is driven by it. Hope plays heavily in all of our lives. *I hope that girl I met in the bar calls me back. I hope I hit the lottery and get out of poverty. I hope my little boy recovers. I hope we can have peace in the world.* Well, I hoped something would happen for me. I hoped the heavens opened up and show me the way. I hoped I would find someone who would believe in me the way Tim did and allow me to just be myself on the air, and most importantly, I hoped I would just get a job so my wife and I would not have to struggle so much.

I was on unemployment and food stamps. I can't tell you how degrading it is to stand in line, and everyone looks at you with those pitying eyes, which seem to say, "Poor thing. You have to use food stamps to eat."

Cracks were already appearing in my marriage. I'm sure the unstable nature of my career didn't help. I give Steph a lot of credit for putting up with the uncertainty. It's hard to have your roots ripped up every six months and go on a radio wild goose chase, only to repeat the whole process, but that's the nature of the business.

Gary at KOPA, Phoenix, Arizona.

When we were all young and trying to make our mark as DJs, packing up our car and heading out to the next station was typical. It was a rarity when, finally in my career, I stayed in the same place for over thirty-four years. The tapes kept going out, and finally I got a call from Steve Rivers at KOPA AM and FM in Phoenix, Arizona. He liked what he heard on my audition tape and wanted to hire me for mornings. Time to pack up our shit again and hit the road.

We rented an apartment, and I got ready to go on the air. The studios were located in the affluent area of Scottsdale, not far from where tv star Bob Crane had an apartment. Bob, who started in radio, oddly enough, in Connecticut, was the biggest star in television at the time playing Colonel Hogan on *Hogan's Heroes* (1965). A few years before I arrived in Phoenix, Bob was found murdered in his apartment with his head bashed in and an electrical cord around his neck. Scottsdale police never solved the murder, but there was rampant speculation that his departure had something to do with him videotaping his sexual conquests, and building his library.

Steve Rivers was a great programmer, but a very strange guy. Not free with his emotions or opinions, he spent most of his days locked in his office, rarely coming out. What the hell did I care? I was working again, and doing mornings! What Steve didn't tell me was that I was to do mornings on KOPA AM, not the giant, popular FM station. KOPA AM was a dog. It was shit. It had no listeners and felt like AM's forgotten child. I begged Steve to use me on the

FM, but I couldn't sway him. I got off the air, saw him in the hall and said, "Did you hear that bit I did at 7:30?"

He just smirked and keep walking. I knew he wasn't even listening. I was just a body, a placeholder, just some schmuck he put in there so there was at least a voice on the air. *How about some input? I'll settle for anything.* I was miserable. (Years after I had left that station, I ran into Steve Rivers, and he admitted to me, "I made a real mistake with you putting you on the AM." *Gee Fucko, do you think?*)

AM station for not, at least I was working, and I made the best of it. I consoled myself by pranking Jay Stone, one of the FM jocks. I love him and his approach, and he had the voice of God. He didn't really adhere to the typical time and temperature approach but ad libbed everything and made the most typical formats sound fresh and new.

I figured out how to rig up one of the studio mics next to his so that when I turned it on, it would only be heard in his headphones, never over the air. Then, I waited until he was on the mic and on the air, and I started making snide remarks about whatever he was saying. He was doing a public service announcement about some pancake breakfast for some charity, and I opened my mic and added, "Well that's going to suck." It totally derailed him. He paused and didn't know where the hell it was coming from. That escalated in the days that followed, with me doing Ed Sullivan and Richard Nixon impressions in his headphones. Every time it happened, he frantically started hitting every switch in front of him trying to shut me off, all the time cracking up. He eventually found out it was me—and loved it—laughing through whatever he was talking about as I spoke into his headphones.

Chapter 14

Finally, Hartford

"Arthur Godfrey is coming in to cut a commercial, and I want you to get one of the production studios set up."

I was stunned hearing Steve. "Arthur Godfrey? *The* Arthur Godfrey?"

Godfrey was a radio and tv host, who was wildly popular in the 1940s-1960s. He hosted *Arthur Godfrey and His Friends* on network tv, and was the first one to deliver a folksy, conversational style that sounded like he was just talking to *you*. He arrived at the station, I ushered him into the KOPA studio, set him up with headphones, rolled tape, and listened in the next room. His voice was still strong, but he struggled to get through the commercial. He finally said, on mic, "God damn it, I can't breathe!" He was fighting emphysema and lung cancer caused by decades of smoking. He died a few years after that recording session.

The whole time I was working at KOPA, I was sending out tapes. The station was another dead end, and the sooner I got out the better. Hard to say, but if I had been employed on KOPA FM, my career path would definitely have taken another direction. Barely settled in Phoenix, I got an all too familiar call, this time from Andy Bickel, Program Director of WBT in Charlotte, North Carolina.

Gary in the studio at WBT.

Gary's WBT appearance at a mall.

Gary doing a live "drop" on the air at WBT.

Gary Craig WBT billboard.

Gary Craig clipping that introduced me.

"I love your tape," he told me. "I'd like to talk to you about doing the morning show down here."

We had a series of phone calls, then settled on an agreement. I should have met him first. Back at KOPA, the newspapers got wind of me leaving and published the story which forced General Manager Chuck Artigue to make a statement to the press. "Gary is leaving. He hasn't told me yet, but I know he's leaving. I'm elated for Gary, he will fit in that station in Charlotte."

How did he know I'd fit? That statement was just saving face, like when someone is let go at your job and they issue a memo that says, "So and so is leaving. They were a great employee and we wish them success in their next job." Well, if they were such a great employee, why are they leaving? All bullshit. Why can't people be totally honest? "So and so was a complete nightmare, and we had to let them go. We hope he can solve his problems before the next job." Andy Bickel was another strange bird. There was something about him that just wasn't right, like a strange man with a lot of secrets. I just couldn't put my finger on it. Sitting in his office a week before taking over the morning show, he told me, "I want you to do what you want on the show. Be creative, get ratings."

That was all I needed to hear. I attacked the show like a warrior on a mission. I studied everyone else in the market and zoned in on all their weaknesses. WBT spent a fortune promoting me. There were print ads, tv spots, and billboards everywhere that said, "Get

Gary's billboard stunt, living in a box to raise money for charity.

up with Gary" with a caricature of me peering out of a coffee cup with the station call letters on it. There were newspaper articles and tv interviews. I was everywhere. I took advantage of every opportunity to get out in public. I hosted Halloween contests, bowlathons, live remotes, and the Charlotte Summer pops.

I lived in a little shack next to a billboard for a week, and I broke the *Guinness Book of World Records* for handshakes at Carrowinds amusement park, 12,000 in less than six hours.

Paul Ingles was the sportscaster on the morning show, and he was quickly pulled into my routines, and when needed, provided a voice or two for my bits. He was more of a cohost than he was a sports guy. We had a good chemistry on the air.

I staged plenty of stunts. I took listeners up in a hot air balloon, and I slept on top of a billboard day and night to raise money for charity.

One day after I got off the air, I was blindsided by Bickel, when he called me into his office and said, "I don't want you to do any more bits. No more comedy. Just read the cards and keep the music going."

"But that's not what I was hired to do."

I protested, but it was no use. For some reason—and who the hell knows why—he wanted to subdue me on the air. I can only speculate that it had nothing to do with ratings, only that I was getting so much attention that I overshadowed the others, and he didn't like it. I only lasted nine months.

I was offered two jobs, the afternoon drive at K101 in San Francisco and the morning show at WTIC-FM in Hartford. News of my departure at WBT spread quickly. All the local newspaper guys jumped on it. Mark Wolf, who had a tv/RADIO column in *The Charlotte Observer* wrote, "With great disappointment and some anger, I could not believe Gary Craig would no longer greet my early mornings with his dynamic humor and talent. It not only made me smile, but laugh out loud when alone in the kitchen preparing my family's breakfast. What a loss to me and others at home and on their way to work who I know enjoyed a smile before starting their grinding jobs and daily activities. I know a great many Charlotteans who are just as disappointed as I and feel they have lost a friend indeed."

Just to be fair, Wolf also printed a comment from a listener: "Thank you WBT for really caring about Charlotte. You finally got rid of Gary Craig."

I'm sure Charlotte didn't know what to make of me. I was a New York boy with a sense of humor to match, and I was never concerned with being politically correct when it came to my delivery. They got more than they bargained for. The people who lived there sometimes prefaced their comments with, "You Yankees come down here, and . . . ." Yankees? Honey, the Civil War's been over for years, get over it!

In another Mark Wolf column, I was quoted as saying, "I'm sorry it turned out this way. I think I've done an honorable job for them and worked very hard to build an audience. I'm sorry I wasn't given a little bit more freedom to do the kind of job I wanted to do."

WBT General Manager Bill Jennings was forced to make a statement. "Craig was a damn good talent, but he just didn't work here." More covering up the truth.

Four months after I took over the morning show at WBT, the paper released the latest ratings. "WBT regained an edge in morning drive time with Gary Craig's 20.8 percent of the metro audience in the 6 to 10 a.m. time period. Thus, WBT can proclaim that newcomer Gary Craig toppled the former share leader Robert Murphy of WAYS and WROQ." I guess it didn't really work there. Idiot.

In one weekend, I flew to San Francisco, and then on at last to Hartford, Connecticut to meet in person with the program directors of those stations. After the nightmare experience that resulted from making a deal only over the phone with Andy Bickel, I wasn't about to make that mistake again.

The studios in San Francisco were, as you would expect, impressive. San Francisco was a major market, and to be offered the afternoon drive show was quite a coup, but something just didn't sit right with me. Call it a gut feeling. After meeting the program director, and taking the tour, I was brought back into his office. He had a big grin on his face. "Well?" he asked, shaking his head as if he knew what my answer would be.

I said, "Yeah, I don't think so."

"What? What do you mean you don't think so?"

"I think I'm going to take the morning show job in Hartford."

"Are you nuts? Don't you realize more people will hear you in an afternoon here than in a week in Hartford?"

"Yes, but I have a feeling that six months from now, you won't be here, and I'll be out of a job."

He just shook his head and laughed. "I'm not going anywhere."

"I've already made up my mind," I said.

"Okay. Your funeral."

Sometimes it's good to follow your gut. Almost six months to the day, the whole staff there was fired. I had one last blurb in the Charlotte paper: "Gary Craig who was pushed from WBT's morning show before he could jump begins June 29th as the new morning man at WTIC-FM in Hartford Connecticut. 'Everything happens for a reason,' said Craig, who was fired even though his show was top rated because WBT officials thought his style wasn't right for the station." I had commented, "WTIC wants me to do the things I do best, the humor and the bits. Here at WBT they tried to change me around to what they thought a morning man should be."

In June 1981, I was sitting in Arnold Chase's office at WTIC-FM on the Gold Building's 19th floor. I had been told, "Do whatever you want, just get us ratings," but I'd heard that before. (In all the years I worked there, they never went back on their word and gave me a free hand to do whatever I wanted. With that freedom, they enjoyed having a #1 morning show, more or less, for over thirty years.) I was hired for $38,000 for one year. I thought it was all the money in the world.

That one-year contract turned into two, then groups of three. I was back in battle again, and vowed to do whatever was needed to become #1 in the market, even if it meant working day and night to defeat the competition.

"Who's my competition?" I asked Arnold.

"Brad Davis."

Davis did the morning show at WDRC AM. (At this writing, he's still there.) He had pretty good ratings, but not a cutting-edge, comedy-driven morning show. He wasn't the personality holding the cards in the market.

That honor went to Bob Steele, who was holding down mornings on our AM station, WTIC 1080. When I arrived in Hartford, he had over a 40 market share, a number completely unheard of. That means, 40% of everyone listening to morning radio listened to Bob.

Gary, John, and Bob Steele.

When I tuned in, I couldn't believe hearing a guy break all radio rules—dead air, corny jokes, and bits that made no sense. In short, I was astounded that he had any ratings at all. What I didn't consider was that he'd been on the air for over thirty years. (I believe Bob still holds the record for the longest running morning man in America.) People grew up with him, trusted him, and considered him a friend, that voice coming a speaker in the morning that told them everything was still alright, Bob is on the air.

I once asked him, "Bob, how do you explain your high ratings?"

He looked at me and said, "Kid, when you sell hot dogs on the same corner long enough, pretty soon everybody comes to you for hot dogs."

Bob was a very funny guy with a dry sense of humor, corny as it was. One day he was walking down the hall, and I looked at him. Something about him didn't look right . . . something wrong with his ears. As he passed me, I saw that he had cardboard coverings on both ears, and printed on the outside of them was "Bullshit Protectors." I laughed out loud.

It didn't matter that Brad and Bob were on AM stations, and that I was on an FM. I considered that *everyone* was my competition. I spent a week listening to all other morning shows in the market and quickly realizing that I could pick them off pretty easily. I didn't hear any creativity or innovation, the DJs were sticking to the old time and temperature model. I pulled into town with a proven bag of characters that, slightly tweaked, would serve me perfectly in the market:

Brucie the Hairdresser became "Rusty Hinge," the doorman. In the theatre of the mind,

Rusty sat downstairs in the lobby of the Gold Building and called up to the studio every day, a bit that went right to the edge.

Hyram Lush was my drunk character, which was my version of the greatest drunk act in the world performed by Foster Brooks.

Thor the Engineer, who grunted and talked in gibberish, throwing in a recognizable word here and there.

Major Minority muscled his way into the studio on a regular basis to go off on words in the English language that bothered him, like "ass-fault".

Biff Kennedy was the over-the-top game show host.

Vito Knuckles rounded out the cast as the self-appointed morning show hit man.

In the beginning, it was just me and John Elliott. Then, Roger Stafford started doing traffic, and Kathy Francis was responsible for the weather. Chemistry on the radio is an uncertain element. (These days, when they put together morning teams, great care is taken to ensure that the people they throw together "gel" before they hit the air.) I had no choice in the matter. John was here five years before I arrived and was doing news on the morning show for the guy I replaced, Bob Simpson.

I was heading downstairs from the 19th floor and, at the elevators, I was introduced to John, and we rode down together. We looked at each other and said the same thing. That was the beginning of our "in sync" relationship that would last for over thirty years.

For the first time in my radio career, I finally found a company willing to give me free reign to do the type of radio that, up to this point, I had been hired and fired over repeatedly. I used this new power to make a big noise in Hartford. We hit the air running and never looked back. I knew I had to get out and meet people, so I started saying on the air, "I'm your *yes* man. You're having a fund raiser and you need someone to host it? You call me, and I say *yes*. Need an auctioneer? I'll say *yes*."

As you could imagine, I had many calls for me to appear. Most people that need a radio personality to help them in their project have to call the station and make a formal request for one of the DJs. There I was, automatically volunteering for any task up front.

On July 9, on one of the hottest days of the year, I sat out front on a 3000-pound ice cube, broadcasting live. I wore scuba flippers, had an arrow going through my head, and held an umbrella. When the ice cube, which we claimed was the world's largest, started to melt

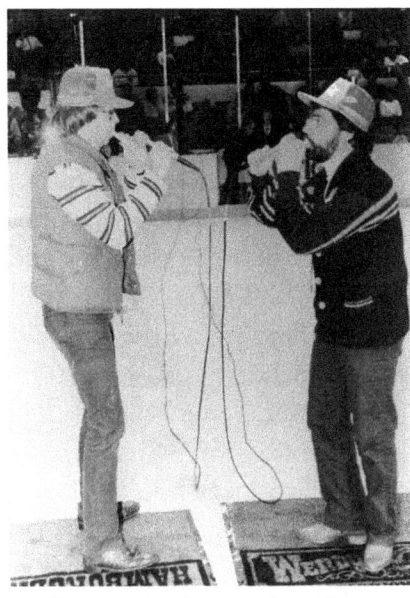

Gary, John, and Roger Stafford, traffic reporter.

Gary and John hosting Kazoo Night at the Hartford Civic center.

Gary chasing after steer at a rodeo, fall 1981.

on Main Street, we handed out snow cones. That was the first in a long line of stunts we pulled over the years, some of which got me into real trouble.

If I was the Johnny Carson of the morning show, John Elliott surely became my Ed McMahon. We didn't even work in the same studio, and didn't see each other when we were on the air, yet our timing was perfect. Shortly after I started, I launched what was to become the morning show's monster benchmark: the Dirty Joke of The Week. Each week on a Thrusday, I gave the joke's first part on the air but edited out the dirty punchline. Listeners had to call in for that. In the beginning, the jokes were pretty mild. "What's the difference between your wife and your job? After five years, your job will still suck." You could actually get away with telling that entire joke on the air now, but then my jokes got dirtier and dirtier, and I started including more words from the punchline on the playback.

A few weeks after I started The Dirty Joke of The Week, I was called into Arnold's office. "Sit down, Gary. We're getting a lot of complaints on this dirty joke of the week you're doing. You need to stop."

Here we go again! I thought, but I said calmly, "I'll tell you what, give me just two more weeks, and if you keep getting complaints, I'll stop doing the bit."

Two or three weeks later, the same people that had been complaining about it were the same people that were now calling in trying to get the punchline.

I got a call from a secretary. "I'm secretary for Judge [so and so]. He won't start court until he has the punchline, so can you give it to me please?"

The phone lines on Thursday morning became jammed. I had to eventually leave the joke for the receptionist at the front desk to give out the punchline, which made me laugh. Can you imagine the conversation? "Good afternoon, WTIC AM and FM. How may I help you? Yes, the punchline is 'both spend more time in your wallet than on your dick.' You're welcome. Thanks for calling."

Pretty soon after I started The Dirty Joke of The Week, an older lady called in to me for the punchline. When I delivered it, she let out the most outrageous laugh I've ever heard. The following week, she called in again, only this time, I named her "The Laugher." Her real name was Viola Willey. She was a staple every week for years until her death in 2007. After she passed, I stopped doing the joke because she was so tied into the bit that it wasn't the same without her. I also ran out of jokes. I've told every dirty joke that ever existed.

The nearest bathroom in the WTIC-FM studio—the only bathroom for everyone—was located right outside my studio door. If I had to go bad, I could put a long song on, go do my business, and be back on the air before the song ran out—except for one day, when I was struggling with a stomach disturbance. I clogged the toilet. I still had some time left on the long song that was on the air, so I came out opened the hall closet, and grabbed a wire hanger to snake into the toilet and unclog it. I thought I had succeeded, and I flushed again. Everything overflowed onto the floor like a shit volcano. As I was exiting, one of the sales weasels brushed by me to go in, but I grabbed his arm. "I wouldn't go in there. Some asshole clogged the toilet, and now it's all over the floor!" Always cover your ass. Bob Steele, the most listened to morning man in America, hated me ... at first.

Can you imagine some kid on the air telling dirty jokes or how a company could condone that? In time, he saw I wasn't going away, and in the first rating period I jumped to the #1 position. He came to accept me, and we became very friendly.

Bob had a grandfatherly, home town image on the air, but off the air he cursed like a sailor. One day, I saw Bob walking by my studio, so I motioned for him to come in. I was on the air *live*, but I turned to him and said, "Hey Bob, how's it going?"

Standing in front of the other mic, he said clear as day, "Well, if any son of a bitch around knew what the hell they were doing, we'd have a radio station!" and then he walked out.

I paused, turned back to my mic, and continued, "7:40 now on Tic . . . ."

I guess he found out that he had said those things on the air, and he was horrified. From that day forward, any time he popped his head in my studio, he always asked, "Are you on the air?"

On another day, he came into my studio and asked me, "Gary, do you know anything about this live ad I'm supposed to do?"

Why he thought I would have the answer to that question was beyond me, because I was on the FM and had nothing to do with his commercials. "Sorry Bob, I don't know anything about it."

He got completely red in the face and, as he walked out into the hallway, I heard him say, "Well, does any cocksucker know what's going on around here?"

That was a huge joke for years. To this day, I'll walk into the TIC newsroom filled with employees and just say, "Does any cocksucker know what's going on around here?" Always gets a huge laugh, so Bob, wherever you are, thank you. On Sunday August 16, 1981, *The Hartford Courant* printed, "Gary Craig, WTIC's new morning man, is making a nationwide name for himself already. First, Craig isolated the instrumental track of the Oak Ridge Boys' "Elvira" and dubbed in his own new lyrics with the new title "Fruit Flyra" and sent copies of the parody to California stations, several of which immediately added it to their rotations. Craig followed that up with "Air Traffic Controller Blues," an all original piece that found its way onto Charles Osgood's CBS network show and was distributed coast to coast."

What I didn't know after making those songs was that John Elliott could also sing. In fact, he spent his younger years in various bands performing throughout New England. Once I knew that, I never recorded another song without him. We whipped out a parody song at a moment's notice to follow a news story that everyone was talking about. Almost every time we finished a tune, one or more local tv stations requested a copy to feature on the evening news. We could do no wrong. John and I took every opportunity to make an appearance somewhere, no matter how crazy or bizarre it might have been, including lassoing cattle a rodeo, sitting in a dunk booth at a fundraiser, or passing out 2,000 kazoos at a Hartford Whaler game at our WTIC-FM Kazoo Night. In the 1982 Saint Patrick Parade in Hartford, I put together a "drill team" with all the station's personalities, which included cordless electric drills that would spin a 45 rpm record as we marched.

In 1982, we were to host the premiere of *Rocky*. John and I came up with the idea of not just welcoming our listeners and showing the film, which up to this point had been the norm, but rather to stage big production numbers in the theatre prior to the film. We ran down the aisle in boxing gloves and robes, as the theme played,

At the premiere of Rocky, with Gary and John.

and then had a "Rocky Talk Off" with listeners, who tried to impersonate Sylvester Stallone.

When we hosted the film, *Staying Alive* (1983) starring John Travolta, we walked down the aisle in white suits and swinging paint cans, and we wore the jackets open to reveal shirts with glued-on chest hair.

One of the biggest movie premiers we hosted was for *Return of the Jedi* that was held in the largest theatre possible at the time. This production had to set the standard, and we went all out. I created a custom soundtrack that led up to a battle in the front of the house with Yoda fighting Darth Vader. In the darkened theatre, the audience heard the music, then heard Vader's voice, then Yoda's, as John and I battled it out in the proper costumes with light saber swords. We topped ourselves.

1982 was a big year for another reason: our daughter, Rachel, was born on May 4. I was a dad and over the moon. Everything I did in my life up to that point was just a rehearsal. Now I was determined even more to work harder, make it bigger, and to try to never let my family down. I remember years ago my goal in life was to make $50,000 and to live in a $50,000 house. I was hired at WTIC-FM for $38,000 a year. I thought it was all the money in the world.

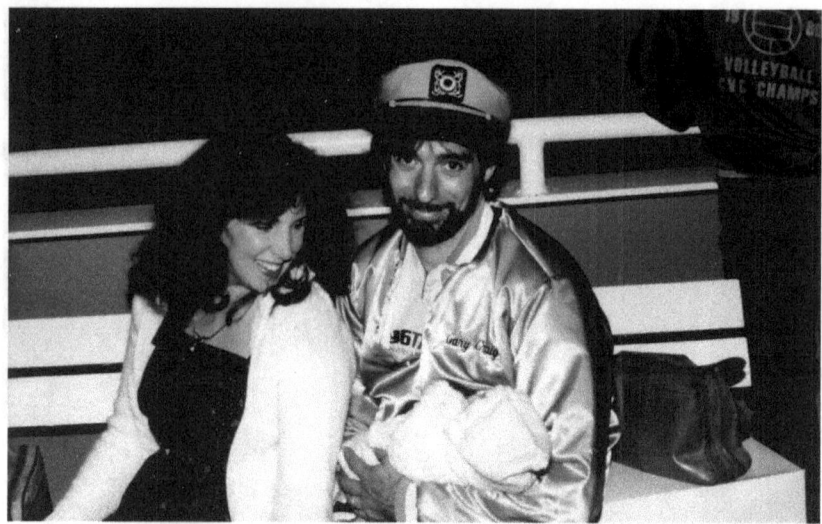

Gary, Steph, and Rachel on a radio station cruise.

Rachel, our newborn, with me.

Steph and I bought a house in Simsbury and settled in to family life, but I was driven. That drive would eventually take a toll on my life and marriage. I think I've mellowed a little over the years, but I must have been a son of a bitch back then. You couldn't tell me anything, and the freight train known as Craig and Company gave me the power to call my own shots on almost everything. I

GARY CRAIG

Gary setting handshaking record at Carrowinds Amusement Park in Charlotte.

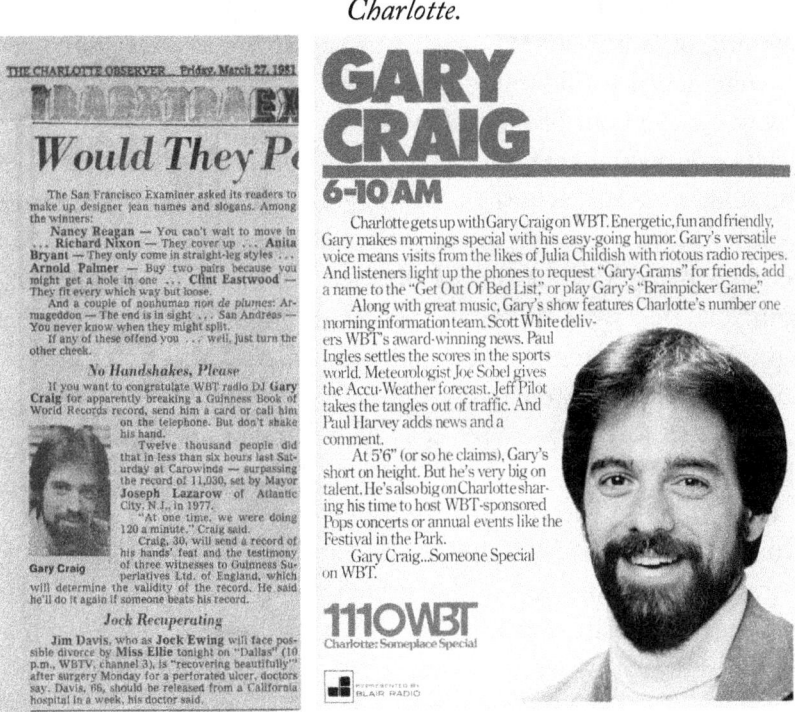

KWBT newspaper clipping.

Gary Craig KWBT promotion flyer.

Gary setting a second world handshaking record at The Big E.

was originally signed to a two-year contract, which included me working on Saturdays. When it was time for renewal, I informed management I would only sign to work five days a week. The sixth day was kicked out of the next contract.

My judgment hasn't always been on point. I was in New York shopping at FAO Schwartz, the biggest and best toy store in the world. As I was meandering around the store, there was a crowd of people looking at something. I elbowed my way in to see what was going on. They were all looking at a tv set, and there were animated figures moving across the screen. I asked what it was, and someone said, "It's called Nintendo. It's an electronic game."

I watched for a few more seconds and then said, "That's stupid. It'll never fly."

1982 was also the year I seized the opportunity to get into the Guinness Book of World Records by, once again, breaking the world handshaking record. This time it was at The Big E, the Eastern States Exposition fair, on Sept 25, 1982. In a completely white tuxedo and wearing white gloves, I barely took any bathroom breaks, as I shook 15,000 hands in 6 hours and 25 minutes. By the time I was finished, the white gloves I was wearing were pitch black.

Steve Goldstein, our Program Director during that time, recently weighed in on his experience with Craig and Company. "Gary ran a bit driven show for years with characters like Rusty Hinge the Doorman, but as that style of radio started to fade, Gary did what few could do—he rebuilt himself and the show into something that was content-driven and discussion-based, focusing on pop culture. There aren't too many people who can do that successfully; there was a lot of carnage along the road of shows that never adapted. That is the sign of true talent, and the ability to "read the room." One of the biggest events I have ever been involved with was the World Handshaking record. Watching thousands come by and shake Gary's hand to be part of a world record was crazy impressive. Good thing Gary had lots of pairs of gloves. People had cotton candy, twice cooked potatoes, and who knows what else on their hands."

The ad screamed, "Gary Craig and John Elliott, WTIC-FM's Morning stars will sing your musical message in person FOR ANY OCCASION. Bottle of Champagne included!" Another one read, "Gary Craig has found the perfect valentine gift at G Fox, if you can name it, you can win it."

The station spent a fortune promoting the morning show. There was a massive amount of print ads and tv commercials. We held

Gary Craig's first stunt at WTIC-FM sitting on a block of ice on a hot day.

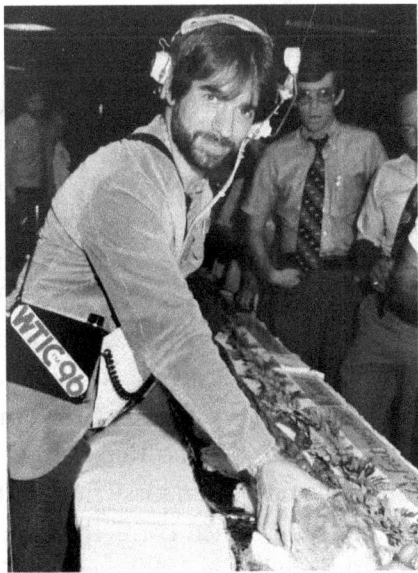

Gary Craig arrives at WTIC-FM first remote with longest hero.

Gary Craig 96.5 WTIC-FM promotion card.

Gary on the air at WTIC-FM, playing the kazoo along with the music.

snow sculptures in Bushnell Park, and rode live elephants through downtown Hartford. In September 1983, I made the front cover of *Hartford Magazine*.

When Ringling Bros. Circus came to town, John and I were made honorary ring masters. There wasn't any group or event that didn't want us to host. There were banana eating contests, pizza eating contests, and on hot days during the "Summer Freeze Out," we handed out 5,000 frozen treats during National Ice Cream Week at the old State House. I hosted on the CPTV auctions, and John and I joined *Disney on Ice*, in costume trying to skate across the ice without breaking our asses. In 1983, the film *The Right Stuff* debuted, and John and I donned space suits and walked around downtown handing out tickets. Recently in Evansville Indiana, Elton John threw a curse-laden hissy fit and stopped a concert cold because his piano wasn't tuned correctly. I don't know how we talked him into it, but back in the 1980s, we convinced him to send us a pair of his shoes. Then, we held an event in the Hartford Civic Center's center

Gary and John riding live elephants in a Hartford circus.

Gary as "The Great Garnac" on the front cover of Hartford Magazine 1983.

Gary, John, and Program Director Steve Goldstein at a banana eating contest.

court a la Cinderella to find someone whose feet would fit into the shoes. John and I wore court jester costumes.

We invented stunts that were so popular they had to be repeated year after year, including "The Egg Drop." Reserving a cash prize, we instructed our audience to come up with some kind of contraption that would catch a raw egg off the roof of a tall

Gary, John, and air staff in a "Summer Freeze Out" news clipping, with John as Ringmasters for Ringling Bros.

At The Right Stuff ticket giveaway, with Gary and John in space, downtown Hartford.

building without breaking the shell. Leading up to the event, listeners would call in describing their inventions which we would either encourage, or shoot down by informing them, "There's no way that's going to work." At high noon, John and I showed up in bird costumes and began the competition. We had a huge crowd, and the event was covered by every tv station in town.

Another promotion that brought us great buzz was "The Dash for Cash." The promotion began with the first listener to call in to

Elton John's shoes promotion and finding feet that would fit the shoes. *The Egg Drop stunt, with Gary and John in chicken costumes.*

the station and state the number of commercial-free songs played consecutively. They won $100 and a chance for his or her name to be picked out of a drawing to dash for cash. Then, winners were taken to a bank vault, where $96,000 in cash was spread out on the floor. The winner then had 60 seconds to pick up as much cash as they could, run to the room's end, and deposit the money in a large drum. Our first winner was Carol Freeman of Windsor, who scooped up $11,722.00. The station sounded big. We had voice-over star Ernie Anderson do all of our station announcements. He was the voice-over announcer on T*he Love Boat* tv series (1977-1987) and a dozen other network tv shows. He had the voice of God, and made the morning show sound like it was emanating from New York rather than Hartford. (Years ago, I found every session he ever did for the station on reel to reel tapes. I transferred them to audio files to preserve them. He was also notorious for dropping the F bombs during those sessions, and I have them all.)

Ernie charged the station based on how many promos he voiced for us. One promo, one price. Three promos, another price. I got this great idea to scam Ernie in such a way that I could get more promos out of him without paying the extra charge. I wrote a promo that just kept going on and on and included all kinds of words that I knew I could edit out and construct extra promos for the morning show. I heard him on one of the tapes voicing the piece, and he stopped in the middle of it and said, "What the hell is this? What do they think, I'm fucking stupid? I know what they're doing here. They're just going to chop this up into multiple promos."

The greatest promo that he voiced, though, was the one for our 10,000 song. This was a massive promotion that hooked the audience along all summer long. Ernie would say, "965-TIC-FM. The $10,000 song! It's $10,000 just for a song! When you hear "Hey Jude" by The Beatles, just be caller 96 and you'll win ten grand! The $10,000 song, in the red hot summer of 965-TIC-FM." This was nuts! Every radio was tuned to the radio station because we never told the audience when the song was going to be played. Could have happened anytime. Listeners have told me that had to carry radios around with them at all times just so they didn't miss it. This was a brilliant promotion, because it gave the entire audience a chance to win the money. Usually, radio contests are short, and for the most part are won by what we in the business call "contest pigs," people that basically just sit by the radio and their phone calling in to win things. When we figured out the same people were winning over and over again, we implemented a new policy, which was that they were ineligible if they had won anything in the last thirty days. Subsequent promotions involved giving away a brand new car one year, to giving three new cars away during one summer. We were in the fat 1980s. Money was no object, and Craig and Company was a money printing machine. If there was something I needed, some piece of equipment, all I had to do was ask, and it was purchased. Need a machine that will make my voice sound like a midget? It costs $900? No problem. That money train would eventually end and would be replaced with, "Sorry we have no budget."

John Elliott and I are like an old married couple. Over the years, we've annoyed the shit out of each other, but for me the bottom line is that I've worked with a lot of people in radio, and John is great at what he does. He got to the point that he knew what I was going to say before I said it. He instinctively knew how to set me up for a big punchline, and that hasn't changed today.

As soon as I found out that John could sing, we started turning out a lot of material. One of the first things we produced was a "wake up song." John and I sang the lyrics, leaving blanks where I would read listener's names live over the music. We ran this every morning, and the phones lit up like a Christmas tree. People loved not only hearing their own names on the air, but the names of coworkers, and people they loved.

Over the years, I would update the tune and make necessary changes to reflect new people joining the morning show. The most popular wake up song versions was the second incarnation, sung to the tune of "Bye Bye Blackbird." It began with:

"Time to get up out of bed,
pull the sheets right off your head,
wake ... up ... Hartford.
Craig and Company is up,
go pour the coffee in your cup,
wake ... up ... Hartford.
All of Cathy's weather will astound you.
Roger looks at traffic all around you.
Newsman John extraordinaire.
Morning news will curl your hair.
Connecticut, wake up.

Huge hit.

On the heels of the new wakeup song, I added another feature, "The Wakeup Call." At an appointed time, I gave people a few seconds to move a radio speaker over the ear of someone who was sleeping. I paused, and then, at the top of my lungs, I screamed, "WAAAKE UUUPPPPP" for as long as my air held out, which was a long stretch. (I can still pull it off today if I wanted to.)

We didn't stop there. Over the years, we turned out over 40 parody songs, many of which aired nationwide. In 1991, we released a cassette entitled, "Craig and Elliott's Greatest Hits, Over Ten Years of Madness." Anyone have one? I have only one copy. If you're into the show, this is definitely a collector's item. On that tape, you'll find such songs as "The Christmas Song"; "I saw Daddy Kissing Santa Claus"; "I'm all Fed Up"; "Cabbage Patch Revenge"; "Hey Hey We're Sea Monkeys"; "Our Ramps"; "My Guy"; "One Night in Hartford"; "Air Traffic Controller's Blues"; "The Kind I Like To Eat-a"; "The Summerwind"; "Quailhouse Rock"; "Bye Bye Baker"; "The Duke of Oil"; "Kuwait Kuwait"; "Gary Be Good"; and both "Wakeup Songs".

Just like the acting bug, I haven't really gotten the singing bug out of my system. I've been trying to do it since I was five. I've sung with trios, bands, and orchestras. I have always wanted to record a mini album, maybe five or six songs. Maybe when I step down from radio, I'll have time.

Better yet, another fantasy of mine has been to open a little nightclub, where I take the bandstand at night and croon to a small, enthusiastic audience. I'll add that idea to all the other ideas swirling in my head.

There was never a stunt too stupid for us to try. Michael Damian, the soap opera actor, was coming to town. He played Danny Romalotti on the soap opera, *The Young and the Restless*. We were going

Michael Damian roll around in honey for cash, stunt promotion with Gary and John in bee outfits.

Gary and Rachel.

to appear with him at the Hartford Civic center, and I wanted a big crowd there. So, we cooked up an absolutely asinine promotion: we wanted to coat people in honey, then have them roll around the floor on top of money, and whatever bills stuck to them, they would get to keep. Not only did people show up to do it, a ton of people arrived to watch this insanity. Of course, John and I were in bee outfits and always in character. What did two idiots in bee outfits and even bigger idiots coating themselves in honey have to do with Michael Damian? Not a damn thing. John just recently reminded me that I poured honey on the head of a guy that was wearing a trench coat ... and he turned out to be homeless. How the hell was I supposed to know he was homeless? The guy got so pissed off that he threatened to sue the radio station. Way to go, Gary!

As soon as my daughter, Rachel, was able to speak, I pressed her into service and made her a part of the show. She was the sweetest thing you ever heard. I brought her down to the studio and put her up on a chair in front of the mic. I said a line, and she repeated it. She did an introduction for me, or John, or announced a bit. The audience loved her, and brought up her name for years to come.

The problem was, if I wasn't on the air, I was in the production studio for long hours producing material for the next day's show, or I was out making numerous personal appearances. I wasn't spending a lot of time with my wife and daughter. I was trying to provide for them, but lost sight of the delicate balance of work to home life. I was especially absent from Rachel's life, and I deeply regret it to this day. Someone wise once said, "When you're on your death bed, you're not going to say, gee, I wish I could work one more day."

The small cracks in my marriage to Stephanie became wider. I don't recall what kind of husband or father I was. That's something others would have to comment on. I could beat myself up, or just chalk it up to ambition, but in any event, what I've created over the years, according to the people who have tuned in, has value, and I'm proud of that.

The radio station had a lot of power in terms of "favors." We played the music, and artists benefitted from the fame and fortune that the country's DJs created. So, when we needed a favor, record companies were inclined to do something for us, because we did a lot for them. In the radio world, the suits had to be careful with that, because it bordered on "Payola," the term for the radio debacle from the 1950s and 1960s from record companies actually *paying* stations to play their records. On numerous occasions, we held events where major talent was brought in to entertain. One year, we launched "The School Spirit" contest. Local high schools were encouraged to send us postcards to tell us why they wanted Bobby Brown and The New Edition to come to their school and do a concert! You have no idea how many cards came in. It was a competition between schools, as to who had the muscle to pull it off. The rivalry between high schools was huge, and every single school who could hear our signal seemed to be into it. We received so many cards that we had to stop counting them. The only way we could calculate was to weigh them. A clear winner emerged.

On the evening of the performance, the place was packed, not only with students and teachers but the entire air staff and media. John and I introduced the TIC radio personalities, and then Bobby Brown and The New Edition. The place went nuts, and the kids raced up to stand in front of the stage to get a close look. Bobby and the boys came out, and we waited and waited for him to start. Nothing. Bobby picked up the mike and started admonishing the kids at the stage to get back.

What? What the hell is he doing? These are his fans!

Whitney Houston and Gary outside her dressing room at The Bushnell.

Bobby kept this up for quite some time, actually saying, "Unless all of you get back 10 feet, we're not going to start."

I was livid, standing in the wings, and I said out loud, "That little prick! I'm going out there to tell him if he doesn't start immediately he can take his little shit band and get the fuck out of here."

The staff had to hold me back, I was so angry. We played his music every day, we promoted the band on every level you could imagine, and he pulled this! Management stood around wringing their hands. I didn't care. If someone's mistreating anyone on the staff, or our audience, they were going to hear from me. That's the way I've always been. I'm a son of a bitch from New York. Luckily, Brown simmered down and started the show, and the rest of the night went off without any further problems.

Another great evening was the night we brought in Whitney Houston. At the time, she had just a few hits and was on her way up to superstardom. She was beautiful, and I think it's safe to say, to this day, that very few have approached the level of her talent. She was finishing her set, and I lined up the air staff at the bottom of the stage stairs.

I said to her manager, "When Whitney comes off, if she can just pause for five seconds, we have a photographer here to snap a photo with the staff."

He looked at me and said, "Nope."

"Nope? What do you mean nope? It will only take a second."

"Sorry, no pictures."

We *paid* to have her perform, her music was in heavy rotation on the radio station, and I just couldn't believe him. How could someone we were helping to make famous not stop for a second so we could have a picture that most certainly would be carried by the local press for even *more* publicity for Whitney. *Maybe it's just her manager*, I considered. *Maybe I can just grab her for a second when she steps off the stage*. Sure enough, she finished, walked down the short set of stairs, saw all of us standing there with the photographer, and with her nose up in the air, walked by and exited the building. I never forgot that.

Fast forward to several years later. Whitney was by then a huge star with a slew of Grammy Award-winning hits. We were giving away tickets for her show at The Bushnell. Yes, we were still promoting her. What choice did we have? We couldn't ignore the biggest artist on the planet, but that night back at the Parkview still was stuck in my craw. Everyone knew me at The Bushnell. I was able to come and go as I pleased. I grabbed a photographer, and when we entered the building, I asked the stage manager where Whitney's dressing room was.

"Second floor, first door to the right," he answered.

Up we went. When I was in front of her door, I told the guy with the camera, "Just get ready. I'm going to knock on the door. When she opens it, snap the picture."

That's exactly what happened. I finally got my photo. I know, so infantile, but she should have taken the picture when I asked for it.

There were other unspeakable promotions.

How far would I go to get publicity? Mike Evans had a story about Kevin Costner, who did full frontal nudity in the film, *For the Love of a Game* (2015), and when they screened it in front of test audiences, people were laughing. So, they reshot the scene with Costner wearing a robe. Mikey asked, "Gary have you ever done a full frontal in a film?"

At first, I said I had *never* done a nude scene, but then I remembered *Playgirl*. There was a news story that the magazine was going

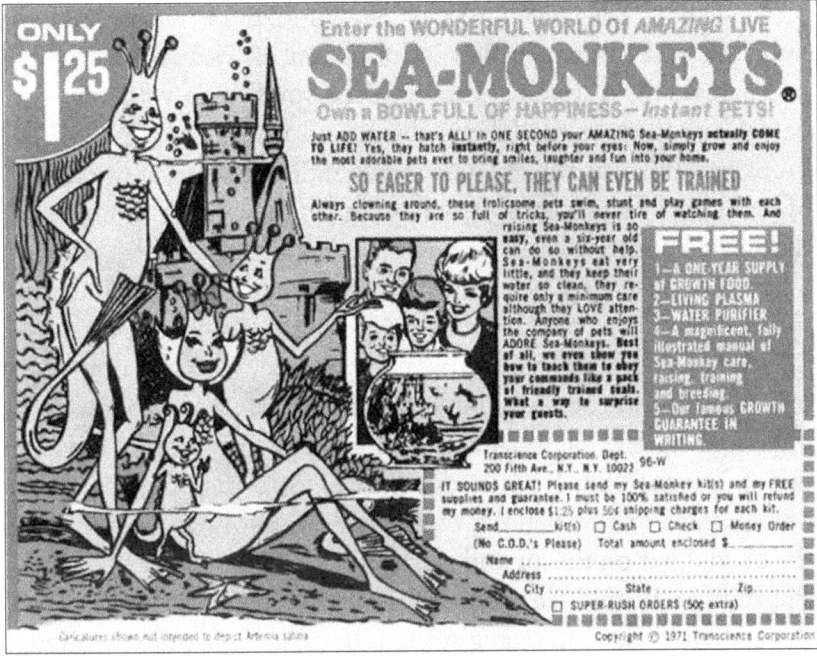

The famous Sea Monkeys ad.

to do a featured, nude spread of radio personalities across the country. We found a local photographer to do the shoot. It was to be a sort of cowboy theme. We brought in bales of hay, and then I struck various poses completely nude. In one of the shots of me laying down on top of a bale of hay, Stephanie's hand can be seen on my thigh, but the shot I was certain to get me into the magazine was one showing me standing with a big grin on my face and a 45 rpm record on my dick. Creative right? I mean, I was a DISC jockey, so why not shove my shlong thru the hole? I never got a call, and the photos were never published in *Playgirl*.

No matter what stunt we tried, people showed up to see anything. Nowadays, I'd have to set myself on fire and give away $5,000 cash for someone to be interested enough to come and watch. I grew up looking at that ad on the back of comic books advertising Sea Monkeys, an illustration of them swimming around a fish bowl with human-looking smiles on their faces. The ad went on to describe how you can watch them hatch and grow right before your eyes, and even teach them how to do tricks! I always wanted them. My mom wouldn't buy them for me. I think she brushed it off by saying, "Gary, we don't need any monkeys in the house." The kit came with water purifier and a packet of "Sea Monkey Eggs. Just add them to water, and in no time you'll have your very own pets. Give them names! Feed them, and watch them grow!" Sea monkeys. This was the greatest merchandising scam in the history of scamdom. They weren't monkeys at all; they were nothing more than brine shrimp. Well, I remember reading these ads, and then eventually there were Sea Monkey tv commercials extolling the virtue of having your own bowl of swimming and smiling pets.

I sent away for the kit, a grown, damn man, who was now going to hatch his own Sea Monkeys. The kit arrived, and I followed the directions to the "T." I got on the air and told everyone what I was doing and that I would do updates as to the progress. About a week later, lo and behold, there were some things swimming in the bowl. I got on the air and started doing "Sea Monkey Updates." Pretty soon, I could see them clearly, and I gave them names. I told the audience that I had taught them to talk. Then, in high-pitched voices, I carried on conversations with them on the air. Stupid right?

John Elliott and I even came up with a song promoting the bit and the tour on the air. We took "Hey, Hey, We're the Monkees," the theme song for the tv show, *The Monkees*, and I rewrote the lyrics and renamed it "Hey, Hey, We're Sea Monkeys":

Here we come,
Swimming past your face
Get the funniest looks from,
Everyone in the place.

Hey, Hey, we're Sea Monkeys,
People don't think we exist,
You can say what you want to,
Just don't get us ... mad.

We were born,
From a comic book kit,
We don't know what our sex is,
We don't give a ... darn.

Hey, Hey, we're Sea Monkeys,
You can hatch us, too,
But you'll be busy cleaning,
Monkey sea, monkey doo.

Hey, Hey, we're Sea Monkeys,
Humans think we're a joke,
We're contaminating
The water in Holyoke.

We look gross,
Swimming nude in our glass,
If the song is offensive,
You can kiss our . . . .
Don't eat a Sea Monkey,
Your breath will smell like fish
We're too busy breeding
We make the water swish.

But wait . . . there's more. The bit got so popular that I finally announced that I was taking them on tour. Yes, The Sea Monkey Tour '85." We set up the appearance at the local mall at high noon. I had the bowl covered with a cloth. Hundreds of people showed up to get a look at these frolicking frisky funny creatures that I had been featuring for weeks. A line of people filed past the bowl, and as I lifted the cloth, they peered in smiling and just shaking their heads. "That idiot Gary Craig did it again . . . sucked us into another ridiculous stunt that we just couldn't resist." There was an old guy standing there, who leaned into one of the promotion people, not knowing they worked for the station, and looked at me and said, "Look at this damned idiot. He's probably hopped up on cocaine!"

So many people came out to see the Sea Monkeys that I fully intended to extend the tour to other places, but a day after that first appearance, one of the other DJs, asshole-jealous that I was getting giant publicity just from a bowl of brine shrimp, snuck into my office where the bowl was, poured rubbing alcohol in the water, and killed them all off.

Chapter 15

Hair Gone Tomorrow, Here Today

John and I were unstoppable. There was the Craig and Company ratings, and then there were all the other stations in the market fighting over whatever was left. No idea was ever too crazy for us to implement. The subject of my thinning hair had been a long-running joke on the morning show, because I always shared everything about myself with the audience, warts and all be dammed.

I was watching the news one night and saw a piece on this guy in New York, who was supposed to be the top hairdresser in the city, and who was now fitting bald men with the best toupees money could buy. I came up with this crazy idea to load a bus filled with bald guys and go to New York to find them solutions for their bare scalps. I called it "The Hair Quest Tour." We had people send us their photos, and we selected all the bald guys that made the cut. I got the bus, had t-shirts made, and selected three or four places that we'd visit.

I asked our promotion director at the time, Lisa Namerow, if she could get us any press on the tour. A few days later, she said, "I got you on *The Regis and Cathy Lee Show*."

"What? Are you kidding?"

"No. They heard about what you're doing and they think it's a riot. They want you on."

On taping day, they sat the guys in the audience according to their degree of hair loss. The guys just starting to lose hair sat in the back row, then they progressed down to the baldest guys in the front row. On the show that day was Richard Simmons, who, when we posed for pictures, lifted me off the ground.

Comedian Richard Lewis was also on, and he told Regis, "Even the bus that brought them here had bald tires."

I was brought on as a guest, and I brought props that included a special comb I made. All the center teeth were gone except for

Gary with Regis Philbin and the Hair Quest promotion.

Gary with Kathie Lee.

some at either end. I told Regis that it was a special comb for guys who still had a little hair on the sides.

After the taping in the morning, we had a little down time until we visited the hair joints, so we parked the bus on Broadway. I got out onto the street with a megaphone, shouting, "See the ninth wonder of the world, a bus full of bald guys, only 50¢ admission." I actually found people willing to pay me to take a look.

The third hair place we visited was Sy Sperling's Hair Club For Men. In the 1980s, he was the king of hair replacement. While all of us visited, I was ushered into a private room, and as previously arranged, was getting fitted for a hair replacement system. Sy's wife ushered me into a private room and took various hair samples. "You'll have to come back," she said. "Your replacement system has to be made."

We all returned to the Bald Tour bus and headed back to Hartford. All in all, a great day.

Years later, the morning show was doing a remote down at Disney in Florida. We were on the air, and I saw Regis walk by. I shouted, "Hey Regis, Gary Craig from CBS. How about a few words?"

He turned to me and said, "What do you think, I just fell off a turnip truck?" and kept walking. *Was it something I said? Was he thinking, Oh there's that schmuck that was on my show?*

Once again, I was tugging on the sleeve of fame. The very next weekend, I had to go back into the city to have my hair system installed. I brought my friend, Seth Darvick, with me. We planned to stay over, just in case something went wrong with the hair and I had to adjust it before I came back home. Once again at Sperling's, I was ushered into the private room, where Sy's wife was ready for me. I just loved the fact that they call the thing a "Hair System," when it was nothing but a toupee that just attached to your existing hair. I sat down in the chair, and Sy's wife pulled out the piece. She started weaving what looked like twine in and out of the hairpiece edges, and then basically tied it to my side hair.

"How do I wash this thing? I asked nervously.

"Oh, you just lift up the front and get some soap in there and shampoo it like your real hair."

Yeah, well, my *real hair* was now buried under this thing on my head. It was as if someone had attached a hat permanently to my head.

"What happens when my existing real hair grows out?"

"Oh, about every four to six weeks, you have to come back and have it tightened."

She worked on me for what seemed like two hours to get it to look just right, and I was thinking, *How the hell am I going to be able to get this to look this good on a daily basis?*

Seth and I grabbed a cab. I said to the Jamaican driver, "Hey what do you think of my hair?"

He looked at me puzzled and said, "Uh, yeah mon, it looks good."

"I just had it attached. It's fake."

"You can't even tell!"

That night in the hotel room, Seth gazed at me laying on the bed flat on my back like a toppled statue and staring at the ceiling. "What are you doing?"

"I'm sleeping on my back all night," I replied. "I don't want to mess up the hair."

In the morning, when Seth took his first look at my head, he burst out laughing so hard that he lost air and no sound came out of his mouth.

I staggered to the mirror. Apparently during the night, I had rolled over, and now the hair system jutted straight up like a spear or as if a small animal had crawled under it during the night and just died there. I immediately called The Hair Club and demanded that they take the thing off.

We got to their office only to find the waiting room filled with guys who had the worst-looking hair I'd ever seen: they were all in there for their periodic hair-hat-tightening. Some were so bad that they looked like their dead animal had slipped almost to the side of their heads or like they were wearing a beret.

In no time, I was back to my true self, but I kept the hair hat and used it many times deliberately wearing it like a beret in public just to get a stare or a laugh. One time, Darvick and I were walking down a street and I stopped at a restaurant window and saw people dining inside. I put on the hair beret and just stood there like a poster boy for Toupees Anonymous.

Bill O'Reilly visits Craig and Company.

Gary with Bon Jovi.

Gary with Lorraine Bracco.

Gary with Huey Lewis.

Jerry Mathers "The Beaver" visits Craig and Company.

Joey Pantoliano Joey Pants visits Craig and Company.

Kelly Clarkson at a WTIC-FM concert.

Michael Buble with morning team, Gary, John, and Christine.

Richard Thomas (John Boy on The Waltons) visits Craig and Company.

Valerie Harper (Rhoda) visits Craig and Company.

Weird Al visits the studio.

Chapter 16

More Stars Than There Are in Heaven

We have interviewed, hosted, and hung out with hundreds of celebrities over the years. Most have been nice, some . . . not so nice. I have found that stars at the top of their game are the easiest to talk to, and stars that are on their way up are animated and the most open, but stars that are on their way out begrudgingly do interviews and are not much fun. Luminaries that came up to the studio were always fun, which included some near miss opportunities. One morning, promotions came into the studio and said, "We have this vocal group that want to come in and sing for you."

I said, "Vocal group? No. Nobody gets on the morning show unless I know them."

"Well, we're going to start playing one of their songs on the air next week, and the label thought it would be nice to have them on."

"What's their name?" I asked. She rattled off a name I had never heard of, so I relented. "Okay, but they get one tune and that's it!"

Mclean Stevenson and Gary at WTIC-FM.

Gary, John, Program Director Dave Shakes, and McLean Stevenson.

In walked these four guys. I introduced them, and after they finished their song, you could have picked up my chin from the floor. I had never heard harmonies like that in my life. I begged them to do one or two more songs. Soon, "End of the Road" reached the top of charts worldwide, Boyz II Men's first #1 single.

One of our craziest in-studio guests was actor Mclean Stevenson. He played Col Henry Blake on M*A*S*H. I don't know why he was in town, but about five years had passed after he ended his role on M*A*S*H. He was a riot and completely disrupted the entire show, never answering a straight question, always with a comeback and a punchline. He went into another studio when John was doing his news, and on an open mic, every time John mentioned someone in the news, Mclean made a snide remark about them. John said,

Gary and John backstage with Phil Collins right before he went on.

"Soviet Union leader Mikhail Gorbachev just said—" and McLean piped in, "He's got a stain on his head, and he's a complete idiot. Who cares what he has to say?" Hilarious!

John and I hung out with Phil Collins backstage one night at The Civic Center. We talked about many things—the music industry, and other artists, and he couldn't have been more down to earth and humble. Then, he glanced at his watch and said, "Oops! Gotta go do the show, mates," and he was gone.

Bob Sagett with Craig and Company at Disneyworld in Florida.

Gary and John partying with Merv Griffin at Paradise Island.

Spanky McFarland from the Our Gang/Little Rascals comedies at Merv Griffin's party.

Ian Ziering with Gary.

The morning show traveled to many locations to broadcast live. We were down in the islands and attended a private party thrown by Merv Griffin. That man knew how to throw a party! He was sick as a dog that night, but still came down to schmooze with his guests. When we stopped for a photo, I remember touching the back of his jacket with my hand and I could feel that he was soaking wet. At that same party was Spanky McFarland, famous as child actor "Spanky" in the *Our Gang/Little Rascals* comedy films. This was a weird sensation standing next to him, this guy, who had entertained me when I was a kid.

We've broadcasted live from Disneyworld, Universal studios, The Grammy Awards, New York, even Hedonism in Jamaica—a wild place—a resort where anything goes. There were gorgeous male and female social directors, who were rumored to keep individual guests, shall we say, very happy. All you had to do, was ask.

We got up at 4:30 one morning to go down to our broadcast site, and just as we started to set up, an all-night toga party in the night club ended and half naked, drunk guests in bed sheets, spilled out onto the property. There were parties going on 24/7 the whole time we were there.

Some star notes:

Howie Mandel: a funny and strange man, but a riot. He came to town, and Diana and I went to see his show. Afterwards, we went backstage to say hello. We all know now that he's a germaphobe, but we didn't know that then. They ushered us into a room that was pitch dark. It was obvious that there were other people in there with us, but all of a sudden, we heard Howie in the darkness say, "Hi everybody!" Then, he proceeded to continue the meet and greet in pitch black. Hilarious and weird.

Bill Maher: another strange one. I went backstage to see him after a show. He was sitting at the end of the room, eating. I went to shake his hand, and he refused. Could it be he had the same hang-ups as Howie? Barely looking up from his food, he finally said, "I have to go. I have a hooker coming to my hotel room." Funny, but I wondered if it was true.

George Forman: The champ was great. We had him in our studio. He picked me up with one arm, John with the other.

Jewel: I went to interview her and was told by her "people" not to look at her directly in the face when we were interviewing her. *What?*

Weird Al: I was having dinner with him one night at Carbones in Hartford. I made a bet that if he walked into the adjacent dining room that nobody would know who the hell he was. So, he went there like a waiter and topped off all the water glasses to almost overflowing. He came back to our table, and looked disappointed because . . . I won the bet.

William Shatner: A good sport. We played him a parody we did of his Priceline commercial, and he laughed his ass off.

Robert Goulet: No sense of humor. He didn't think the "Goulet Joke" was funny.

Leslie Nielson: He even used his famous fart machine over the phone when we interviewed him.

Kelly Clarkson: She licked my face, as we took a picture together.

Ian Ziering: The *Sharknado* star was riding in a limo with me in the middle of summer, but the car had no air conditioning. The two of us sat in the back sweating like pigs.

My friend, Seth Darvick, visited me in the studio one morning, and he had brought me a little gift, a bottle of "Morning Breeze" that he had found at some joke shop. He remembered the story I told him of how I used it back in the KIKX days on Paul Lotsof. Apparently, I didn't get that prank out of my system, because I was willing to try it again a few minutes before John was to do the news. Our studios weren't together; his was way down the hallway in a little room. I ran down there, opened the door, and sprinkled a few drops. At the top of the hour, news time, Seth and I were laughing our asses off, because we knew what it smelled like in there. I told him, "You better get out of there before John comes down."

Immediately following the newscast, John came into my studio and said, "My news studio has a very foul odor. Do you know anything about it?"

Of course, I denied it at first, but then I couldn't let the charade go on any longer and owned up to it, but added, "It was Seth's idea. He brought the bottle."

That would have been fine if it had ended there, except that the ventilation system at the radio station drew in the foul air and then distributed it to all the other studios. Soon, the odor was wafting through the entire radio station so badly that men with white hazmat suits were called in. Gary Craig—what a child!

By 1984, my marriage to Stephanie had taken a last breath. There was unfaithfulness on both sides, but I took the responsibility for most of the demise. I was too focused on my career to pay attention or even notice what was going on at home. Rachel was barely two years old, and once again, my family history repeated itself. I later asked Rachel if she ever remembered living in the same house with myself and her mom. She didn't. I suppose that was a good thing, in terms of Rachel thinking the arrangement was the way it was supposed to be. I always thought that "you have to work on a marriage" was true, as the popular saying went. After working hard all day, coming home and *working* on the marriage was the last thing I wanted. I always thought that, if the relationship was right, then it should be easy; the home and the relationship should be a sanctuary not a mine field.

Stephanie had gladly packed up and followed me from one radio job to another, unselfish and never complaining, yet now that I was finally experiencing success, our relationship was coming to an end.

The divorce was hard on me. I could no longer see my daughter every day, tuck her in, or be there on the spot when she learned new things and discovered the surprises of life. I had to get up every morning at 3:30 a.m. to do the radio show, so she couldn't be with me every day. Mostly, I could only see her on the weekends and holidays. For the longest time, at the end of my visit and after I dropped her off at Steph's house, I drove away weeping in my car. Eventually I learned to live with that, but, it was devastating. I tried to make it up over the years, but I can't make up lost time or get it back. There are no re-dos, there's only here and now.

That same year, Michael Jackson and his brothers embarked on "The Victory Tour," based on The Jacksons' new album, *Victory*. It was supposed to be 55 concerts in the U.S., followed by a European tour. No songs from the album were performed, because Michael refused to rehearse them. After all, it wasn't his music. He didn't need the money, and he only agreed to even do the tour because his brothers needed money.

The tour pulled in $75,000,000, a new record at the time. Fans came to see Michael, because few would shell out big tickets prices to just see his brothers. At the U.S. tour's conclusion, Michael announced that it would be the last time he would ever perform with his brothers, and promptly cancelled the European leg.

Through the record company, John Elliott and I secured two tickets to see the show at Madison Square Garden in New York. Fans were fired up. We grabbed a bite and headed over to The Garden, where we had great seats. The audience was filled with *crazed* Michael Jackson fans and the requisite Michael Jackson clones, those people that dressed like him, looked like him (short of plastic surgery), and danced like him. I'm sure they were hoping Michael himself would get a glimpse of one of them and bring them up on stage. We heard an explosion, followed by a large flash of light that bathed the stage, where there were bodies in silhouette against the bright backdrop. Then, the floodlights fired up all at once, as the first note of the first song showed all the Jacksons taking that all too familiar Jackson Five stance. The place went nuts. This was a thrill. Michael was still flying high from his *Thriller* album, but a majority of the songs were from *Off The Wall*. Nevertheless, it was still in my Top 5 all-time great concerts. Usually, I don't attend events at night during the week, because I have to get up at 3:30 a.m. the next day to do the morning show, but this was Michael Jackson, and I couldn't let that opportunity slip away.

Driving back to Hartford, we had been on the road for quite some time, and I didn't recognize anything along the road and started getting concerned. Soon, we were passing farms and cows. I said to John, "I don't remember seeing cows on our way to the city."

"Oh yes. Cows. I remember them. We definitely passed cows."

An hour later, we were still driving, but by then I knew for sure we were lost. A while later, I saw what looked like a toll booth up ahead. "Thank God!" I said, as we approached and pulled up o the lady "Hi. We seem to be lost. How far are we from Hartford, Connecticut?"

She looked down from her booth. "37 miles."

"No, *Hartford, Connecticut*. How far from *Hartford*?"

"37 miles."

I drove off. *No way in hell we were 37 miles from home.* We roamed around upstate New York for two and a half more hours, finally realizing that we had made a wrong turn somewhere. 37 miles my ass! We finally made it back, but unfortunately, there was no time to go home. We had to go right to the studio and on the air. (I wish I had a tape of that show. Operating on zero sleep and drained brain cells, I was completely loopy, but the concert was worth it.

Throughout the 1980s, I managed to land in a few national projects. I was a featured extra in the tv soap opera, *As the World Turns*, in a nightclub scene, where the principle actors were walking through the dining room and stopped right behind me to do their lines. For some reason—and don't ask me why—I stopped eating and just held a fork up in the air with a carrot speared on it. Nobody does a carrot on a fork better than I can.

In 1986, I landed a speaking role on another tv soap opera, *One Life to Live*. I played a reporter. I had about five lines. This was known in the business as a "Five and Under." There are three categories of performance for actors. There's the "extra," where you might be seen walking around or standing in the background, and maybe the camera sees you, maybe it doesn't, but there are no spoken lines. There's the "featured extra," where you definitely get screen time, maybe in a small scene with only a few actors in it, or maybe the camera focuses on you for a reaction, but there are no spoken lines. Then, there's the "principle," where you can have five lines or under, all the way up to a supporting role or star. Isn't it funny how you can look at a photo of yourself from years ago and cringe? In *One Life to Live*, I had hair nearly down to my shoulders and a mustache. What was I thinking?

In 1989, I went to Chicago to visit my friend Steven C Brown, who was working on radio there. I stayed at the Marriott Hotel downtown, and Steve came over one day to hang out. Being like-minded and bored, we ran down to the drugstore and bought some balloons. My room was 14 floors up and above a cab stand at street level. What better way to amuse ourselves than to fill the balloons with water and drop them from the window. The cabbies were standing outside their cars shooting the shit, and we figured out how to throw the balloons out the window in such a way that they hit the cabs. Do you have any idea what water-filled balloons sound like when they hit the hood of a car from 14 stories up? Like small bombs. We carefully peered out to get our bearing, making sure we weren't seen, and then let them fly. We waited a few seconds, and then BOOM! Screaming and cursing erupted from the street below from the poor cab drivers down there polishing up their cars so they looked pristine for the day's work. You would think that since I twice drove cabs, I would have had some compassion for them. Nope, just two radio assholes entertaining themselves. Soon, all the cab drivers were looking up at the building to figure out who was dropping the bombs, but at that point we weren't even looking out to see where the hell the balloons fell. We were laughing our asses off, and we kept doing it until ... a knock on the door. I closed the window just before a big burly hotel security guy walked in.

"What up?" I asked.

"Some clowns are throwing water balloons out their window."

Steve answered, "Gee, what stupid idiot would do that?"

The security guy went over to the window, opened it, and peered down.

The two of us didn't say a word.

He closed the window.

I said, "Hey, I'll keep an eye out for these idiots and let you know if I see anything."

He shot me a look that said, "You fuck, I know it was you guys," but he had no evidence and left.

We had another good laugh.

I was the classic example of a clown, but I was plagued by depression. Entertaining people and laughing on the outside, but dying on the inside. What was I supposed to do? I had to keep going. I had no other choice. I wasn't trained to do anything else, and I knew, at least, that I was good at what I did. Whatever world I created, I molded it by myself. It was my reality good, bad, or indifferent, I had to deal with it, and for the first time in my career, I questioned what the hell I was doing and who I was doing it for. Many mornings driving to work, I mused, *What if I just steer my car into that oncoming truck right now? It will be all over in a second.*

I literally had to kick myself in the ass to get up, go in, and do the show. I would have much rather succumbed to pulling the sheets over my head and just vegetate in bed, never imagining that those feelings, as years went on, would become less frequent and severe. Some days other than speaking on radio, I went days without saying a word to anyone.

Eight days before Christmas in 1985, and I was feeling sorry for myself, because I knew I wouldn't be seeing Rachel for the holiday. The deal I originally made with Stephanie was that she would have Rachel for Christmas, but I would have her for another holiday during the year. But the holidays, Jewish or not, is when you're supposed to be with family, and Rachel was the only family I had in Connecticut. All of my other family was in New York. Of course, I was feeling down about the situation, but then I reasoned, *At least Rachel is being treated right, and she's with her mother.*

"What about kids who have *no place to go* on Christmas?" I asked the next day on the air. "Why don't we have a party for children who have nowhere to go on Christmas day?"

We Are The children Party snow machine.

We Are The Children Santa.

We Are The Children Elves.

We Are The Children Gary, with Jesse Branche.

Aaron, Hannah, Diana, and Gary at We Are The Children.

Aaron, Hannah, Diana, and Gary.

People thought I was nuts.

"You're not going to be able to pull it off in eight days," I was told.

I love it when people tell me I can't do something, because it gives me the fuel to go full speed ahead and make it happen. The first call I got was from Jesse Branche, who basically said, "Gary, whatever you need, or need to do, I'm with you."

I aired the call.

More calls came in from people in every walk of life. Rob Gottfried—Rob the Drummer—was next offering a full band to entertain.

Food was donated, a costume shop offered free costumes of cartoon characters for people to wear, toys were collected, and phones rang off the hook from people who wanted to volunteer. The Holiday Inn in downtown Hartford said, "Use our space free to throw the party."

I couldn't believe that what started as just a mere thought on the air turned into a freight train that couldn't be stopped, as if the people of Hartford had taken over and made sure this dream became a reality.

Eight days later on Christmas Day, we had a party for about 130 kids. That on-air thought gave birth to the biggest party in America for abused, homeless, and poor children, and would continue for the next thirty years, staged as The We Are The Children party on every Christmas day. The event had become a well-oiled machine. We hosted one thousand kids, dozens of costume characters, indoor carnival rides, air slides, 300 elves, a 10-piece live band, food, Santa, and, of course, each kid left the party with about six new toys—that's about 6,000 toys. From the day after Thanksgiving until Christmas day, we fired up the community on the air, and although in some years I would have my doubts whether we'd get everything we needed, we always did.

Every year, a group of talented musicians step up and lend their extraordinary gifts such as Rob Gottfried, Tom Majesty, Dave Stoltz, Neil Gottfried, Dave Negri, Jimmy Biggins, Erriene Grieco, Bill Holloman, Mike Thrower, Gregg Allen, Diane Mower, Nancy Sousa, John Colby Liza Colby, Gabriel Colby, Bev Rohlehr, Barbara Fowler, Joe Grieco, Karin Barth, Rob Zapulla, Gordon Cohen, Polly Messer, Billy Durso, Desiree' Bassett, Bob Laramie, Tiny

Joe Eleazer, and Jeff Pevar. A special thanks to Joby Rogers, who for many years, through his performance as Michael Jackson, put smiles on the faces of every child and adult. I am forever indebted.

I just wanted to do something nice for children. I wanted them to know that, no matter what was happening in their lives, at least one day a year, somebody cared. I told myself, *If I just made some kind of impact on one child, that if they, years later, passed it on and did something good for someone else, I will have done my job.*

My payoff came years later. I walked up to a volunteer, shook his hand, and said, "I just want to thank you for giving up your Christmas to be with these kids."

He said, "No, it's me who has to thank you. You see, I was a child at your first We Are The Children party, and I told myself that when I became of age, I would become a volunteer for these kids." Wow. Full circle.

Chapter 17

The Diana Drug

At the second We Are The Children party in 1986, I met Diana at the Holiday Inn, downtown Hartford. She and her daughter, Shannon, had volunteered to work at the party. As Diana told the story, her friend, Wendy, who was the Food and Beverage Director at the time, asked, "Do you want to meet Gary Craig?"

Diana said, "Sure. Why not?" I walked up to them in my tuxedo, and Diana remembered that I was very aloof and completely impressed with myself. When I walked away, she turned to Wendy and said, "What an asshole!"

Wendy replied, "Yeah, but you'll be dating him in six months."

"You're so full of shit."

"Nope. You will. I saw the spark there."

At the time, I'm sure her observations were right on the money. Our first *actual* date was for lunch at the Wadsworth Museum cafe. I had arrived first, and I was seated at the table when Diana arrived. She marched up, saw me sitting there, and said, "When you're on a date with me, you wait to be seated."

What the hell am I getting myself into? I thought, but I was wildly attracted to her, and there definitely was some spark there.

Shortly after that first meeting, she showed up at the radio station looking for a job, without an appointment to see anyone, but she was determined to get hired. She planted herself in the lobby and said she wasn't leaving until someone saw her. The tactic worked. She was finally interviewed, which led to a sales position. I didn't even know she was in the building.

One morning, during a long break in the show, I emerged from the studio and there she was walking down the hall. My eyes followed her killer body all the way down the hall. I was hooked—not that I wasn't hooked before, even for a short period of time—but I felt that there was something was different about her, yet I couldn't put my finger on it.

In those days before text messaging and emails, we passed written notes back and forth, starting out innocent enough, but those soon got progressively more teasing and sexual in a way that would soon never be tolerated in any company.

One morning, after I knew she had had too much to drink the night before, I opened the studio door and shouted to her, as she walked down the hallway, "For someone that had too much to drink, you're sure walking okay!"

She responded, "Why don't you broadcast it to the whole world?"

"Maybe I will!"

Minutes later, and maybe for the first time ever, I regretted what I had said. I went down the hallway, found her in a meeting, stuck in my head and said, "I just wanted to say I was sorry for the comment." I ducked out and returned to the studio.

One other person in the conference room was stunned and asked Diana, "What did you do to get him to say that? He never apologizes for anything!"

From that point on, we were nearly inseparable. Our mutual sexual desires were insatiable; we were screwing in the car, elevators, building stairwells, and restaurant restrooms, but . . . our passions were balanced with intensely hot fights. If we weren't getting it on, we were fighting. I sometimes wrote her off completely, only to rekindle the romance a few days later. In 1988, the Craig and Company brand was red hot. I had, by that time, been on the air for seven years, and had more or less been #1 in the ratings during that time. Diana and I thought that we should come up with something to trade on that name. The two of us had adopted an all-natural diet, and at the time there were very few places to go to eat that would offer the kinds of food we were used to. That's when we got the brilliant idea to open a restaurant and call it Craig and Company. Why not? Everyone already knew the name, and I was a giddy idiot thinking, *Every time I open the mic and say the show's name, it will be like a free ad for the restaurant.* The fact that I didn't have the first clue as to how to run a restaurant didn't faze me. Besides, Diana had experience working at the Sheraton Hotel in Hartford in Food and Beverage.

We started looking for a location and found a space on the 2nd floor of 57 Pratt Street in Hartford. When we walked into the space, we were shocked to discover that there was already an entire restaurant there that looked like a 1950s diner complete with a counter, old-fashioned stools, tables, chairs, and equipment, literally everything we needed to start a restaurant.

Jonathan Cohen, whose dad owned and managed the building, was going to give us everything for $25,000. If we set out to find a space and had to furnish everything that was already there, the cost would have been four times that amount. Jonathan told me, "Originally, it was Jack Robbins Deli, which was huge, but then came Captain's Kirk's Galley, not so huge."

I grabbed it.

We concocted a menu and boasted that nothing on it was made with preservatives and everything was "all natural." (Of course, today, "all natural" means nothing and is somewhat of a scam. Today it has to be "organic" at the very least to carry some weight.) We believed in what we were doing, and I guess my theory of free promotion for the place every time I opened the mic rang true.

Soon, Craig and Company became the best little secret in town. We served breakfast and lunch. It didn't take long for lines to form out the door and down the stairs at lunchtime.

Jonathan also recalled, "You were going around to each table with a megaphone asking people if they were enjoying their food . . . hysterical!" We also developed regulars, who just had to come in for a specific menu item.

Celebrities in town, who were looking for alternatives in food, occasionally found their way to us. Lenny Kravitz came in for breakfast one morning, and actor David Patrick Kelly from *48 hours, Twin Peaks,* and *The Black List* came in for lunch on a recommendation from his hotel concierge.

Customers got their choice of two soups made from scratch every day. Also The Great Pretender, which was a homemade veggie burger; pizza on all natural shells on multi-grain or sourdough; and Gary's own brown rice—my original recipe—sautéed in toasted sesame oil, scallions, garlic, tamari, and ponzu, with your add-ins of

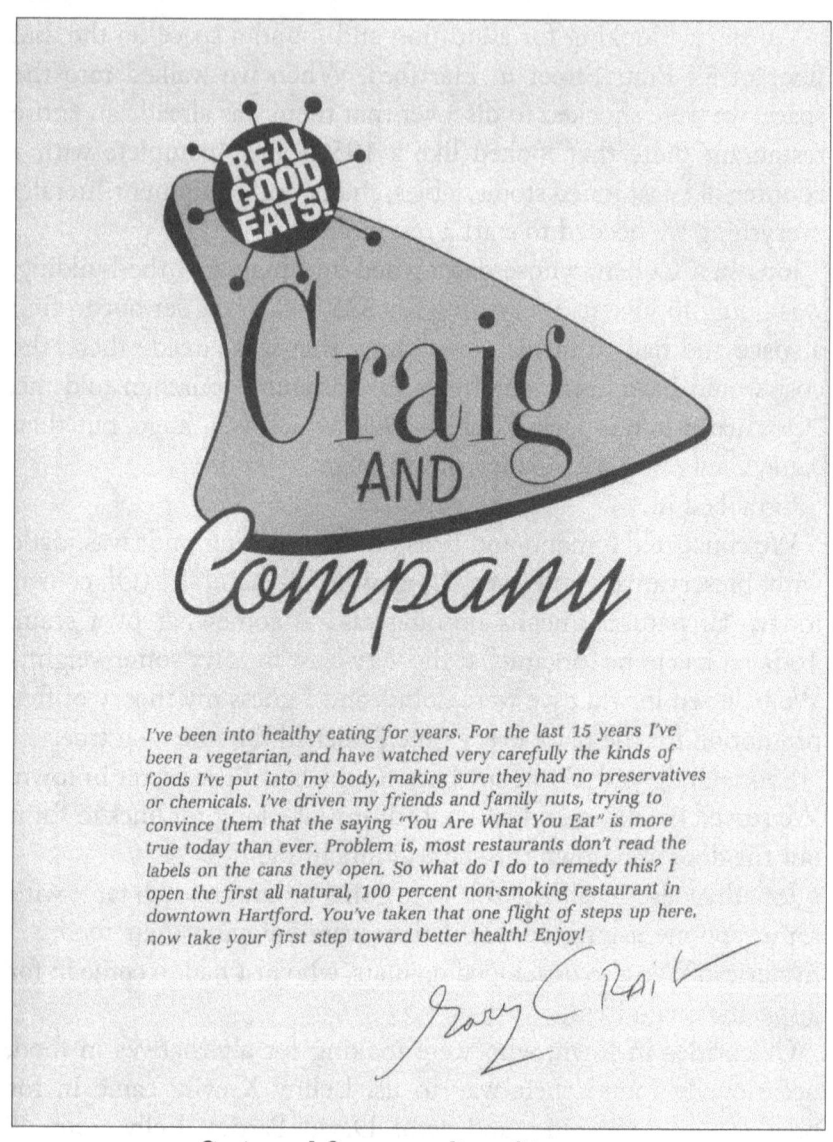

Craig and Company diner front menu.

tofu, veggies, or chicken. This was a wildly popular item. We even had all natural sodas sweetened with fruit juice.

We were way ahead of our time, so far ahead that we couldn't sustain it. First of all, we couldn't serve dinner. Once the office building closed at day's end, we closed. The second problem was that, at the time, we had to buy all our ingredients in small jars and cans because the "all natural" items had only been available to retail customers.

Luncheon

(Please check our boards for Daily Specials)

Original Recipe Homemade Soups (2 offered daily, check our boards)
Served with fresh whole grain rolls   1.95 Cup   2.95 Bowl

"Great Bowls of Fire"
Natural Meatless Chili with a kinder, gentler flavor   3.50

Sourdough Garlic Bread
Hot, Crusty & Cheesey   2.50

"Are, Uh, You Gonna Eat That Sandwich?"
– from "DINER" the movie

The Great Pretender – Served with sliced tomatoes, pickles, and lettuce over a grilled patty covered with melted cheese. This natural energy packed patty is created from a variety of grains, nuts and exotic spices and herbs on a whole grain bun, giving you an exciting alternative to the burger blues   4.95

Tuna Salad - with reduced fat mayo & fresh dill   4.95

*Chicken Salad - reduced fat mayo, celery and spices   4.95

Smoked Turkey - with lettuce and tomato on whole grain bread   4.95

The Great Veggie Meltdown - tomatoes, cucumbers, sprouts, lettuce, mushrooms covered with cheddar or mozzarella cheese**   5.25

Sea Hunt – The search is over! Our seafood salad is packed with the freshest ingredients, spices, and a dab of lite mayo. Served in a whole wheat pocket or your choice of bread.   5.25

Grilled Cheddar Cheese-crispy on the outside, gooey on the inside - like mom used to make on your choice of bread.   4.25

The Dynamic Duo - 1/2 of any one of the above with soup or salad   4.95

Tabouly - a Middle Eastern Salad made with grains, chopped tomatoes, and exotic spices served in a pocket bread   4.25

Hommos - a Middle Eastern Paté made with chic peas, sesame butter, spices served in a pocket bread with sprouts and lettuce   4.25

*Our chicken and chicken stock are free of chemicals and preservatives
** Our cheese is soy based and cholesterol free
All sandwiches served with chips & garnish

"Just The Fax" – Fax us your order for speedy delivery or pickup
Our Fax # is 524-8464

Craig & Co. is available for Private Parties Monday – Saturday.
Call 249-2772 for Details

Craig and Company diner lunch menu.

We couldn't buy a gallon jar of anything all natural, so our food costs went through the roof.

By the late 1980s, I was still living alone in the house that Stephanie and I owned in Simsbury, but before long, Diana and Shannon moved in. Shannon was a sweet girl, and the three of us more or less lived in harmony. That idyllic picture was about to be shattered. On the night of December 28, 1989 Shannon had gone out with some

Salads

Garden Party - *lettuce, tomatoes, cucumber, mushrooms, celery & carrots, Garden Fresh & Delicious* — 3.25
Sea Cruise - *Organic Natural Pasta, topped with the Seafood of the Day* — 4.95
The Charlie Chan-*Stir Fried Chicken in tamari, garlic & fresh ginger served up on a bed of greens* — 6.25
Tuitti Fruitti - *fresh fruit salad (seasonal)* — 3.25
Gary's Own Brown Rice - *sauteed in toasted sesame oil, scallions, garlic, tamari and ponzu* — 3.75

Add Ins: Tofu .50
Veggies .75
Chicken .95

The Hot Pasta of The Day!

(Check Our Boards)

Sourdough Garlic Bread
Hot, Crusty, & Cheesey — 2.25

Pizzaria

100% natural pizza shells, sourdough, multigrain, and sourdough rye topped with old world sauce and mozzarella, baked on stone to golden brown perfection! (serves 2) — 6.00

Toppers:
Mushrooms .50   Onions .50   Sausage .75
Sun dried tomatoes .75   Tomatoes .75

At the Fountain

Assorted Natural Sodas *sweetened with fruit juice, caffine & sugar free* — 1.25
Lofat Milk Shakes - *the finest quality natural ice cream or non-dairy dessert blended with lo-fat milk and fruit sweeteners to create a frosty treat to send you back to the future!* — 2.75
Bottled Spring Waters — 1.25
Iced Tea — .95

Mom's Pies

Assorted fruit pies baked to perfection using the purest ingredients and no preservatives!
Ask server for selection 1.75 per slice

Craig and Company diner salads.

friends for the evening. Nothing about that evening was particularly unusual. The weather wasn't bad, and there weren't more people on the road than usual. At around two o'clock in the morning, there was a knock on the door. I groggily roused myself out of bed and walked downstairs to find two police officers at the door. Seconds later, Diana joined me at the door. We were told there was a horrific car accident and that Shannon was in the hospital. As Diana raced

"Wake Up Little Suzie"

Start your day with whole grain cereals sweetened with fruit juice, fresh eggs from native grain fed hens, nitrite free bacon & breakfast sausage, and fresh all natural breads.

2 Fresh Eggs any style, toast — 2.25
2 Fresh Eggs with breakfast potato, toast — 2.95
2 Fresh Eggs, breakfast potato, bacon or breakfast sausage, toast — 3.95

Omlettes
(Check our boards for Daily Specials)

3 Farm Fresh Eggs with cheddar or mozzarella cheese*, toast — 4.25
Add Ins: 50 ¢ea

Turkey*   Peppers   Sundried Tomatoes
Bacon**   Mushrooms   Tofu
Sausage***

* Our cheese is soy based and cholesterol free
** Naturally cured and nitrate free
*** Made from turkey and selected spices, no preservatives

Organic Oatmeal with cinnamon and raisins
Served with 100% natural Vermont maple syrup-creamy, hot and delicious — 2.25
Crispy Cold Cereals - Corn Flakes, Raisin Bran, Rice Crispies
Naturally sweetened with fruit juice — 1.45
    With fresh fruit — .25
Old Fashioned Waffles
With 100% pure maple syrup, just like grandma used to make — 2.25
    With fresh fruit — .25
Flapjacks - old fashioned and all natural - hot off the griddle
Served with a hint of cinnamon and pure maple syrup — 2.50

—————————"A Real Basket Case"—————————
Basket of fresh natural rolls & pastry, juice & coffee

Beverages

Fresh Ground Coffee — .55
Assorted Teas — .65
Decaf Coffee — .55
1% Milk — 1.10
Fresh squeezed Orange and Grapefruit Juice — 1.50
Assorted Natural Juices — 1.40

On The Side

Bacon or Breakfast Sausage — 1.25
Breakfast Potato — 1.25
1 Egg — .25
Whole Grain English Muffin — .25
Cinnamon & Raisin English Muffins — .85

"Just The Fax" - *Fax us your order for speedy delivery or pickup*
Our Fax # is 524-8464

Craig and Company diner breakfast menu.

upstairs to get dressed, I searched the officer's faces for some sign of hope ... and I didn't see any.

One said, "It's serious," and at that very moment, I knew she was gone.

I reassured Diana all the way to the emergency room and told her not to worry, that everything would be okay, even though in my heart I knew that it wouldn't.

Shannon.

When we arrived, a doctor came out to greet us. "We did everything we could do, but she expired."

Diana collapsed on the floor, screaming.

I didn't know what to do. I'd been through divorce and bankruptcy, but even those paled compared to this. She wanted to see Shannon. We went into the room where they were keeping her and gazed on her lifeless body. It was all I could do to hold Diana and myself up. This was a horror for a parent. This was not the way it was supposed to be. The parents were supposed to go before the kids.

In the weeks that followed, it was a constant struggle to keep Diana from going over the edge. I was ill-equipped to deal with the situation, but I had to, because I had no choice. Diana had to be medicated just to be able to sleep. During the times the pills wore off, she bolted upright in bed, crying to tell me that it was all just a dream.

I was the one handling picking out a casket, arranging for the flowers, and other details. Shannon's biological father, Diana's ex-husband, never showed up to help. Diana and I weren't married, just living together, but if anything happened to any of my kids—married or not—you can bet your ass I would have been on the first flight out.

Having to navigate through this tragedy with Diana still goes down as the hardest thing I've ever done. This loss changed Diana, as well, and had a lasting impact on our lives. To her credit, she picked herself up and moved forward, one of the strongest people I had known.

One year had passed since we opened the restaurant, but Diana's heart was no longer into running it. Who could blame her? It was a very sad and rough time. Because of that and other roadblocks, so we decided to close the restaurant.

On January 5, 1991, we were married.

Chapter 18

I Own You

No matter how popular you are, or what your act may be, eventually you cease to be relevant. A younger version of you is waiting to step into your shoes. You're hot, you're hot, you're hot . . . you're not.

Here were the four stages of my career:

Who's Gary Craig?

Get me Gary Craig.

Get me someone like Gary Craig.

Who's Gary Craig?

I'd done my share of live work as a DJ in private clubs, resorts, and even weddings, but soon after I arrived at WTIC-FM, I more or less gave it up and left it to the guys that did it for a living. I didn't have the time, or the equipment, to pull it off, and frankly had little interest in pursuing it, because the few such jobs that I accepted turned out to be royal pains in the ass. I had to rent the equipment and find the music, and by the time it was over, I made little profit.

"Is this Gary Craig, the disc jockey?"

I didn't recognize the voice on the phone. "Yes."

"My son is having his Barmitzvah and he wants a DJ there for the music, and he only wants you."

I thought, *No way am I going to do this!* But out loud I told him, "Well, that's very flattering, and I appreciate that, but I don't do that kind of work anymore. I can give you the names of some great local DJs who will do a terrific job for you."

"No. He only wants you."

"Really? It would be ridiculous. I would have to charge you a fortune. For the money I'd have to charge you to come out, you could go out and hire an entire orchestra."

"Money is no object. Name your price."

I figured I'd have to make it an outrageous amount so he'd just go away. "1,000 an hour, with a 3-hour minimum, for a total of $3,000."

He didn't miss a beat. "Fine!"

After he gave me the date, time, and venue address, I thought, *Holy shit, what did I get myself into?*

I rented two turntables and an amp, pulled as many records as I could find, and schlepped out on the appointed evening. I hated it, but what the hell, he was paying $3,000 for three hours. Diana offered to help and came with me.

I hadn't done this kind of work in a long time, but I thought that I just kept the music going, and catered to the various guests making requests, I'd be alright. A song was spinning on one a turntable, when this young man walked up to me. I recognized him as the Bar Mitzvah boy.

"I want you to play a song for me."

"Sure thing. Just as soon as this song is finished, I'll put on your request."

"No, *now!*" he insisted.

"I can't stop the song that's currently playing, but I promise as soon as it's done, yours will be the next."

He leaned close to me and said, "Look, my dad is paying. *I OWN YOU!*"

He owns me? I couldn't believe what I had just heard, and I didn't know what to say, but Diana did. She whispered in my ear, "This is the last one of these you're ever doing."

In 1989, I went out to Los Angeles to visit my friend, Jeff Cahn, a film editor, who had had a great career editing numerous network tv shows. He was working for Universal Studios at the time. This was the operating studio in Hollywood, and although there wasn't a theme park there, they did have guided tram tours. Jeff wanted to show me where he worked, but he wasn't actually scheduled to work that day.

"How the hell are we going to get on the lot," I asked, "if I don't work there?"

"You put a film can under your arm and you walk right on."

"What? What if someone asks us for credentials, or asks what the hell we're doing there, or asks us who we are?"

"Look, the studio lot is filled with people walking around, and a lot of upper management, and the studio heads are young guys. Nobody would dare ask us who we are because we could be their bosses."

He was right. Each of us slipped a film can under our arms and we waltzed right onto the lot. As we were walking around, I saw a prop wishing well that obviously was used on some film, and I also saw a tram coming filled with tourists. So, I crawled down into the well and hid until the tour neared. I popped up suddenly and started waving at everyone. The tour guide, who was talking into a mic, was struck speechless and didn't know what the hell to make of it. I wasn't part of the tour. Jeff was doubled over laughing his ass off.

As we continued the tour, we quickly realized that the studio just wrapped filming on *Back to the Future 2*. Most sets were intact and amazing. I didn't grab any artifact and I didn't take any photos, which I kicked myself for later.

One of my contacts was coming up for renewal, and I had asked for a substantial raise, based, of course, on my ratings and what I was bringing in value to the station. At the time, I was negotiating with Station Manager Tom Barsanti, a great guy, but he was suddenly singing the blues about business. "You know, business is down. The station is not making as much as it used to. I think you've reached the top of your pay scale for Hartford."

I knew this was a game, but he was holding the cards on this one, yet I doubted that business was off. The morning show was on fire, and ratings were solid. One morning, I came in to get ready to go on the air, and I picked up the operating log, which was printed out every day and contained all the radio commercials that were to be played that day. Something was attached that should have been removed: extra pieces of paper showing the actual dollar amount that clients were being charged for their commercial on the morning show.

Hmmm... interesting. I grabbed an adding machine, and I added up the amount just for *that* morning—thousands of dollars—and I then multiplied that by how many days a year I was on. Got the total.

After I got off the air, I grabbed the log, walked down the hall to Barsanti's office, and stuck my head through the door. "Ha ha ha! Hey Tom!"

He looked up and smiled.

Gary as Grandfather in The Nutcracker.

"Will ya look at this? It's that extra piece of paper attached to the log that spells out how much the station is making on the morning show. Gosh, it's crazy! It comes out to about $3 million a year!"

The smile drained from his face.

I got my raise.

Tom recently weighed in. "When we brought Gary in from Charlotte, we knew he was a serious talent. Little did we know that decades later he would still be going strong. I think that Gary, working alongside the legendary Bob Steele, a totally different kind of talent, helped Gary see how being consistent pays off."

One day in 1990, the Hartford Ballet called and wanted to know if I would like to appear in *The Nutcracker*. *Okay, they're looking for publicity. I get it, but what the hell am I going to do in that show? I'm not a dancer.*

They wanted me to play the butler, which just entailed me prancing around the stage in costume and hitting certain marks on the stage synchronized with the music.

"No problem, I could do that."

I went to a few rehearsals, and then appeared in one show. Of course, I talked it up on the air, which is what they were looking for. In every city in the country, the Arts were taking a major hit. Funding was drying up, and organizations had to fight to stay alive. I was happy to do it.

The next year, they called again asking for my commitment. I told them, "I'm flattered that you thought of me again, but I've already appeared as the butler, and I see no point in repeating it."

They wanted me to do the grandfather role. This was a totally different animal. The grandfather has a huge dance number with the grandmother.

"But, I'm not a dancer."

"You'll be fine. Come to rehearsals and we'll walk you through it. Nothing to worry about."

Yeah? Famous last words. I was terrified! *What if I screw this up? It's in front of a live audience. It's not like taping a bit for the morning show, that if I screw up, I just record it again. Here, I get one shot, that's it.*

I went to many rehearsals, and it was choreographed down to the last step according to the music. On performance night, I couldn't think of anything but counting the steps in my head. In the end, I pulled it off. As soon as the number ended, I breathed a sigh of relief and then started having fun with the character. There were no spoken lines, so when my back was to the audience, I waved my hand back and forth fanning the air in front of my behind, as if grandpa just passed gas. Even over the music, I actually heard laughs from the audience. That was the first and last time anyone has done that in *The Nutcracker*.

During the morning show's history, *Craig and Company* did a lot of tv commercials. In our If You're Not Laughing campaign, we had Viola Willey, who was known as "The Laugher," in four commercials. I also produced a spot where a laughing Mark the Shark was dragged from a courtroom. Then, there was the time John and I got decked out as drag queens.

Viola Willey, The Laugher, who called in every Thursday for The Dirty Joke of The Week.

Disney also flew us down to the theme park in Florida to shoot a special spot promoting Michael Jackson's appearance in their 3D film short, *Captain EO* (1986). Disney had built an entire futuristic set, with us on the commander ship's deck.

On September 26, 1991, my son, Aaron, was born. People talk about milestones in life, particular moments that are the highlights of one's existence. It has to be when your kids are born. First was Rachel, and now this precious, smart, adorable boy, who made me realize that I had to keep going so that he would have a future. He was, and still is, sharp as a tack. Brilliant technically with electronics, he never read an instruction manual.

Diana and I settled in with the new baby, and for the first time in a long time, I saw happiness in her eyes. She loved him more, I believe, than life itself.

1993, and I was months away from the expiration of my current contract, but I'd been in this exact place many times before, always living in limbo, always insecure about the outcome and whether I'd be renewed. Certainly, I was making money for the company, but this was radio, after all. Most radio personalities typically might

Captain EO shoot with Gary and John.

Aaron and Uncle Bob.

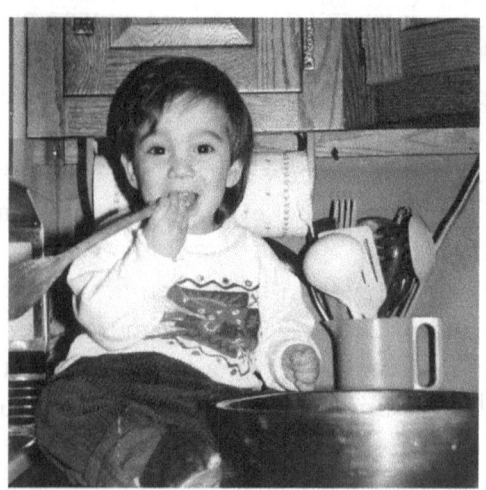

Aaron as a child.

have a run of several years, and that was it. We couldn't make any financial plans in the event that I might suddenly be out of work. At each signing of a new three-year contract, I breathed a sigh of relief, but then the old insecurities would creep in when I only had a year left. 1993 was different. I was rising high. I had a terrific run, and I was still clearly the #1 one radio personality in the market. The ratings said so.

After a Friday morning show, I was summoned to the office of General Manager Gary Zenobi to "Talk about my future." I was ready. I had compiled a list of my salary requirements and other points that I wanted in the new contract.

I sat down in Zenobi's office, where he was flanked by Program Director Tom Mitchell.

Zenobi said, "This morning's show is your last. We're taking the radio station in another direction."

I hadn't seen that coming and was blindsided by his "bullshit-speak" for "We really don't have a reason, but we had to come up with something." It really didn't make much sense at the time to get rid of the guy who's #1 and making the company millions, but in retrospect, I got it. I had some run-ins with Zenobi where I didn't back down, and I had pointed out in glaring fashion why I thought he should quit radio and go sell used cars. As much as his decision was personal, it was also a bad business decision.

To make matters worse, Zenobi also informed me, "We intend to enforce the 'Covenant Not To Compete Clause' in your contract."

The Covenant Not To Compete Clause is an old legal instrument that was originally used in the scientific community to protect companies from researchers or scientists that left one company to go to a competitor. They agreed not to work for a period of time for any competing firm, and not to reveal any secrets, so as to not damage their former company. How and why it was adopted for the radio industry was always a mystery to me. What the hell secrets did I know? None. I came in, entertained on the radio, and left. Nevertheless, this clause was in every contract that I signed, and the company was planning to hold me to it, which prevented me from working at any radio station within 50 miles of WTIC-FM for a period of six months. If I was under contract and marched

Footnotes

Rally 'round Gary Craig

Listeners and competitors reacted Tuesday to WTIC-FM's firing of longtime morning host Gary Craig. Fan Leslie Nyberg, 29, of Barkhamsted got 23 signatures at her office in West Hartford on a petition saying "the undersigned hereby protest the firing of Gary Craig." She said she planned to get more and give them to the station.

On Monday, with Craig's contract due to expire Aug. 15, WTIC-FM management told Craig his contract was not being renewed and his 11 years on the air were over. Craig expressed anger afterward, saying he had not been given a chance to say goodbye to his listeners and thank them. The non-renewal was a hot topic on morning FM shows Tuesday — and Craig's chief FM competitor, WKSS-FM's morning host Jeremy Savage, even said he wanted to offer Craig a chance to say goodbye in a WKSS appearance. Craig said in a phone interview later, "I am flattered that my comrades in radio have responded so warmly." He said he was not sure whether he would appear on Savage's show, but "I'm not totally opposed to appearing as a guest on somebody's show. After all. . . . I'm a civilian now."

News clipping reaction of my firing at WTIC-FM.

WTIC will appeal Craig job decision

WTIC-FM will appeal a judge's decision allowing the station's fired morning host, Gary Craig, to seek on-air jobs with Hartford-area broadcasters, its lawyer said Friday.

A WTIC executive Thursday had left unanswered the question of whether the station would try to counter a Hartford Superior Court decision Wednesday that granted Craig's request to be freed from a "non-compete" clause in his old contract. The clause said he could not do on-air work within 50 miles of Hartford for a year after Aug. 14, the last day of his contract.

For his part, Craig had said Thursday, "It's over."

But Friday, WTIC's lawyer in the case, Albert Zakarian of Day Berry & Howard, said, "It is not over 'til it's over. We are going to be seeking post-trial relief" — including filing an appeal, and a request for a stay of Wednesday's decision during the appeal. A stay isn't automatic.

News clipping WTIC-FM appeals the judge's decision.

into the manager's office and proclaimed that I was quitting and taking a job across town at the competitor, I could see the rationale of enforcing the covenant, but they didn't want me, and in the same breath, they didn't want anyone else to have me either. I didn't think that was fair. I had a right to make a living and support my family. What really pissed me off was that after being on the air for twelve years, I wasn't afforded the courtesy to at least say goodbye to the audience that supported me for all that time. They were probably afraid to let me continue for the little time I had left on my contract, and they probably made the right decision. No telling what I would have done on the air.

I didn't rant. I was very calm. I stood up and said to both, "Well, hold on to your nuts boys, I'll see you in court."

I walked from the office, went down the hall, quietly packed up my things, loaded them into my car, and drove home to give Diana the news. Local tv stations and newspapers all covered my departure. Jeremy Savage, who was the morning man on my main competition, WKSS-FM, said he wanted to offer me a chance to appear on his show as a guest and be able to say goodbye to my fans. There was another problem. The annual We Are The Children Party had grown into the biggest party in America for kids on Christmas day. Because promoting the party on the radio was key to its success, I was at a loss on how I would pull it off again. I quickly saw how important the event was to the station, as there were no attempts to help me continue the event. Their attitude was "Yeah, screw the kids, as long as we get Gary out of here."

WKSS stepped forward to help me promote the party so it could continue. Because I was bound by the Covenant Clause in my WTIC-FM contract, I couldn't appear on the air on any station, even as a guest, but ... the Covenant Clause didn't pertain to Diana. She could appear anywhere on my behalf, and that's exactly what she did.

Diana went on WKSS to announce that the station would be sponsoring the party. She read this statement from me: "To all my old radio friends, and all my new ones. The business of radio politics prevents me from being on the air with you. But I would not let anything get in the way of a cause I strongly believe in."

I had gone on to say in a *Hartford Courant* interview that I felt "WTIC-FM (up to that point), never really supported the party, and that it was a source of annoyance to them."

They used to call me into the office and tell me I was devoting too much air time. Tom Mitchell, the Program Director at the time, said, "That's not true. This is such a tremendous event for the children, that we support it as we have in the past." Really? Then, why was I kept off the air and not able to see it through? More bullshit, but WKSS saved me that year when they got their whole station behind it.

Chapter 19

On the Beach

"On the beach" is a radio industry term for being out of a job. I suppose I knew that my fears about not having my contract renewed would eventually become a reality, but after all those years of employment, I faced a tough time. We hadn't saved a lot of money, yet the bills were still be rolling in.

Diana said, "We'll fight them. They can't prevent you from working after they've let you go."

"What are we going to fight them with?" I countered.

My contract said exactly what I couldn't do. Besides, we didn't have the money to hire an attorney.

Diana won a wrongful death suit over the loss of Shannon, and so we immediately allocated funds for an attorney to fight my termination. I had strong mixed feelings about this. On one hand, I wanted to show WTIC that I wouldn't be knocked down that easily, but I considered, *How can I use this money?*

We had no chance of surviving if I allowed WTIC to keep me from working for six months. Nobody took on WTIC. If they did, they didn't win. WTIC had deep pockets, and the local attorneys knew that all too well.

I relented, but one by one, each lawyer in town backed away from taking my case. Maybe they didn't want what they perceived would have been a devastating loss on their score card. Just as it looked like we weren't going to find someone to represent me, Attorney Tom Heslin said yes.

What followed his acceptance of the case was a grueling three weeks of testimony, as WTIC paraded one expert after another in front of the judge to support their claim that allowing me to go to work for someone else in the market would cause then irreparable damage.

Sometime later, Tom Heslin was asked by another lawyer how long he was on his case.

"Three weeks," Tom answered.

"What are you on, a murder trial?"

"No, a non-compete action."

At trial, when I finally took the stand, the station's attorney did everything he could to rattle me and get me to snap, but I was as cool as a cucumber.

As I got off the stand and sat back down next to Tom, he leaned over and said, "You're a hell of a witness."

Day in and day out, as the trial dragged on, I could see that the judge, who didn't understand most of the technical jargon used by the other sides' attorney, started to exhibit a glazed-over expression and seemed to be tuning it all out. The testimony on both sides finally came to close, and I was exhausted. We weren't going to know the outcome right away, because the judge would have to render his decision.

Diana convinced me to take a break and get out of town. We went down to Florida, where we had a place in New Smyrna Beach, a custom-built home right on the sand. This time more than ever, I felt so lucky to have a place like that to be able to recharge.

Two weeks later, the phone rang, and I heard from my attorney, Tom Heslin. "The judge ruled that the Covenant Clause with the not to compete order was invalid, and that in general, you weren't privy to any secrets that could be of a damaging nature to WTIC. In fact, it's your case that's now making Covenant Clauses in the State of Connecticut illegal. You're on the books!"

I had won, and I was free to go back to work. Diana and I were elated. When news of my victory hit the news outlets, all stations in the market made offers for me to work for them. In an effort to win me over, the manager of a station owned by Merv Griffin asked, "Do you want me to have Merv call you?"

Two executives actually flew down to Florida to talk to me in person. One was David Pearlman, who owned WZMX in Hartford. He had just recently purchased the station and changed the format. The other manager was Tim Montgomery, who was running WTIC's main competition, WKSS-FM, (the station that had rescued my annual We Are The Children Party). I also received calls

WKSS caricature.

from other stations, as well, but in the end, I went with WKSS, who offered the best salary.

Once again, I found myself starting all over again at another station. This is the life of a DJ. Most of the time, a DJ's run at any job is more likely to be just a few years, but I was already known in the market, so I just had to reinvent myself.

1993 was also another milestone. Our daughter, Hannah, was born. *How could a complete screw-up like me produce such beautiful children?* I thought. Hannah was a sweet soul of a child, who touched us with just her smile. Hannah has my sense of humor. She gets it. She's picked up my brand of cynicism that gives her that edge in her approach and view of life. *That* I will, for better or worse, have to take credit for.

When your kids are young, you're constantly working, thriving to make a better life for everyone. When you're older, and you start checking the score, you just wish you could go back and spend more time with your children when they're young. You can't. You can never go back. You just hope that somehow they think of you as a good parent. There is no handbook. You have to make your own way.

At WKSS, my show was rebranded as "Craig in the Morning" and they teamed me up with Robin King, who was already at the station working another shift. We hit it off on the air, and I think ours was a great combination.

Jay Beau Jones was in the driver's seat, one of the great radio programmers, (and still to this day a good friend). With me on board now, WKSS had the ammunition to bring down WTIC-

FM. Jay Beau and I were always conspiring on ways to screw WTIC over. This is what radio stations do. We're always in a ratings war. We thought nothing of sending a crew out to cover competing radio station's bumper stickers with our own, or to show up at the competition's live broadcast with our own van and prizes, or to stop them from getting tickets to their core show from a local concert promoter before they did. We even complained to the FCC when they did something we knew wasn't kosher. I mocked their radio campaign slogans on the air and broiled them for a bit their morning show did, trying to diminish their impact.

One day, Jay Beau called me into his office and said, "Hey buddy, WTIC has just hired a new morning team and they'll be on the air in a couple of weeks."

"Yeah, so?" I answered, unconcerned.

"They're names are Kelly and Kline, and their benchmark bit is prank phone calls. I think you should start doing them on the air and steal their thunder."

A benchmark bit is a repeating gag gimmick like Johnny Carson's Carnac, or Jimmy Fallon's "Thank you notes," a popular routine only tied to that personality.

Post office eggravated by station's little yolk

By JON LENDER
Courant Staff Writer

The people at WKSS-FM thought their promotional stunt was eggciting.

But the U.S. Postal Service considered it eggregious, eggnoble and eggainst eggulations.

This messy situation began to emerge Monday morning when Gary Craig, newly returned to the Hartford airwaves on the station that bills itself as KISS 95.7 FM, hatched a plan for a publicity stunt.

He announced on his morning show that he would give $500 to the first person who could mail a raw egg to the station in a regular letter-size envelope. The catch was that the winning egg had to arrive intact, as in unbroken. It could be padded, but everything had to fit in one envelope.

This apparently proved difficult. Tuesday morning, there were isolated reports of unsuccessful entries whose contents ran out and caused collateral damage to nearby envelopes, which were then delivered to people who did not like being

Postal service frowns on stunt

Continued from Connecticut page

the butt of KISS' yolk.

Two eggrieved individuals called The Courant to complain.

The Connecticut District office of the Postal Service, here in Hartford, received at least one phone complaint. An official from the Postal Service called KISS to express concern about the station's inducing the public to mail items that could damage expensive automated mailing equipment or other pieces of mail, said KISS promotions director Larry Hryb.

Linda Crabb, manager of communications in the Postal Service's Connecticut District office, said she believed that to be true.

Postal regulations deal at length with the improper mailing of items such as combustible substances. There is no specific reference to poachable substances, but, Crabb said, "there are several different references in what we call our Domestic Mail Manual that specifically address harmful matter — and harmful matter can be anything that is likely to destroy, deface or damage mail or postal equipment, or to harm postal employees."

The bottom line: "The mailer is responsible for the proper packaging of the mail," Crabb said — which means the packaging should keep the material from breaking or leaking. She said postal authorities would not like this to happen again.

Anyway, while KISS personnel said they were sorry if anyone's mail was damaged, they were fairly crowing that about five dozen entries arrived in Tuesday morning's mail.

Hryb said a winner will be announced this morning. Perhaps someone named Al Bumin or Sal Monella.

WKSS egg stunt news clipping.

Thank you letter from Johnny Carson.

"I'm not too keen on the idea of using somebody else's bit," I said.

"Just think about it."

I did. The more I thought on it, the more I realized Jay Beau was right. This would totally screw them over. Stealing that benchmark bit from Kelly and Kline before they even arrived in the market was sheer brilliance.

Gary Craig's "Phoney Phone" crank calls were born, a benchmark bit for me that I would do every week for years, eventually producing enough material to release 6 CD volumes. Shortly after Volume 1 was released, I read in the paper that Johnny Carson was going into the hospital for some kind of operation. He was always my favorite. I packaged up that CD along with a note and mailed the package overnight to him. The note read, "Johnny, you've entertained me for years, and if you need a laugh during your recovery, just pop in the CD."

I didn't expect a response, and I also didn't even expect it to reach him, but stars always have "their people" weed through all their mail, filtering out what they think they should or should not be given to them. Out of the blue, a letter arrived that was signed by Johnny himself. It read, "Dear Gary, thank you so much for your note, and sending a copy of your CD "Born to Make

Chris Lemmon with Gary and Robin King in the studio at WKSS.

Crank Calls. I look forward to listening to it. Thanks again, your thoughtfulness is appreciated. Best wishes, Johnny Carson." Soon after I took to the air with WKSS, I pissed people off with a stunt I cooked up, announcing one Monday morning that I would give $500 to the first person that could mail a raw egg to the station in a regular letter-sized envelope. The catch was that the winning egg had to arrive at the station intact and unbroken. It could be padded, but everything had to fit in one envelope. This proved more difficult than it sounded. On Tuesday morning, there were isolated reports of unsuccessful entries from contestants that had mailed packages that caused collateral damage to other envelopes being mailed. The US Postal Service was not pleased, sighting the possible damage to expensive automated mailing equipment, and the violation of the rule of mailing that no package could contain "material of a harmful nature that is likely to destroy, deface, or damage postal equipment, or harm postal employees." Luckily, they didn't take any action. If I had tried that stunt today, I would be arrested. As it turned out, five dozen entries arrived in the mail, and a winner was announced—Sal Monella from Rocky Hill!

Pranks weren't just relegated to just the "Phony Phone" crank calls. I took every opportunity to get into the papers, or push the show to the edge just short of being sued, jailed, or taken off the air by the FCC. Somehow, I found out that Chris Lemmon, the son of actor Jack Lemmon and a successful actor in his own right, was living in Connecticut. We tracked him down to his address in Glastonbury. At the time, we had some hot concert tickets or a big prize to give away, and I offered it to the first listener that would go to Chris's house and get him to open the door, in person, live on the air. Sure enough, a listener took the bait. They were on their cell phone when they got to the house and we had them on the air live. (This is something we probably wouldn't attempt to do today because of the liabilities of having someone on the air live, and they might drop a few F bombs, even though most radio stations these days are on a seven second delay.)

"Ok, we have so and so on the phone with us and they're walking up the driveway of Chris Lemmon's house," I said, on the air. "Are you near the door?"

"Yes, I'm almost there," he answered. "Ok, I'm at the door now and I'm ringing the bell."

We waited a few seconds, and the door opened . . . with Chris Lemmon standing there in a towel! We heard him ask bewildered, "Yes?"

The listener babbled, "I have Gary Craig on the phone, and if you say hello, I'll win a big prize!"

Lemmon said into the phone with mock anger, "Thanks Gary . . . thanks a lot!"

Bingo! We scored a great prank and the listener won a terrific prize.

Shortly after that stunt, we had Chris Lemmon up to the studio for an interview, and we became friends. At the time, he was starting production for a show called *Thunder in Paradise* (1994), which costarred Hulk Hogan and super model Carol Alt. "Yeah, I'm going down to Florida in a few weeks to start shooting," Chris said.

"Really?" I answered. "I'm going to be in Florida in a few weeks."

"Well, why don't you come visit me on the set?"

They were shooting at Walt Disney World. When I arrived on the lot, I was met by Producer Kevin Beggs. He brought me inside their production offices, where I hung out for a while. Suddenly, in walked this guy with a bad wig and in costume, doing a terrible Fidel Castro impersonation . . . Chris! He was getting ready to shoot a scene. It was a riot, and the set had a great fun vibe. I met Hulk Hogan—the "Hulkster"—and Carol Alt, and both were very friendly. Once you're on a set, the stars just assume you belong there and usually act accordingly.

Producer Kevin Beggs and I became friends. He was only one of the Junior Producers, but a few years down the line, he called me. "I'm producing this show, and there's a part in it for you that I think you'd be great in. Would you be interested? We'll fly you out and put you up."

I didn't have to even think about it. "When do I pack?"

The show was *Baywatch* "Wet and Wild" (1995, Season 5, Episode 22). I had three or four lines in a scene, where I played an announcer in a daredevil motorcycle jump show. Big stretch, huh? We shot the scene right on Venice beach. There was no security whatsoever. In fact, the director walked up to the sand, and said, "Hey, you girls want to be in this scene?"

"Sure!" they said.

That's how he filled the frame, so loose that I couldn't believe it. I was on my mark, I'd memorized my lines, and the director sat on his big rig and swung into place, with the giant camera right in front of me. He said, "Now Gary, when we start the scene, I don't want your eyes to wander past this point," and he showed me physically how far past the camera lens I can turn. All of a sudden, like in a movie, everything went into slow motion for me, and I thought, *What is better than this? I'm on the beach, I'm the focus and shooting this scene for a national tv show, and I'm getting paid for it! All the stars bitching about this and that are literally out of their minds. This is not work. Digging a ditch is work!* We wrapped the scene, as the sun was starting to slowly come down.

The assistant director walked up to me and asked, "Can you stay a little while longer? The director wants to put you in another scene."

That, my friends, is how luck sometimes hits those of us in show business. (Kevin Beggs later became Chairman of the Television Department at Lionsgate.) I'd been on national shows before, such as *As The World Turns* and *One Life to Live*, but this was different. *Baywatch* was a huge worldwide phenomenon and a lot of people saw that episode.

In 1993, Vsevolod Shilovsky, a Soviet and Russian film and theater actor and film director, arrived in Connecticut to shoot his film, *The Verdict* in Canton, Connecticut. Someone made a connection with the WKSS, and I was cast in the role of a tv reporter. I just think they needed a location to shoot a scene that *looked* like a tv studio, so that's where the connection to the radio station was created. It was a bare bones, run and gun production. Only one guy, a production assistant, spoke English. The rest of the crew, including Vsevolod, who was starring in the lead role, also didn't speak a word of English. During production, they borrowed my car, which they crashed and ultimately had to pay to get repaired. The strangest thing about that film was that it didn't matter what lines I actually spoke on camera, because they later removed my voice and dubbed in a Russian-speaking voice actor. I was, as I recall, in three scenes. One was shot in the radio station's parking lot, the other one in a WKSS conference room, which came off extremely cheesy. It was supposed to be the set of a television news show, but they left the WKSS banner up behind me. Ah, those Russians—they just didn't get it.

The final scene was shot on location in Canton. An English-speaking assistant explained what the scene was about. "The hero is reunited with his love interest, and you are the reporter on the scene. You walk toward the camera, and just make up dialogue. It will be replaced later in post-production."

The actors were set, camera was ready, and the director said in Russian, "действие!" (pronounced dey-stv-iye), which meant "Action!"

As the camera dollied up to me for a close-up, I made up dialogue like he had instructed. I said, "I've got a boil on my ass, the size of Chicago. You wouldn't believe the size of the thing. I can't even sit down. I need an extra pair of pants just to carry it around."

The director yelled, "порез," (pronounced "porez"), which meant "Cut!"

I saw the assistant convulsed with laughter. He walked over to Vsevolod and told him in Russian what I had said, and *he* cracked up!

When it came time to release the film, they renamed it *Prigovor*.

In November 1994, O. J. Simpson, a former National Football League (NFL) player, broadcaster, and actor, went on trial on two counts of murder for the June 12, 1994 deaths of his ex-wife, Nicole Brown Simpson, and a restaurant waiter, Ron Goldman. The country was riveted to Cable News Network (CNN), as they watched the live coverage of his Ford Bronco chase prior to him turning himself in, and now the trial was about to begin with, again, live in-court coverage. The sordid details dominated the news every day. About two weeks prior to the beginning of the trial, I got a call from a guy named Mike Evans. He was promising to cover the daily proceedings with unprecedented access in the courtroom. I didn't know this guy from Adam, but he had an attractive offer. "Use me for a week on the air free. I'll do a live report every day, and you can see if you like it." Apparently, this worked on many stations around the country.

I took the bait. "Mikey," as I started calling him, was terrific. During the trial's entire run, he was *in* the courtroom and presented our listeners a point of view that nobody else had.

After the trial was over, Mikey transitioned to a daily Hollywood gossip-type of report, and we decided to keep him. Glad we did, because he became a daily fixture and feature that listeners always mentioned.

At the O. J. Simpson trial's height, we found a doppelganger for Judge Lance Ito, the Los Angeles County Superior Court Judge that had presided over Simpson's trial. By then, Ito was in the country's collective consciousness, as America was riveted to the courtroom television coverage every day. Jbeau Jones and I went to Tim Montgomery and asked for the money to bring Ito's double in. We had to fly him to Hartford, and we paid his fee of $1,000. I had to laugh, because I was sure that any time Montgomery saw me and Jbeau walking into his office, he thought, *Oh no, what now?*

Mike Evans.

Suzane Northrop.

We got our money's worth out of the Ito doppelganger. While we were on the air that morning, they paraded him around making appearances. That night, Scott, Ito's double, and I brought him to the Hartford civic center. We even had enough time to shoot a TV commercial with him supposedly in his judge's chamber dancing around while listening to WKSS on the radio.

It was a lot easier pulling off pranks and stunts back then. WKSS wasn't owned by a conglomerate; it was basically a "mom and pop" operation. If we needed something, we just walked down the hall and made the request. (Years later, if I need an extra roll of toilet paper, I was told, "Let me run that by legal.")

Scott Pitek was my producer at WKSS. Scott was known as "Rocky," his nickname given to him by a radio station in New York. He had that New York attitude that I love, because I also spoke

David Pearlman.

the language. One day, he came into the office and said, "Hey, I've got a great guest for you."

"Who is it?"

"Her name is Suzane Northrop, and she talks to dead people."

"Get the fuck out of the office."

"No really," he insisted. "We had her on the air in New York. She's amazing!"

I relented. "I'll give her 10 minutes, but if she doesn't dazzle me, she's out of there."

Suzane was on the air with us for two hours, and I begged her for a return date. There have been a lot of skeptics out there, and I know that listening to her sounded crazy. How the hell can she communicate with people who have passed over? But she has a gift.

Judge Lance Ito's lookalike.

In all her on-air visits, she was able to tell people things that would have been impossible to know. One morning, she was on the air with us talking to a listener on the phone, and Larry Herb, who was our Promotion Director at the time, walked into the studio to watch her work. Suzane stopped talking and turned to Larry and said, "Your dad is in the studio with us. He's holding a fishing pole. He wants you to know he's okay and you have to let go." Then, she continued the conversation with the person on the phone.

I looked out the corner of my eye and saw Larry slumped to the floor and crying. We came to find out that his dad used to take him fishing every week and that Larry still had extreme grief over his passing.

I can repeat that same scenario in dozens and dozens of stories of Suzane's readings. On one of her appearances on the air, Diana called during a commercial break.

I said, "I have this lady on the air with us, and she apparently talks to people who have passed away. Do you want to talk to her?"

Diana was hesitant to talk about Shannon. Finally, she agreed.

I told her, "It has to be on the air, because she doesn't have the time to talk to you privately."

She agreed.

I didn't tell Suzane who she was or who she wanted to talk about, so I began, "Diana, you're on the air with Suzane Northrop. Go right ahead."

Suzane said, "Hi Diana. Who do you want to talk to?"

"I'm calling about my daughter, Shannon."

"I feel she went quick, Diana—a BOOM, and she was out of here." (As you recall, Shannon was in a car crash that took her life instantly.) Suzanne continued telling Diana other things about Shannon that she had no knowledge of.

Just amazing and weird things happened around us when Suzane was in our presence. On many occasions we had Suzane over for dinner at our home the night before her morning appearance the next day. Electrical disturbances, and things not working properly, were common. One time, Suzane and some of her promotion people came for dinner, and the conversation at that dinner party was enlightening, amazing, and eclectic. Somehow, we got into a conversation about Ouija Boards, just a lighthearted discussion of how we used to have them as kids and whether anyone thought that the triangle in the center *really* was being moved by something or did we kids move it and made believe that it worked.

Suzanne weighed in. "You should stay away from Ouija Boards. They're dangerous."

"Dangerous?" I asked jokingly. "Come on, it's just a toy!"

"No, you're inviting entities into your house that you don't necessarily want."

I didn't believe it and tried to reason even further that it was just a board game invented to entertain. Just then, for no reason, a filled wine glass placed in front of another guest shattered and spilled. We all gasped, and when I looked over at Suzane, she just had a smirk on her face. Point made. (To this day, she makes the trip from New York twice a year to be on the show.) There is a part of me that thinks it's all bullshit, but I don't know how Suzane could be telling people the kind of accurate details about their lives. Even some of my relatives have come through from time to time, and I miss these people, so maybe it's hope that tends to make me want to believe.

The Snapple drink company announced they were holding a contest for people to come up with their own jingle extolling the virtues of the beverage, and winners would get their creation aired all over the country. *Wouldn't it be great*, I thought, *if I could come up with something that would score a win? The other stations in the market would be forced to play it, and it would be a very special "Up yours" to WTIC-FM knowing they were airing me yet not realizing it. After all, all radio stations are whores . . . they'll never turn down money.*

I went into the studio and whipped something up, never really thinking I would win, but sure enough, I did. I knew ahead of time when the jingle was aired, but I had to keep it to myself. I wanted the stations in the market to be running the commercial with my jingle in it for several weeks before I let the cat out of the bag. Then, one morning I opened my mic and said, "You know that Snapple jingle that's on the air that all the radio stations are running? You know, the one that says, Gary Crattick of Windsor? Yeah . . . that's me. What a riot.

The Hartford Courant ran the story:

Trickster Gets Snapple Jingle Played On Radio

October 17, 1994 By MARIE K. SHANAHAN, Courant Staff Writer

If you've been listening to the radio lately, you may have heard a new Snapple All-Natural Beverages commercial on a number of Connecticut stations. It features a jingle submitted by a man from Windsor, Gary Crattick.

The singer—of sorts—is the latest addition to the nationwide family of ordinary people, who get their songs in the commercials starring "Wendy the Snapple Lady." But what local radio listeners and competing radio stations don't know is that Gary Crattick of Windsor is no ordinary person. He is actually Gary Craig, the morning radio personality from WKSS-FM (95.7). (Craig really does live in Windsor. He moved there a year ago.)

"One of the great fantasies of a morning man is to get his voice on other competing stations without them knowing it," said Craig, "and I did it legitimately."

An added bonus: Snapple paid Craig for the jingle.

The commercial is now on a national 12-week run in radio markets in Los Angeles; New York; Chicago; Portland, Ore.; and of course, Hartford. It's been heard on the Sebastian show on WCCC-FM (107) and also on WHCN-FM (106).

"Snapple should enforce the playing of all their commercials, including mine," Craig said sarcastically, "because local stations probably won't play it anymore once they find out it's me."

This isn't the first trick Craig has pulled—or tried to. In June 1993, he and a cohort submitted a fake wedding photograph to *The Courant* as an intended publicity stunt for the radio station. In the picture, Craig was dressed as the bride, wearing a wig, high-collared dress, and long gloves. *The Courant* realized a prank was afoot and did not publish the photo with its wedding announcements.

Craig, whose legal name is Arthur G. Gopen, got this latest idea after interviewing the Snapple Lady a few months ago. Wendy Kaufman had told him how an ordinary person could submit a jingle.

Kaufman was in Hartford last week at a WTIC-FM (96.5) party and knew nothing of Craig's commercial entry, he said.

His jingle, created in the WKSS studio "with the perfect blend of cheese,'" was completed in about 40 minutes, Craig said. All the tune's background sounds, like the bass and the trumpet, were made not by instruments but by the announcer's voice.

Craig made sure not to make the recording sound so professional as to scare Snapple off. He also made sure not to use his own name, "just in case,'" he said.

Craig, or rather Crattick, found out about a month ago the Snapple people were interested in his song after Snapple's New York office called.

"[Snapple] must get thousands of jingles every week," he said. "The odds of getting picked are zero to none. I was very surprised when they called me."

"All the things we were doing on the air added up to big ratings," Jay Beau recalled. "With Gary's help, KISS went to #1 12+ beating WTIC FM. First time in history that had happened. I was the first PD in history that beat WTIC FM."

What's equally impressive, WTIC had a better signal than WKSS in Hartford, but there was a fly in the ointment. Aside from the remuneration, Tim Montgomery, operating partner and GM of WKSS, had made me a promise. I wanted the morning show to be syndicated. There were several morning shows in the country that were successful in getting their programming on other stations, and when I signed my three-year contract, Tim assured me that it would happen, but as time wore on, I saw that more than likely it wouldn't. I kept reminding Tim what he had promised, but he never addressed it. Six months before the contract ended, Tim called me into his office and told me he was working on the syndication, but by then it was too late. I had decided that I wasn't going to renew my contract. Management tried everything to get me to stay. Don Law, one of the owners, came down from Boston to try to talk me out of leaving, but I had already made up my mind. I was about to make another move.

Chapter 20

Second Time is A Charm

David Pearlman, who owned WZMX, had unsuccessfully tried to hire me three years earlier. He had since formed a company called American Radio Systems. He and his partners rolled WZMX into that company ... and then they bought WTIC AM and FM, my former employer.

John Elliott, my former WTIC morning show partner, had planted a seed with David that my contract with WKSS was coming to an end and that I might be persuaded to return to WTIC-FM.

I took a lunch with David in Boston. I came prepared with a list of "must haves" if I was to consider a return to the morning show after having been previously dumped so unceremoniously by WTIC and having sued them over my contract's Covenant Clause. As I went down this extensive list, David said "No problem" after each item. The last item on the list was a deal breaker: someone was still employed at the station that I wanted gone ... Gary Zenobi, the guy that had dumped me nearly four years earlier.

David said, "No problem."

When Zenobi learned that I was coming back to the station, he quit.

Because of my earlier lawsuit against WTIC-FM, Covenant Not to Compete Clauses about not working for competition to compete were eventually made illegal in Connecticut, but that was a bit down the line. I made the deal with David to come back, but because I wasn't fired from WKSS and had just walked away after my contract expired, I had to honor *their* Covenant Clause that was in my WKSS contract.

At Eagle 93.7 in Boston, I met Eric Caldwell, who was the Producer of a show without a morning guy, but he had a girl named Lorrie anchoring the show. David Pearlman's solution to work around my Covent Clause on my WKSS contract was to stash me in Boston for six months and doing the morning shows at Eagle

93.7. After I arrived, Lorrie, Eric, and I increased our ratings spectacularly within six months.

I begged David to let me stay in Boston, but he said, "We need you too much in Hartford."

That was a bit of letdown, because I knew if I was able to stay in that market, I would have most certainly duplicated the success I had in Hartford.

In 1996, I insisted that David let me bring Eric with me as my Producer on my return to WTIC. I walked back in and it was a little weird. Bill Stairs was the Program Director, and there was an orientation being held in a conference room for all new employees and current employees that had made the cut and survived the station's recent sale to American Radio Systems.

Until that day, only management knew that I was coming back, so when I arrived, it was a bit of surprise to the rest of the staff. What was uncomfortable was that as I was turning the corner to enter the conference room, I passed my old office and saw Kelly and Kline packing up their things to leave, and they saw me come in. I felt bad, in the same way years earlier when I replaced Jeremy Savage and took over mornings at WKSS. In the years I had been at WKSS, I beat Kelly and Kline in the ratings easily. I worked at it night and day, in the battle trench.

Coming back to WTIC-FM, I realized that, once again, I needed to reinvent myself. That meant discarding most of the old characters listeners were used to hearing, such as Rusty Hinge, Major Minority, and others, but I brought back The Crazyman, using the same voice that I had used for years as his character on tv and radio. Characters were not the way to go. This time, I had to be real and appeal to every demographic. It couldn't just be two guys on the radio anymore. I needed a female cohost.

We launched a nationwide search, and started getting cassette tapes from all over the country. Back then, radio personalities taped themselves right off the air and sent those tapes out to try to land jobs in markets larger than their current town or city. Two months went by, and with each new batch of tapes, prospects seemed hopeless. I could tell in the first thirty seconds if someone had it or not, and if they didn't, I tossed the tape. Just when I was ready to resign

Christine, Gary, and John, the second time around.

Craig and Company: Gary, John, and Christine.

myself to the boy's club, four more tapes came in. I was the only one listening to them. I went through the motions of giving thirty seconds to three of the tapes before they wound up tossed, too, but the fourth tape was different. I heard real talent. She had an incredible voice, sounded intelligent, possessed a great laugh, and was obviously wasting her time doing a show in Lincoln, Nebraska. Her name was Christine Lee.

I ran down the hall to management. "This is it! I found her! She's the one!"

We all listened to the tape again, and everyone who heard it nodded in agreement.

"Well, let's see if we can get her out here," Stairs said.

Christine arrived, and we saw for the first time that she was on the heavy side and wore the worst wig I have ever seen. I had this misguided, preconceived notion of what she might look like, thinking, *She'll show up, be a blonde bombshell, and be great for personal appearances. She'll give the show a boost!*

Nobody saw us on radio, so what we delivered on the air was what counted. After her visit came to a close, I took her to the airport, and she was mulling over whether she was going to take the job or not.

"You know," I said, "You might want to think about losing some weight."

I knew the second the words came out of my mouth that it was a critical mistake. What an asshole I was, but it was too late to shove the words back in.

A day or two later, Christine called to tell me that she was passing on the morning show.

John and I went on damage control, calling her every day, apologizing for the idiotic comment, and begging her to take the job. She finally accepted, and about a month later, she was on the air.

Throughout my tenure at WTIC-FM, I went through many program directors. Every time a new one came in, he tried to "lay down the law" to me with, "We're going to have air check seasons every day." Those were meetings where they played back show recordings and gave me constructive or destructive criticism.

Of course, I always answered with, "Uh, not going to happen. If you have to meet with me every day to go over my show, I'm the wrong guy for the job."

Soon they always realized the best thing for them was to just leave me along and let me do my job.

WTIC Program Director Bill Stairs was one of the strange ones. When he first came to the station, he brought his daughter with him every day for the first four weeks, and she spent the entire day in his office on his couch. I thought that was odd. *Bill, get a baby sitter, or better yet, why isn't she in school?* There were other problems with him. He made knee-jerk decisions that made no sense. One day, he proclaimed, "Beepers for everyone! Everyone has to be available to me day and night!"

Astounded, I argued, "You need to get ahold of me at two in the morning? For what?"

There were other things, like the time I was on vacation and he issued a memo that said I wasn't coming back. There was the time he told John Elliott, "You will eat my shit if I tell you to."

John said, "Uh, can you come with me and repeat what you just said to General Manager Susanne McDonald?"

I started sending Bill emails that said, "I'm on to you," and "You're not fooling anyone," and "Your days are numbered here."

Finally, I marched into Suzanne's office and told her to get rid of him. Two weeks later, he was gone.

Steve Salhany was the Promotion Director at the time of Bill's departure. At that year's company Christmas party, Suzanne walked up to John and me and asked, "I'm thinking of making Steve Salhany program director. Do you have any objections?"

We didn't. Steve was a great guy with an easygoing management style. He basically left me alone to do the show as I saw fit. I just thought it was funny that Suzanne needed our approval before she offered the job to Steve.

President Bill Clinton was coming to town for an event at Mohegan Sun. Of course, I'd been impersonating him for years on the show. Every woman in America was in love with him, and Diana was no exception. When it came to women, he was like a magnet; all he had to do was walk into a room, and the excitement women felt was palpable.

"I want to go see Bill Clinton," Diana announced.

"Why do you want to see Bill Clinton?" I asked.

"Because he's hot."

This was easy enough to arrange. I always had a great relationship with the casino, so we arrived in a special room that was filled with about a hundred people waiting for Clinton to arrive. John, Christine, and I were part of the press corps and we were cordoned off a

Bill Clinton with Diana.

Bill Clinton with Gary and Patrick O'Connor.

few rows back. I called Diana, who was up in the room, and told her to come down and I would get her in.

She came down and saw where I was, grabbed champagne that was being served for the VIPs and walked to the front line right in before the stage. Clinton arrived like a rock star, and the place went crazy. He reached down and shook Diana's hand, walked down the front row to do the same, and came back to stage center.

Diana asked, "Mr. President, would it be alright if I got a picture with you?"

"Of course," he answered, grabbing her hand and pulling her on stage with him.

By then, I was there with the camera to take the picture. Diana's dress matched Clinton's tie. I grabbed a shot, and I also took one of him with my producer at the time, Patrick Seton O'Connor.

Later on after the event was over, I remarked, "How great is that? You got a picture with Clinton."

Diana answered, "Yeah, it was great. He rubbed his hand over my ass."

"What?"

"Yes, he rubbed his hand up and down my back, and then he ran his hand over my butt. I'm commando—no panties—so he did it again and gave it a little squeeze. I wasn't angry. I just had to laugh, and thought, *How many asses has he massaged?*"

Chapter 21
Berle, Caesar, and Bill

Gary and Milton Berle.

Gary with Sid Caesar.

I saw an advertisement for a traveling celebrity roast show that was coming to the Oakdale Theatre featuring Milton Berle and Sid Caesar and some other comics from that time. An argument could have been made that Milton Berle really was too old for our demographic, but I believed that an icon like him really transcended age groups, and unless you've been living under a rock most of your life, you knew who "Uncle Miltie" was.

We had him on the show. He was funny, touching, and great. Of course, I would have been remiss if I didn't ask him the most important question about whether the story about the size of his dick was true. This was a legendary show business tale about his manhood that had been flying around for years. Celebrities have claimed to pull him into men's rooms and demand that he drop his pants to show them. "Roastmaster General" Jeffrey Ross claimed to have been taking a leak next to him one day and saw that it was huge.

"Miltie, is it true about the size of your manhood?" I asked.

All he did was laugh, but it was the kind of laugh that said, "Yeah, well, if I were there in the studio, I'd show you."

I had another interesting connection to Milton and Sid. Both celebrities had dined in my grandfather's restaurant, Moskowitz and Lupowitz. I grew up seeing their pictures hanging in the restaurant, and now I possess all those vintage photos. Both of their pictures were taken in the early 1950s, and Milton's showed him sitting next to a hot brunette. I got a ticket to the show, and I arranged to go backstage, thinking that they might want to have their pictures copied. I printed them out and had them framed. When I arrived in the doorway of Milton's dressing room, he looked up and said, "Gary! Come on in. Great to see you!" as if we'd been friends for years. He was sitting on a couch surrounded by a group of people.

"Milton, I brought you a little present, thought you might enjoy it," I announced, handing him the photo. "It was taken in my grandfather's restaurant, Moskowitz and Lupowitz."

He held it up and said, "Look everyone, look how young I was!"

It was a touching moment. No jokes, just him looking back. He didn't address the hot brunette sitting next to him, but she wasn't his wife!

Next, on to Sid's dressing room. He was alone, and he looked rather frail. I handed him the picture. He was puzzled at first, but then something came back to him. "I know this . . . I know this place . . . this is Moskowitz and Lupowitz!" he proclaimed.

I couldn't believe it. *What a memory!* I thought.

Then, he dropped a bombshell. "I was married in the restaurant."

I had never heard that story. Nobody in my family ever told me that fact. Nine years later, my cousin, Phillip Anzel, son of my actor uncle Hy Anzel, said that Shelley Winters was also married in the restaurant. Amazing.

Meeting Miltie and Sid, for me, was of great significance, because those two men single-handedly invented "appointment viewing" and motivated more people across the U.S. to buy tv sets than anyone else, back when Milton's *Texaco Star Theatre* and Sid's *Show of Shows* dominated television viewing for years. Imagine people buying a tv set just to see one or two shows that everyone was talking about? It was like someone getting Netflix today just to watch *House of Cards*.

At WTIC-FM, Gary, John, and Christine were the new order, well-oiled machine, and Christine breathed new life into Craig and Company. An amazing talent, she was one of the very few people who could routinely crack me up.

I continued to do crank calls and released 6 new CDs throughout the 1990s. Crank calls got us into plenty of trouble, and Christine took credit for some of it just through association with me. Once I had mastered a Bill Clinton impression, Christine and I did a series of "Clinton Calling" bits. I had read where Elizabeth Taylor was in the hospital, and I wanted to see if I could get through to her. Christine always played Clinton's secretary, because it made sense that he would have someone calling for him. If I just called people as Bill Clinton, it wouldn't have been believable, so Christine's voice was first heard saying, "Hello, I have the President of the United States on the line for Ms. Taylor."

They told us to call back in five minutes, because she wasn't ready to speak to anyone just yet. We waited and called back. They were expecting the call, and they put me through. A very sweet voice answered, "Hello?"

"Hello Elizabeth, it's Bill Clinton."

"Oh, Mr. President, is it really you?" she asked.

"Hillary and I are thinking of you, and wanted you to know that when you recover, we'd love to have you up to the White House for lunch."

"Oh, that would be wonderful."

Soon after that, we ended the call. We were all dumbfounded that we even got through, and more shocked that she bought the whole bit. I'm assuming some listener called the *National Enquirer* and tipped them off to what I had done, because the next week, we were in the publication. "Shock Jock Gary Craig takes advantage of an ailing Elizabeth Taylor" a headline screamed.

Shock Jock? I've been called a lot of things but never that. I left that moniker to Howard Stern. I thought I was doing Elizabeth a favor by lifting her spirits and giving her something to look forward to. Alight, so I was just looking for a great bit, but I could have taken the phone conversation south and really been cruel, yet I was completely respectful.

As soon as that *National Enquirer* hit the stands, *American Journal* dispatched a van to my house. The doorbell rang. I looked out through the window to see the truck and a guy standing outside with a camera on his shoulder that I could see was on because the little red light was on. I never opened the door, but instead called John. "You're not going to believe this, but *American Journal* is outside of my house right now getting ready to ambush me."

John said, "They're outside of my house, too."

That wasn't the only time when "Clinton Calling" got us into trouble. I had read in the news that Walter Cronkite had injured his knee. I also knew that Bill Clinton had fallen down some stairs at golfer Greg Norman's house and sustained a similar injury. This fact opened the door for a call to Walter Cronkite. So, once again, Christine played the secretary for The President, and this time, we got right through to Walter. The call went flawlessly, except I made the mistake of letting him off the hook at the end of the conversation. "Walter, this isn't the President, I'm actually Gary Craig at WTIC-FM."

Cronkite let out a tiny snicker and hung up. I thought that was the end of it, but later on that day, the receptionist at the front desk called me at home to give me the message that Walter Cronkite had called the station and wanted me to call him back.

I called John, and said, "Walter Cronkite called and wants me to call him. What the hell does he want?"

"I don't know," John said, "but you better call him back, but conference the call so I can listen in."

I dialed the number for New York. They put me right through. I had no idea what to expect. Walter got on the phone and said, "Is this the Gary Craig that called me earlier today?" He sounded mad. "Why in the world would you do such a thing?"

Now I felt two inches tall, as if being reprimanded by my father. I had to offer a reason why I would do that to the most respected newsman on the planet. "Well sir, I knew if I had just called you as myself, I would have never gotten through. I really admire you, and just wanted a chance to get you on my show."

"If you had just asked for an interview, I would have given it to you. I don't know why people your age do what you do. I should sue you for what you did, but I won't."

I meekly answered, "I'm sorry sir. I just wanted to talk to you."

He hung up.

I had just pissed of Walter Cronkite! I became paranoid about the call, and not only didn't we air it, but I went ahead and erased it! That was dumb, but at the time I wasn't sure if he was going to make good on this threat to sue, and didn't want any evidence.

I have shocked and pissed off hundreds of people in New England and around the country with my Phoney Phone cranks calls. I once called a new mom and told her that I was from

City Hall and the name she used for her baby has been revoked because the quota for that name has been filled. I've ripped my glass eye out of my head, and had it fall on the floor. I've drilled my own teeth on the air. I've called people to tell them, "I'm home, naked, and thinking of you."

We shocked a wife by telling her that her husband had been let go because he was caught having sex on a desk with his secretary. I called my dad's gas company to tell them I had a terrible gas leak, which was actually me not being able to control my farts. They turned off his service. When I called some veterinarians to tell them "my bee is sick," they just hung up on me, except for the last vet, who told me to shove the bee up my ass. I pretended to be Yoda from the *Star Wars* film series and called an 800 sex chat number looking for some action. One prank call had to do with my cat getting stuck in a motorized litter maid litter box, complete with all the screeching and screaming of the cat. I tried to get some help from someone when my penis was on fire. My head has been allegedly stuck in a fence, a bucket, and an oil can.

Taking slogans literally, I once called Olive Garden restaurant and thanked them for paying for all my relatives because their slogan was, "When you're here, you're family." Staples lost their patience with me after I called and asked for a bunch of shit they didn't have, and then I reminded them that their slogan was "Staples, yeah, we have that."

My character, Julius Johnson Jr, has called the people that make raison bran to tell them "I counted them, and there aren't two scoops of raisins in the box."

Of course, Dr. Psychovet, the sick veterinarian I portrayed, made a series of calls about the puppies, the kitties, the bunnies, the bats, and who knows what else. Our duo act, the Midgets of America (MOA), Shorty and Stinky, did their own insane group of calls.

I was arrested for one crank call that was initiated by a husband that gave me all the details about his house and that his wife kept her underthings in a hat box. She was the target, but she was at work at the time. The bit was that I would pose as a cable guy, call her, and describe everything in the house as if I was inside . . . but it went terribly wrong. When she answered the phone, I, of course, knew her name, and told her I was "Stew from Cox Cable," and I stated her exact address, then went on to tell her we had a surge problem at her house and that her cable service was going to be out for about three weeks.

"Three weeks?" she asked, alarmed.

I went on to tell her that the surge blew out a bunch or capacitors and couplings, and I used a bunch of mumbo-jumbo technical terms, because "I used to be an electrician," I stated. Then, I said,

"I had to go up to the roof and tear away part of it, but don't worry, because "I used to be a roofer and we'll get that taken care of. In fact, I'm calling you from inside the house and some of your outlets got blown out."

"You're inside my house?" she asked in a panicked voice.

"Oh yeah, I'm inside the residence, because . . . I used to be a locksmith." I started to point out the home's content room by room. "Yup, there's the green chair, the Sony big screen tv, and, oh, there's a kitty. Here kitty kitty. Now I'm in your bedroom. What's this, a hat box? Oh, you have some very nice lingerie in here."

She said, "Uh . . . can you hold on?" Then, she came back on the phone again, but the voice was one of her co-workers *posing as her*. I knew something wasn't right, and it was at that point I told the poser that it was all a joke, that it was a crank call, and to get her back on the phone. What I didn't know was that when she put me on hold, she had called the police to tell them there was an intruder in her house. The Meriden police department came up with sirens screaming and kicked the front door in, only to find a screeching cat.

The police were pissed because they were embarrassed. They decided to make an example of me by calling the radio station to inform me that either I turn myself in or they would come and arrest me on the spot. Management hired an attorney for me. I was taken down to their precinct, fingerprinted, and a mug shot was taken.

When we finally came before a judge, and she heard the case, she had a smirk on her face, as if thinking, *Really? This is what you're bringing me, an idiot who's doing crank calls?* She admonished me for the stunt, and threw the whole thing out of court. My record, fingerprints, and mug shot were expunged, but that year, I sold more Phoney Phone crank call CDs than I ever had. I actually went on to do the call again with 5he same exact information but a different couple, and that time it went off without a hitch.

The first location of WTIC-FM was in the Gold Building in Downtown Hartford. In those studios, I couldn't see John when we were both on the air at the same time, because his news studio was down the hallway from mine. One day, he was excited telling me something that was right out of the news.

I paused and said with a deadpan look, "Well, John, that sucks . . . and anybody that like it also sucks."

John was pissed. He was the ultimate guy to pull shit on because he got mad. Eventually, he joined the rest of us in using that phrase, but didn't get it at the time.

I was in New York in an office building elevator. The door opened and in walked Arnold Schwarzenegger with a few other people. I couldn't believe it. What kind of luck is this? The elevator continue up, and Arnold was standing right in front of me talking in his unmistakably Austrian accent. I just happened to have a recorder on me, which I carried to record stuff "just in case." The doors opened to a massive guy, and out walked Arnold. I decided to follow him. I knew that he had just written a book for kids, and I was determined to get an interview, because when you're on a morning show, you *never* pass on material you can air. I waited a few minutes for him to get where he was going in a gym, and then I walked up and said, "Mr. Schwarzenegger, mind if I ask you a few questions?"

"Sure, go ahead," he said.

"I know you've just written a book for kids entitled—." I didn't have the book's exact title, so I mispronounced it.

Schwarzenegger looked at me and said, "Why don't you find out about it and then ask me?" With that, he walked away.

I was pissed, but years later when I reflected on it, he was right. You go to interview someone, know what the hell you're talking about!

In Christine, I found a female version of myself, someone that was as infantile as I am. Nothing was sacred when it came to who we targeted. Take Scott Gray, for instance, the sports director of WTIC-AM. Every morning at the same time, he was on the air live doing his sports scores, and for the longest time, we were outside his studio, trying to distract him and mess him up on the air. We started out by Christine pretending that she was going to flash her tits.

When he got used to that—and it was obvious that it wasn't going to affect him—I started drawing pictures of giant penises and holding the pictures up to the glass in front of his face. He started losing it, but then get got used to it. So then, I took five or six pieces of paper and taped them together to make one long piece on which I drew a giant cock with the head of it on the last page. We waited for the appointed time, hiding just to the right of his studio. When he got on the air, we slowly started moving the paper across his window, like a movie of a never ending schlong. Slowly, the shaft moved across his window until the giant penis head was in full view. He had to scrap the whole broadcast, and go directly to a commercial.

Peter Drew was our Production Director. They're generally not good enough to host their own shows, so they stick them in a studio and they voice and produce the commercials for the station. Peter was a straight-laced type, and was not only one of the voices heard on the radio commercials but one of the local tv stations also hired him to do their off camera announcements. One day, Christine told me this story about how Peter went to Suzanne MacDonald and demanded that every woman in the building stop wearing perfume. He claimed it was offensive. I thought this was ridiculous. All the women working at the station weren't going to stop wearing perfume because the scent might wind up on his clothes when they passed him. How stupid was that? The request was vetoed by management.

About a week later, I walked into the lunchroom, and the whole place stank of fish. "What the hell is that smell?" I asked.

"It's Peter," they answered. "Every day, he microwaves fish."

"What?" I replied surprised. "Every day?"

I hadn't noticed it because I didn't always walk into the kitchen, but I started going into the lunchroom every day just to check, and sure enough, the smell was there. I wasn't the only one that complained, but Peter's answer to management was, "When they stop wearing perfume around here, I'll stop making fish."

Really? Well, that did it for me. I was going to fix this guy good. I went to a fish market and bought a handful of raw shrimp, and then I cut them into small pieces. The next day was Friday, and at around 5 p.m., when I knew Peter was finished and had left for the weekend, I went into his office and started strategically placing the raw shrimp pieces everywhere: duct-taped under his desk, hidden inside the phone receiver (back when you could remove the mouthpiece), in drawers, and other places you couldn't see. I locked the door for the weekend.

On Monday, the rotting shrimp I had hidden in Peter's office stank so bad that it took them hours to figure out where the smell came from, but he got the message and never microwaved a piece of fish again.

Chapter 22

The Funniest Jokes I Ever Heard

Gary, John, and The Amazing Kreskin.

We interviewed hundreds of celebrities over the years. Most were a joy to talk to, but people always ask, "Who was the *worst* interview?"

Ben Kingsley: he obviously didn't want to be interviewed and was annoyed at answering any questions.

"The Amazing Kreskin": John had just returned from a charitable mission to Ethiopia, and so we asked Kreskin, "John just got back from an exotic location. Can you tell us where that was?" Kreskin answered, "Oh, I could, but I won't." In other words, he was just full of shit, and his act was a magician's scam.

Sandra Bernhard: her people told us before the interview, "No matter what, don't ask her anything about Madonna." So, she called in, and she just sucked, giving nothing but two-syllable answers and refusing to talk about things directly relating to her career. I had enough of the bullshit and said, "So, tell us about the time you kissed Madonna on the lips." She hung up.

Steve Guttenburg: he wins the award for the absolutely worst interview. Why do celebrities agree to do an interview if they don't want to do them? Every question we asked Steve, he was a dick in his responses. Yes, I think he ate a bowl of dicks that morning, and every interview we did after that was always measured on how bad it was by asking, "Was it Guttenburg bad?"

Robert Goulet: Then, there was Robert Goulet. I must have delivered thousands of jokes about him, but a few have been fan favorites, such as the joke not only told on the air many times but in the hallway, in the newsroom, anywhere I could get a laugh. It's a classic: an agent calls an actor he's representing and says, "I've have terrific news, I've just got you into a major feature film with Redford."

The actor excitedly says, "You mean, I'm going to be in a movie with Robert Redford?"

"No, it's Bill Redford, his brother, but it's going to be great, and you know who else is in it? Streep."

The actor says, "Meryl Streep is in the picture?"

"No, it's June Streep, her cousin, but it's a great part for you. And you'll never guess who's doing the soundtrack."

"Who?"

"Goulet!"

"You mean, Robert Goulet is doing the soundtrack?"

"Yup. But that's not the end of the story.

I got a call from the Bushnell Center for the Performing Arts.

Robert Goblet was actually coming to town and they wanted to do an interview. He called in to the show, and the interview was going well, and towards the end I asked Goulet, "Hey, Bob, have you ever heard the Goulet joke?"

"The Goulet joke? No, I've never heard it."

"Do you want to hear it?"

"Sure."

I told him the damn joke. I got to the punchline, "You mean to tell me Goulet is doing the soundtrack?" "YUP." Robert wasn't laughing. Either he didn't get it, or he did get it but didn't think it was funny. He made me mad because I've always thought people should have a sense of humor about themselves. After I told him the joke, the interview went on for a few more comments after I gave him the punchline and then I edited the phone call to make it sound like he hung up on me. The Bushnell Center was pissed off, but I just had to do it.

We had a code on the air. If, while doing an interview, we didn't really give a shit about the call, or they were boring as hell, we said, "Wow" as over the top as possible, which we started saying after every comment some of those stars made.

The other gem that people always ask for is The Bellringer Joke:

A priest puts a sign in the church window that says, "Bellringer wanted." The first day, a little man shows up and applies for the job. The priest asks, "Do you have any experience?"

The little man assures him that he does.

So, the priest takes him up to the bell tower, where the church bell is on the room's other side. The little man gets a running start, runs up, hits the bell with his face, falls out the open window, and falls to the street below, dead. A crowd forms. The priest runs down. He leans over the dead body.

Somebody shouts, "Does anyone know this man?"

The priest says, "No, but his face rings a bell."

Next day, another little man shows up. He has no arms. He tells the priest it was his brother who had the job the day before.

"But you have no arms!" the priest says. "How will you do it?"

"Don't worry," assures the man. He starts off running and slams into the bell, but the impact flings him out the window, he falls to the street, dead.

Priest runs down, and as he leans over the body, someone asks, "Anyone know who this man was?"

Priest answers, "No, but he's a dead ringer for his brother."

Next day, a man with just one prosthetic arm takes the job, goes to run for it, the arms gets caught in the bell's crack, rips it off, he flies out of the window to the pavement, dead. Priest runs down. A voice in the crowd asks, "Anyone know who this is?"

Priest answers, "No, but he had a hand in ringing the bell."

Next day, a man with no arms and just one leg shows up and convinces the priest he can just hop on the one leg and hit the bell with his body. He, of course, misses, falls out the window, falls dead.

"Does anyone know who this man is?"

The Priest says, "No, but I thought he had a leg up on the last ones."

Next day, another person shows up, no arms, no legs, no body, just a head, but he convinces the priest to bring him up to the bellower and allows him to grab a rope with his teeth. The Monsignor pulls the rope all the way back to the opposite wall and lets go. He misses the bell entirely, flies to the window, and falls to the street dead.

"Anyone know who this man is?"

"No, but he should have quit while he was a head."

Next day, a jar appears at the church's front steps. The priest opens the door and sees inside the jar there's a pair of eyes with a note asking for the Bellringer job. The note reads, "Take me up to the tower, throw me at the bell, and put me back in the jar."

The priest takes the jar upstairs, throws the eyes at the bell, and the bell rings louder than ever, but the eyes ricochet off the bell, out the window, and squishes on the ground.

"Does anyone know who these belong to?"

The Priest says, "Yes, and they should have seen where they were going!" (Bonus ending with just a pair of ears: "At least his ears aren't ringing anymore!")

WTIC-FM also hired a film crew to shoot a commercial that was styled after the tv series, *Seinfeld* (1989-1998), and shot on location at the Olympia Diner. The commercial featured the morning team with me, John, Christine, and our producer Eric, and it only ran once, but in the highly publicized last episode of *Seinfeld*, "The Finale," broadcast on May 14, 1998. It cost them a small fortune. (Years later, I produced a DVD that contained all of our commercials and antics on television.)

Most celebrity interviews we did were booked by Eric The Producer, film companies, or concert promoters looking to plug something. One time, we had this giant prize, a trip and tickets to a Super Bowl, too big of a prize to just give away to "caller number nine," so we devised a plan to have the audience get a star to call in

Hannah and Aaron very young.

to the show. We told the listeners the person who got the biggest star to call in would win the trip. This idea was based on the fact that everyone either knows a celebrity or has a relative that knows someone that knows one. We did the promotion for one morning, and someone had Oprah Winfrey call in. That same morning, John Travolta also called in. What were we to do? Who was the bigger star? In the end, we settled on John Travolta.

I don't know why I've been chasing fame all of my life. I suppose it had something to do with wanting my tour on the planet to be meaningful, to make my mark, but as I got older, I always seemed to get wiser as I realized that if I do nothing else, I already made my mark with our beautiful children Aaron, Hannah, and Rachel. That's the proof of what I've accomplished, my family. In my pursuit of perfection on the radio, I am sure, at times, it left a void for my kids and my wife because of the time it takes to be #1. I thank them for standing by me all these years. It wasn't easy.

In 1999, the WTIC-FM radio station pulled up stakes and moved to Farmington, Connecticut. We stayed on the air in Hartford while they built the new studio, and at the station's request, I hand-selected what equipment I wanted, all top of the line, new technology. On the last day before we moved to Farmington, we filled the old studio with shredded paper as our parting gift. We went into the newsroom and got an entire roll of teletype paper, print paper, any kind of paper we could find, and ripped and shredded enough of it to fill the entire floor four inches-high. One of our engineers, Charlie Brown was given the task of cleaning it up. He was supremely pissed.

One morning, we were on the air, when the door to the studio opened and singer Carly Simon walked in unannounced. I was on mic at the time, and I just stood there dumbfounded. *What the hell is she doing in my studio?* I just stopped what I was talking about and said, "You're not going to believe this, but Carly Simon just walked into the studio." Carly had visited one of our other stations down the hallway, and just decided to meander into our morning show. She wasn't promoting a book, a new song, a concert, or anything. Christine got up and Carly sat down in front of me. Like magic, or maybe a ghost, she just floated in, spent about a half hour with us on the air, and left. I do remember we had one of our contests, and when the winning listener called in, I had Carly answer the phone and give away the prize. "Hi, this is Carly Simon, and you just won . . . ." It was a little surreal, to say the least.

We bought a terrific house in Windsor, Connecticut. I put a pool in for the kids, there was a big screen tv in the basement to watch movies, and life was good, but we were concerned with the kind of schooling the kids were going to get, since Windsor wasn't one of the top-rated towns in the education department.

I was perfectly happy in that house, but coupled with the education issue, we got sucked into the "bigger better" syndrome. We looked at three towns: Avon, Farmington, and Glastonbury. We saw everything that was for sale in those three towns, and decided to build a new home in Glastonbury. We found a lot, contracted a builder, and began the long process of making decisions about every little detail, and watching the calendar to try to coordinate our move in date.

The house was almost done, when one day, bad weather hit. A lightning bolt struck at the exact spot where an exposed wire for an outdoor garage light would have been. As a freak occurrence, the lightning entered that wire and ricocheted throughout the structure, burning every wire in the house. They were just about to do the finish work, but every inch of drywall had to be ripped down to the studs so the whole place could be rewired. What a nightmare. We already sold the Windsor house and had to move out.

The "curse of the house" followed us. Many months, and a few contractors later, the house was made right, and we finally moved into an amazing home with every possible amenity. We could stay home and be constantly entertained; we never had to leave.

Making John the brunt of our jokes never ended, even off the air. He had a vanity license plate that said JE-News. That obviously stood for "John Elliott News." Who gets a license plate so everyone knows who he is and what he does.

Christine and I were the opposite of that. We wanted to blend into the background when we weren't on the air. We had enough of that lousy license plate. So, Christine searched on the Internet with Google images and found a Connecticut license plate that had a "W" in it. She printed it off in the exact size as the rest of the letters on John's plate. I cut out the "W" and snuck out of the studio during a long break, and then I taped it to John's license plate so it read, "Jew News." He left the station that day and rode around with it for two days, not realizing what we had done. I was dying thinking about him in traffic, driving around proud with his vanity plate, but now it said "Jew News." We finally had to point it out to him. He was not amused, but we were.

There was a time we tricked him on the air. I opened the mic at 6:30 a.m., and said, "John, we've hired a new intern at the station. 'Hoof' is his name."

John asked, "Hoof?"

As soon as the word came out of his mouth, I stepped on him with "Arted" as in "Who-Farted?" Christine and I were hysterical, but John didn't say a word. Hated it!

Christine and I were the charter members of the Asshole Club. The purpose was to give people we liked—or didn't like, usually—nicknames such as Ish, The Float, Fartman, Yentyl, Egg Salad, The Syrian Terrorist, Ashtray, Pukey da Pukey, The Gossip Pussy, Bald Gary, the Italian Grandmother, Sweater, Drunky the Clown, 6 Feet Under, Dexter, Fecal Fingers, The Alien, Lumpy, K K K Katie,

Sports Center, and The Half and Half. (Oh, come on, you do the same thing at your job!)

You might ask, "How does a guy like Fartman get the nickname Fartman? He was a sales guy. He was in the lunchroom, and asked me a question. Instead of verbally answering him, my response was a fart. I went back to the studio and told Christine the story, and she was in hysterics. From that point on, he became Fartman.

Some names just stuck. Back in the summer of 1989, Mark Christopher was making $6 an hour driving our prize van and handing out T-shirts. I was about to introduce him, and when I opened the mic, I said, "Our prize van is following as 96.5 WTIC-FM number sticker. Here's . . . Mark the Shark." Where that name came from, I have no idea, but he's been Mark the Shark ever since. Now you know.

I don't know why I was so hell bent on getting the morning show syndicated. I suppose it was that desperate attempt to become famous. Foolish idea. What the hell did I want to be famous for? You get too famous, you wind up with TMZ cameras up your ass. When I go out, nobody even knows me anymore. It's great.

I was depressed that WKSS never made good their promise to get my show syndicated, so when I came back to WTIC-FM, it was an item I negotiated as part of the deal. The only difference was, they actually tried to make it happen, but the project was doomed from the beginning, because of restraints that were in place. In pretty short order, Craig and Company was being carried in Buffalo, Baltimore, and Pittsburgh. What we were trying to do was insane. Each station was playing their own music, had their own producer, and carried us live after a song we were playing ended, which we determined should be about 4 minutes and 10 seconds. So, we were on, live as usual, and if our song ended at 3 minutes and 30 seconds, we had to fill the time up to 4 minutes and 10 second. Then, we had to pause to make sure the stations rejoined our show live. It sounded awkward and measured, and sucked all the spontaneity out of the show. In fact, it just sucked period. It's no wonder the whole project tanked.

While we were attempting to make it work, there were some very funny moments. For these stations to agree to carry the show, we had to agree to a certain amount of appearances in those cities. We also had to pander and schmooze to the people in charge of those stations. I wasn't really into yucking it up with a bunch of suits, but if I wanted this to work, I had to agree to it. None of us really took any of it seriously. We were naturally rebellious, and schlepping out to these cities, and we really didn't give a shit about anything. Kind of like now. I don't think any of us actually thought the experiment was going to work, but we went with it anyway.

A guy named Bill Pasha was in charge of the Baltimore station. We arrived to make personal appearances and to meet with the staff, take pictures, and cut some promos. One of the appearances that was arranged for us was at some crappy bar. We pulled up in a limo and told Eric to go check it out first. He came back to the car and told us the place was a dump, but we didn't believe him. *They wouldn't book us into a place like that,* we thought. They did. It looked like it was in the middle of a renovation, with leaky pipes and wires hanging down. We never stayed.

We were required to go to some furniture store for two hours to "Meet and greet fans," but fans never showed up, and the customers that came into the store didn't know us from Adam. We stayed for one hour, and then I said, "We're out of here."

The manager said, "You can't leave! The sign says you'll be here for two hours."

We left and took the sign with us.

That evening, a dinner was arranged with Bill Pasha and the station staff at a local restaurant. Christine got completely sloshed at a spaghetti dinner. She wound up getting on the table top and started dancing. The whole time she was drinking, Bill kept trying to limit the amount of spirits she was imbibing. He finally accused Christine of being an alcoholic.

John and I, of course, defended her, and I started sending Pasha these emails that said things like, "You're not fooling anyone" and "Aren't *you* hiding something?" Our syndication was cut shortly after that. Of course, it didn't help the project that while on the air in Buffalo, Christine said, "Buffalo can kiss my ass!"

A morning show eats up material at an alarming rate. Every day, you have to come up with stuff, and you're only as good as your last show. "Hey, great show today! What are you doing tomorrow?" In no other profession are you judged daily on the strength of your performance. Late night talk show hosts with a team of writers and producers are only on for an hour a night. We were on for four hours every day. It's true that a lot of that time is eaten up by music, but we had to be on, be engaging, funny, informed, and in the loop every time we opened the mic, which averaged out to approximately every 4 minutes. So much time was devoted to creating bits that run in the show, and then—poof!—they're gone. Some can be replayed, but most of the time it was one and done.

I stayed after the show many times and worked three hours on a bit that lasted two minutes, especially parody songs; those are a killer. Being on the radio was the greatest job in the world. I got to say exactly what was on my mind, be completely immature, and got paid well for it. I also knew what was going on in the world early in the morning before anyone got up and tuned us in.

Sometimes, news happened while we were on the air, such as in the infamous attack on the New York World Trade Center in 2001. John had come into the studio and asked me to put him on after a song had ended. He reported, "A small plane has crashed into the side of the World Trade Center."

I walked into the newsroom and CNN had a camera on the building that showed a rather large gaping hole with smoke billowing out. I took one look at it and said, "That's not from a small plane. The whole is too large." As I was saying that, the second jet circled around and slammed into the building live as we all watched. We immediately suspended all music and went live with continuing non-stop reports and coverage. Then, news of other crashes occurred. I became scared because one plane after another was crashing somewhere in our country. I called Diana and asked her to go to the school and take our children home. I felt powerless as everyone did to do anything about what we were seeing.

For days, we covered the events as they unfolded, but eventually, I had to make a judgment call and get back to what listeners expected of all of us on the morning show, and that was to entertain people. It was important for us to at least *try* to get back to normal, whatever that was. From that point on in our lives and in this country, normal changed forever.

Pam Anderson and Gary on the set of Baywatch.

David Hasselhoff on the set of Baywatch.

Gary as a cop in the short film, Thrall Hall.

Gary in Eschelon 8.

Chapter 23

That Nagging Feeling

I never got the acting bug out of my system. I hadn't really done anything since *Baywatch*, except for a local indie called *Thrall Hall*, where I played a cop. I placed my desire on the back burner, but it always nagged away at me. Finally, I had to tell myself to either address it or shut the hell up. So, I went for it.

I had professional head shots made. I joined casting sites and started to audition. Using the footage from a local independent movie that I had appeared in, *Eschelon 8* (2009), *Fishwrap* (2010), and *Rising Star* (2013), I started to form what's called a "reel," little scenes of work I had done. I had no idea what I was doing, and hadn't had any training, but I knew being on the air every day, performing characters, and writing material would help in some way. I wasn't delusional. I wasn't going to become a star, but I wanted to just carve out some special moments for myself on screen, and that would be enough, kind of like what my uncle Hy did.

I hated auditioning. It makes me nervous as hell. I went to New York to some crumby casting office, signed in, and waited with all the other people who had showed up to read for the same role I was going after. When they finally called my name, I went into a little room, where a 20-something kid with a camcorder started the camera and said, "Ok, go ahead." I wasn't really acting opposite anybody.

Once in a while, someone read with me and played the other part in the scene. The whole thing was over in two minutes. In fact, I called auditioning "2-2-2". That'a a two hour drive into the city, 2 minute audition, back into the car and two hours back. Auditioning was brutal. To add to the difficulty level, when I went into the city, I was competing against New York actors, who were there every day trying to get hired.

I landed several roles. Since going after the bug, I appeared on network tv shows and feature films. The acting jobs available for beginners fell into two categories: union and non-union. The two unions were Screen Actors Guild (SAG) and American Federation of Television and Radio Artists (AFTRA), but those two merged into one, SAG-AFTRA. For someone starting out, there were way more opportunities for non-union actors, but the roles were relegated to extra or background work.

The first call I got was to work background on a tv series called *Brotherhood* (2006). I was in a bar scene and walked by the camera once. For that, I was on the set for 8 hours. I arrive on the set, was hoarded into a "holding room," where I and others sat with all the extras and waited until I was called to the set to work. We sat there for hours doing nothing. Many actors brought computers, books, or anything to pass the time. I worked, of course as a non-union player—at the bottom of the barrel.

Principle actors got to eat lunch or dinner first, and got better dressing rooms or trailers, but the experience was wonderful. Background actors set the mood for the scene. We got paid, and the food on set was almost always fantastic.

I was cast to be on *The Good Wife*, I had no idea what I was going to be doing. I drove all the way into New York and got up to the holding room, where I saw sitting there a bunch of actors, all looking strangely just like me. Apparently, in a scene, two rows of perpetrators were going to be seen on a computer screen, like a lineup of criminals. For this, I had to go through make up and wardrobe, and a test picture was taken. Then, we waited while the director looked at the photo. Word came back that he wasn't satisfied with the pictures, so we had to do it again. I couldn't believe it. I was on there for nine hours for a lousy photograph that would be seen on the show for probably five seconds. While I spent long periods in the holding room, I tried to learn what I could from the other actors, like how the business worked. Someone got into a conversation about union and non-union. I found out that in order for actors to join SAG-AFTRA, they would either land a principle role, or work three union jobs as a non-union actor, but get three waivers, a system where a non-union actor was allowed to work a union project by the producers giving them a waiver to be able to appear in the production, and apparently if someone got three of those, they can join SAG-AFTRA.

The following week, I called the SAG-AFTRA office in New York and asked, "I heard that if I get three waivers, I can join the union, is that right?"

The staff member said, "What's your name? Let me look you up in the system to see if you are eligible."

"Oh, there's no way I'm eligible. I only have one waiver now. I would need two more."

"Well, let me look anyway."

"Okay. I'm Gary Craig."

After a few clicks on her computer, she said, "Did you appear in an episode of *Baywatch* years ago?"

"Uh, yes, I did."

"Well, did you know that you were eligible to join SAG that day?"

What? I thought. "No, nobody told me that. So, I'm eligible to join the union now?"

"Yes."

Great news, right? The only thing was, if I had joined the day I did *Baywatch*, it would have cost a lot less than it did years later. I now had to pay the initiation fee, which by the time I knew I could join, was a heavy $2,750. The day that I shot *Baywatch*, it was $700.

I agonized about it for a long time. *How could I justify spending that kind of money?*

I asked Andy Sunseri, a friend at the station, "Do you think I should spend the money and join?"

Andy said, "Are you kidding? It's an honor to belong to that club. You should definitely join."

So, I did.

Robert De Niro, Drew Barrymore, and Kate Becksale were coming to Connecticut to shoot the feature, *Everybody's Fine* (2009). I was cast as a pilot—a short, fat, airline pilot. Of course, since then, I've seen plenty of actual pilots that were that fat, but none that short.

It was an all-day shoot for us up at Bradley Airport in the old Southwest Airline terminal that was no longer being used. I was in a scene with De Niro, as he says goodbye to Drew. I walked by with another pilot. We did the scene over and over again until it was time to break for lunch.

The director said to us, "Now, you can stay in this side of the terminal, but don't walk further, because the other part of the airport is active, and you guys are in costume."

Me and this other actor went to catering to get lunch, and when we were finished, we still had a lot of time to kill, so I said, "Follow me." We started walking toward the active terminal. Our costumes where so authentic that flight attendants smiled and nodded as we walked by, and I was playing it for all it was worth by tipping my flight cap and acknowledging crew members.

When we got into the terminal's other part, we were near a gate packed with people. I said to the other actor, "Watch this." I started walking very slowly, weaving back and forth, as if I was completely sloshed toward one of the gates, as if I was going to get onto the plane. I just stopped short of doing that, then walked back. When I turned around, the other actor was laughing so hard, nothing was coming out of his mouth. I asked, "What was people's reaction?"

"Gaping mouths."

In between takes, I saw De Niro just sitting there sort of mumbling to himself, as if he was talking himself into the scene. Then, when he was finally on camera, his performance was so understated, it looked like he wasn't even acting at all. That was his genius. We watched him do a take, and thought, *That's a nothing scene. He's doing nothing.* Then, when we saw the film, we totally understood what he did, how he finessed the dialogue, and how he owned it.

I was shooting a film in downtown Hartford called *Rising Star* (2013), a lovely independent film, where I played a city bus driver. Again, I was wearing an authentic costume, including the cap that had the exact logo as the actual bus drivers wear. During a break, I walked over to Hot Tomatoes, one of the restaurants downtown, to get something to eat. When I was finished and asked for the bill, they wouldn't let me pay because, as they put it, "We take care of our drivers." Well, since I only had a bowl of soup, I let them pick up the tab.

I always knew that I would be better on the air than anyone I heard. I spent half my life at CBS, and most of that time working on the show in some form, when my eyes were opened. I don't think you can "teach" funny. You have to have it within you. I looked at everything I saw to determine if there's "a bit" in it for the morning show. I tried to figure out how I could twist a news story into

Painting "Life is a Beach"

Painting "Keeping Warm"

Painting "New England Dinner"

Painting "Butterfly Garden"

something funny. *What is everyone talking about?* I ask myself, then try to riff off of that. In other words, I was always physically or mentally working on the show. That's why we were #1 consistently.

Painting "Panda"

Chapter 24

I'm Sick of Looking At It

Some years ago, I bought a Bob Ross painting kit—yes, the "Happy Little Trees" guy. I don't know why I bought it or why I thought I could paint anything. Maybe it was because in Ross's shows he emphasized how easy it was for anyone to paint. The painting kit sat under our tv in our bedroom for literally ten years. One day, Diana finally said, "Are you going to use this damned thing? Cause I'm sick of looking at it. Either use it or throw it out."

I cracked it open, began, and never looked back. I was self-taught. I had no training, but I studied other artists and watched an awful lot of YouTube videos to pick up a technique here and there. I love the old masters, especially Vermeer. His approach to painting light was nothing short of amazing. In the modern painting era, Kincade, of course, was a master at capturing light, as well.

I've never painted the same thing twice, and many pieces I've done, are hanging in other people's homes. Every time I pick up the brush, I feel that I have no idea what the hell I'm doing, and almost every time, I get three quarters through it and come very close to throwing it out. In the last stage of details, the painting always finally came together I was happy with what the painting.

In radio, we were purveyors of bad news. There were a couple of events that occurred while I was on the air that have been forever marked in time. Back then, few computers were in use at most companies. Radio guys got their news from teletype machines, which were just sophisticated typewriters that sent information over telephone wire. The machine typed away all day on long rolls of paper. The newsman came on air near the top or bottom of the hour, ripped off the paper with the stories on it, and just went into the studio and delivered the news. That's where the term "rip and read" came from. Occasionally, when Associated Press wanted to get our attention, an alarm went off, meaning a story had come over that was particularly urgent.

On August 16, 1977, I was on the air in the afternoon at KHYT in Tucson, Arizona. I had just turned my mic off after introducing a song, and I opened the studio door only to hear the teletype alarm. When I went to the machine, I saw that Elvis Presley had died. He was one of the most popular and influential musicians of the twentieth century. I was shocked, and I was the only one on the air at the time. The song came to an end, I opened the mic, and got so choked up that I barely delivered the news.

In 2004, Ryan Jones took over the producing duties at Craig and Company. Ryan was so calm, it drove me nuts. Nothing rattled him. We routinely made fun of him off and on the air, and he just took it, never wavering, never raising his voice. I never saw him mad at anything. Christine and I had full-blown screaming fits in the studio, while he just stood there observing. It was maddening, but I suppose it was good that he didn't add to the drama either. When it came to social media, music, or what was hot or not, Ryan was the guy.

Diana was a huge Jimmy Buffett fan, and her zeal for him bordered on fanaticism. She first saw him at a bar called The Euphoria in Portland, Oregon, in 1977, and basically saw him every year after that. When she dragged me to my first Jimmy Buffett concert, I didn't know what to expect. Oh sure, I knew about his mega-hit, "Margaritaville," but I really didn't know what I was getting myself into. Soon after the concert started, I was asking myself, *What is this all about? Jimmy Buffett can't really sing, and what's up with all these drunken adult assholes with parrots on their heads?* I just didn't get it. I sat there for most of the time with my hands folded, waiting for the damned thing to be over. The second concert she schlepped me to, I softened a bit. *Oh, yeah, well this music isn't all that bad. Not bad.* At the third concert, I was up on my feet with the rest of the dopey people singing the lyrics, and shouting, "Salt, salt, salt!" as if they we all drank from a mind-numbing Buffett concoction.

One year, when I knew he was coming to perform, I got tickets early, but I wanted to do something special for Diana, to get her a meet and greet with Jimmy. I knew that would be a tall order. Mitch Ettess, the CEO of Mohegan Sun, once said to me, "We

Uncle Bob on the street with actor Eli Wallach.

Gary and Uncle Bob.

pay him a million dollars to play our arena, and I can't even get in to see him."

But I had a chip—Jim Vicevich—who had a show on our AM station, WTIC, and he once told me that a good friend of his was a guitarist in Jimmy's band. On a Friday, I went to Jim and explained the whole thing about how Diana was a "Parrothead" and had seen him every year, and we just wanted to see him for five minutes and

Hannah, Gary and Uncle Bob.

grab a picture, and we didn't even need tickets because I already had them. Jim said, "No worries. I'll talk to him and set it up."

I couldn't believe it. *This is going to be an amazing surprise,* I thought. On Monday, I went in to see him and asked, "Well, did your friend talk to Jimmy?"

The smile ran away from Jim's face. "Oh man, you won't believe it. My friend talked to Jimmy and asked if he could just say hello, just for a few seconds before the show, and Jimmy exploded in the guy's face yelling, 'Don't you *ever* ask me to do something like this again!' Then, my guitarist friend said, 'But Jimmy, you don't understand. This is the morning guy at CBS, big local guy, and they're huge fans.' Jimmy said, 'I don't give a shit *who* he is, don't ever bring something like this to me again.' He thought he was going to get fired. Then, a little while later, Jimmy walked up to him and said, 'Hey, I'm sorry I reacted that way, but I can't do it.'"

And that was that. How odd I thought the whole thing was, because if we went to a Buffett show, invariably, somewhere in the concert, he stopped to tell his fans how much they meant to him, and said, "Thank you all for keeping me employed all of these years." I guess all of that was, well, bullshit. Jimmy Buffet? No thanks!

They called him "Bobby, Baby, Booby," my uncle Bob Anzel. I loved my uncle Bob. He was the embodiment of New York. He was Mister New York. He saw every show on Broadway. He knew where all the best restaurants were in the city. He went into Chinatown every week to the secret, out of the way places he knew about to source his own ingredients to make his own Chinese food at home. On the occasions when he didn't want to cook, he rattled off the top of his head which place had the best Dim Sum.

When I went into the city to visit Uncle Bob, we always dined at a place of my choosing, but I deferred to him if I wasn't familiar with the area. He knew the *entire* city. When I came in to do an audition, I told him where it was, and he always lived up to his reputation of being the ultimate foodie. No matter where the restaurant was, he always arrived in fifteen minutes.

Uncle Bob also knew the New York subway system cold. He should have, because he lived in his upper west side rent-controlled apartment for over thirty years. It was crazy walking with him in his neighborhood. He was like the Pope of the upper west side. Every block, somebody walked up to him and said, "Bobby, Booby, Baby, how are you?" as if paying their respects to the guy that knew everyone. Character actors that I recognized stopped him. "You working?" Bob always asked. It seemed to be commonplace that Bob would run into an actor like Eli Wallach, and then spend the next twenty minutes commiserating on the street.

On one particular visit, Uncle Bob and I were walking down the street, and this lady walked up to him and pulled him aside. Usually, he introduced me, but not this time. I was close enough to make out some of the conversation. "I can't fucking even get out of my own apartment," she said. "The press are everywhere, and they won't stop hounding me."

When we finally walked away, I asked, "Who the hell was that?"

Uncle Bob whispered, "That's a friend of mine. She's the one that found Health Ledger dead."

She turned out to be Diana Wolozin, the massage therapist, who found the actor's body.

Uncle Bob knew everyone. Mention a celebrity's name, and he either knew them personally or knew someone that knew them. In the 1960s, he roomed with actor Dennis Hopper, a story he refused to elaborate on. I always felt intellectually inferior to Uncle Bob. I mistakenly thought that he just tolerated me. I mean, in addition to being Mr. New York, he was also a world traveler.

"Where you going *this* year?" I always asked.

"I think I'm going to Spain."

Every year, and often twice a year, he jetted off to some exotic locale. When I was eleven or twelve, I reiterated the question about my uncle, which always was, "Mom, when is uncle Bob getting married?" This time, there was a different answer. "Your uncle Bob is gay." For some reason, it didn't come as a shock to me. It kind of went along with his "live and let live" attitude about everyone. He never judged. The odd thing was, in all those years, I'd never known him to have a partner, unless he had very short, maybe discreet relationships that nobody knew about.

Uncle Bob was diagnosed with stage 4 liver cancer, but he kept it from me, because he didn't want to worry me. Can you imagine? He was the one that was sick, but he didn't want me to worry. This was the type of person he was. He finally told me, "I was having some pain, and I went to the doctor, and I have cancer, and don't worry about it, we'll see what happens." He knew there was nothing they could do to reverse it. At that point, it was just a maintenance of life issue. He held on for a long time.

With each subsequent visit into the city, I saw Uncle Bob deteriorate. He couldn't climb the steps to his apartment anymore, and he needed an apartment in a building that had an elevator. His friend, Josh Leherer, was instrumental in getting him into another apartment that still maintain the same rent he was paying in the apartment he had previously occupied for over thirty years.

In the last year of his life, when I visited, I was seeing a distention of his stomach. One symptom was that his belly filled up with fluid. He had to go to the hospital to get it drained. As these visits were getting more frequent, his doctors actually installed a tube and a valve in his stomach so he could drain the fluids himself. I arrived at his apartment to find him shirtless and watched him drain his stomach. I wasn't revolted by it but glad he was getting some relief. He complained that it would just fill right back up again.

The end neared. His friend, Josh, lived in the building was in charge of coordinating all of his care. Thank god for him. When

Bob learned about his fate, the only request he had was, "I want to die in my own bed in my own apartment, not the hospital."

Josh made that happen for him. The call from Josh came the day before. "I don't know how long he can hold on . . . he's sort of in a coma. The nurse says it could be any time now."

The next day, after I got off the air, I rushed to the city hoping, praying, that he just held on. When I arrived and walked into the apartment, I found Josh, the nurse, and another friend. I walked into Uncle Bob's bedroom, where he was lying in bed, making a moaning sound, with one leg up that he was rocking back and forth.

"He's been in the vegetative state since yesterday," Josh said.

I walked closer to the bed and said, "Bob I'm here." He opened his eyes, looked at me, and said, "Oh, Gary." Then, he closed his eyes again.

Josh told me that the night before, Uncle Bob had opened his eyes and asked, "Am I dead yet?"

My daughter, Hannah, had also become close to Uncle Bob, as she experienced the many spirited and fun dinners in the city with him in those last years. She knew Bob was winding down, but this urgent call to the city was unexpected. I called Hannah and told her that he was probably going to pass very soon. She was understandably upset. At the time, she was attending college at the State University of New York (SUNY) at Purchase. Her arts class was meeting in the city at Museum of Modern Art (MOMA), and she was going to leave the class to race over to Bob's apartment.

I went back into Bob's room, sat down next to the bed, and took his hand. His eyes were closed, and his breathing was erratic. I rubbed his hand and his arm and kept repeating to him, "It's okay, Uncle everything is going to be okay. I'm here. You can let go. Just let go, Bob."

He stayed in this state for quite some time. Frequently, Josh came in and talked to him, reaffirming that he could let go and everything would be alright.

Uncle Bob's breathing became shallow, and with one last exhale, his leg stopped wiggling and he was gone. I watched as all the blood drained from his face and he became white. This event affected me profoundly. I had never seen a person die before. I was sobbing as I leaned over and kissed him on the forehead. I walked out and saw Josh sitting with his hands up to his face, also destroyed.

I called Diana to tell her that Bob had passed. She called Hannah, who was in a cab on her way to MOMA. When she got there, she told her teacher that her uncle had just passed away, and she had to go see him. The teacher bluntly remarked, "Well, you're not going to get credit for today's class." What a dick.

Hannah arrived at the apartment, and I said, "Are you sure you want to see him? I don't want you to get rattled."

She visited with him, and also came out sobbing.

A few weeks later, she was in the city and wanted to sleep in Uncle Bob's apartment. Josh said, "Of course."

Bob meant so many different things to so many people. At his memorial, which I filmed, over 100 friends and family came to pay tribute to an uncle, a friend, and a mentor. A week later, I had to go through everything at the apartment. When he moved that last time, he kept every little and really downsized. I took three pieces of clothing, and I wear them frequently, even to this day. It makes me feel close to him.

I was astounded to find letters he had written to his mother—my Grandma Rose—when he was in California. In the letters, I found out, he missed me terribly and always asked how the little boy named Gary was doing. So, I was wrong all my life about how he felt about me. I can't forget the things I didn't say.

Chapter 25

What the F**k's Wrong With You, Kid?

Gary on the set of Curb Your Enthusiasm.

Gary with Larry David shooting Curb Your Enthusiasm.

I got a call for a role in the *Curb Your Enthusiasm* tv series (2011). Something happened to me when I was on the phone with casting. The day we were shooting the show, I was talking to a production assistant and told him that when casting called me I was eating, some food went down the wrong pipe, and I almost choked to death. When he heard this story, he said, "Oh, you've got to tell this story to Larry." He dragged me over Larry David, and I recounted the whole story.

Larry commented, laughing, "So, your big break comes in, and you almost die before shooting the show!"

As I walked away, the production assistant said, "Don't be surprised if you see that story pop up on one of the episodes."

I was hired as a featured extra in a small scene set back in the 1960s when Larry David was a child. He is caught playing strip poker in a Mister Softee truck with a girl, whose father happens to be the driver. The dad comes back, catches little Larry David in the truck, and kicks him outside to the curb nude!

I was one of the neighborhood wise guys sitting on the apartment building's stoop when the kid lands. We were shooting this on location up in the Bronx. I knew about Larry David, and I knew how this show worked. There was a lot of ad-libbing. I decided to ad-lib a couple of lines (but I wouldn't suggest others do this), and I looked at the kid and said, "What the fuck you doing, kid? Will you look at this fuckin' kid?"

All of a sudden from inside the director's tent in the middle of the street, I heard "CUT!" and saw the director storming toward us. I thought, *Shit! I'm going to get thrown off this project*. He walked up and said, "That was *great*! Do it the same way each time!"

I breathed a sigh of relief that I went with my gut. At days' end, the assistant director said, "We're ripping up your day papers and bumping you up to principal. Go sign your new contract."

That's why you take every project that comes your way because you just never know where it's going to lead. Actually, as in this case, it lead to residual checks, which was lovely.

Boston casting called. They wanted me to come up and read for a new film to be directed by David O Russell, a feature film shooting in Boston based on the ABSCAM controversy in the 1970s.

It wasn't the first time I'd read for a part. I'd been to many, many auditions. Some pan out and some don't. I had to learn to do the audition, then walk away and forget about it. If I sat around and said to myself, *God, when are they going to call me? Am I going to get the part? What's going on?* I would drive myself crazy. I did the audition, gave it my all, and walked away. I knew they were casting me as a mobster, but they didn't send me any sides (those were the lines that only pertained to my character).

I got up there, and every mobbed up actor was sitting there waiting to get in. We learned quickly that the audition was to be all improvisation—no lines to memorize. Thank goodness, I had experience in radio and on *Curb your Enthusiasm*.

A casting director came out and walked up and down the long bench with actors, asking, "Now, you know what the scene is about? Here's what you're going to ad-lib on." She got to me, and I held my hand up and said, "Stop. I don't want to know anything. I don't want any pre-conceived notions of what the scene is. I'll make it up on the spot." I wanted to react in the moment. If I thought about the story too long, it could have taken the spontaneity out of it.

Soon, it was my turn to go in. They told me, "Here's the scene: you're a mobster, a guy wants you to help him build a casino, you have to have the money up front, then you insult his wife."

I said, "Got it. Roll!"

They started the camera, and I ad-libbed an entire scene. They loved it, and had me do it a second time.

The casting director said, "Great job today!"

"Yeah? Thanks."

I forgot about it and went on vacation. Wouldn't you know, four days later, I got a call from the agency that I had gotten a callback.

"I can't," I told them. "I'm on vacation and won't be back for two weeks."

"Okay", she said disappointed. "We'll have to figure something out."

Well, there's goes that role, I thought, but the day I got back, there was a message that they wanted me to come up to Boston that Saturday for another reading.

I did, and there I was in the audition room again.

"Okay, you're going to do the same thing as you did last time."

I thought, *No! I am not going to do the same thing as I did last time.* I created a different scene.

"CUT!"

My heart dropped. I looked up, and sitting at the table behind a computer was director and screenwriter David O. Russell. I didn't even know he was sitting there. He looked up and said, "Now there was a Gold Star face."

I was told by the agency, "Don't make any plans, and don't leave town."

I got the part, playing a character named Jerry Catone. Wow! After weeks of auditioning—improvisation at the first audition, going on vacation, and then giving it my all in my call back in front of Jennifer Peri—and it all came down to that call.

There's was only one problem: I had a torn meniscus in my left knee, but I didn't dare tell them about it, or even address it. I was certain that if I took the time to get an operation, I would have lost the part. Just had to suck it up. I was popping Advils like Tic-Tacs for the entire four days. Standing on my feet for ten to twelve hours a day in intense pain wasn't fun.

A flurry of phone calls came in from every department. Hair and makeup called, wanting me to grow my sideburns long because it was a story set in the 1970s. Even before I knew I landed the role, I was growing them out in anticipation. I had to send them pictures showing the progress.

Wardrobe called. They wanted to know all of my sizes.

The production director called. He had the details of where I would have to be and when.

Three weeks later, I found myself on the set of this great film. It was a four-day shoot up at the Wang Center. They had converted the whole building into a Hollywood studio.

The first scene was taking place in an old grand hall. I walked over to some chairs in front of the stage and sat down. Sitting to my right was Amy Adams. Next to her was Jennifer Lawrence, and sitting to my left was Bradley Cooper. Standing in the corner was Christian Bale, and up on stage waiting for the scene to begin was Jeremy Renner. For me, just for a moment, that was surreal. *Was I*

Gary in his trailer getting ready to go to the set of American Hustle.

American Hustle, with Gary and Armen Garo.

American Hustle, with Gary, Jennifer Lawrence, and Jack.

really here? Yes, I was. I had admired the work of all those actors, and now I was working with them. Would I love to tell them how I appreciated their work? Sure, but there's an unwritten rule on a set: act professional. Don't invade another actor's space unless you're invited.

The whole first day, we worked on a scene where I escorted Jennifer and Jack Huston into the hall with a ton of other dignitaries. We did it over and over again until we got it right. Jennifer was wearing a slinky satin dress that looked like she was poured into it. Not a bad day on set. David O. Russell had an incredible method, very run and gun, and he opened a space in which we could improvise.

The next day, I was in the makeup trailer, and there was the entire cast: Bradley Cooper with curlers in his hair, Jennifer Lawrence on her cell phone, and a complicated transformation of Christian Bale was taking place. I sat down next to Christian and said, "Good morning."

"Hi mate," he answered. "How's it going?"

"Can't be better. How long in the chair?"

"About 2 hours."

Two hours just on his hair—every day!

David O. Russell was a great director, but he has the reputation of being a little bit of an asshole. If you believe stories on the Internet, there's one about the fracas with Lily Tomlin and a leaked video of her screaming her head at him, and him treating her like shit. There was even a story about Amy Adams not being treated well on the set of *American Hustle* (2013) and tension that became so uncomfortable that Christian Bale had to tell him to stop being an asshole.

Then, there's the documented David O. Russell story of George Clooney working on *Three Kings* (1999). George recounts, "David wanted one of the extras to grab me and throw me down. This kid was a little nervous about it, and David walked up to him and grabbed him. He pushed him onto the ground. He kicked him and screamed, 'Do you want to be in this fucking movie? Then throw him to the fucking ground!' The second assistant director came up and said, 'You don't do that, David. You want them to do something, you tell me.' David grabbed his walkie-talkie and threw it on the ground. He screamed, 'Shut the fuck up! Fuck you!' and the assistant director replied, 'Fuck you! I quit.'"

I knew the history of all of this going into the film. The next two days, we worked on the bar scene, where the entire cast visits the mob guys that run Atlantic City. I worked with a great actor named

Armen Garo, who had an impressive list of credits including *The Sopranos* (2007) and the HBO original series, *Vinyl* (2016).

We were all in the scene together, and frankly, I can honestly say that I don't remember any knee pain. I was having too much fun. David O. Russell was a visionary. His directing style was so relaxed yet on the fly. He gave actors generous leeway to be creative, but he had a combative side.

Russel was doing this long, Scorsese-style shot, dollying into the bar, and he told me to lean over and whisper in Jack Huston's ear, which I did, but apparently I didn't hold the movement long enough.

"CUT!" Russel said before the entire cast, "Hey, Gary, you want to be in the movie? You have to wait until I say 'cut' to stop whispering."

There was that line again! The same thing he said to that extra on the set of *Three Kings*, but when he said it to me, it was embarrassing, because it was before the entire cast. My initial reaction would have been to tell him to go fuck himself and walk off the set, and I almost did, but if I had gotten to that point and snapped, it would have been way more than a "fuck you." To my credit, a cooler head prevailed.

On the last day of shooting, Bradley Cooper and I shook hands after finally completed the scene. He said, "Great Job!" At least for me, it was a wrap.

I constantly tried to screw with people at the radio station. Why did I do this shit? I guess it was for my own personal entertainment, and it was funny, or at least I thought it is. It was also very passive-aggressive.

Walking down the hall one morning, I passed an office that had a sales guy sitting there. I leaned in through the doorway and said, "Have you heard?"

"No, what?"

"Oh man, you haven't heard?"

I continued to walk down the hallway. There was nothing to tell, no story, no gossip, nothing, but the way I answered him implied that he was out of it and maybe the only person who "Hadn't heard."

The next day, he got fired! It had nothing whatsoever to do with me or my little joke, but I bet he thought I had something to do with it.

Prince's death at age 57 was such a tragedy. So many amazing talents have checked out early. Another one, of course, was Michael Jackson. Not only was I lucky enough to be an audience member for Prince, but I saw Michael three times. One record company sent out a sequined glove to promote one of Michael's albums. I always held on to it. Why did I save it? Who knows? It sat in my office collecting dust. Every once in a while, I put it on. Did I ever use it for anything? Of course not, until Michael came to Hartford. He was performing at the Hartford Civic Center, and we were going down there to see the show. We took a limo, and headed downtown early. The place was a zoo, with people everywhere, and Michael wannabes dressed just like Michael. Venders hawking various Michael T-Shirts, buttons, and wing dings. I had the glove with me. The car windows were tinted, so no one could see in. As we approached the mayhem, I lowered the window, stuck out my hand wearing the glove, and waved. Suddenly, people rushed the car, wanting to shake hands or get an autograph, because they thought I was Michael!

I have a confession to make. Every time I came off stage from introducing a band or act, I felt like shit. I could just hear people in the audience thinking, Oh here comes those idiot DJs. I had done introductions hundreds of times, and as the morning show host, I was *expected* to introduce acts, especially when it was the radio station's show. Introductions were over in ten seconds, and I handed the mic back to the sound people, then left the stage for the band to begin to play. Slinking backstage, I realized that I really was just a schmucky DJ! I'd been performing since I was 5, and in my mind, I thought, *Somebody should be introducing me!* It was a misguided emotion, because I always underestimated whether what I did had any impact on anyone, or whether it was even worthwhile.

I once posted an update on Facebook that said, "I must apologize to all of you. You're going to have to put up with my abuse a little while longer. I just signed a twelve-month extension on my contract." Many people reacted to this with a collective sigh of relief. They went on to tell me how much the show means to them, and how I was part of their lives. I guess I was wrong . . . *again.*

Chapter 26
WOR

The Gamblings had a death grip on morning radio on WOR in New York.

John B. Gambling first started WOR in 1925, then his son, John A. Gambling, became host in 1959. Then, his son, John R. Gambling, joined the show as cohost from 1985 until his retirement in 1991. In September 2000, WOR cancelled the program.

Somewhere in between one of the Gamblings, I heard that they were looking for a new host for the morning show. I knew the program director, because he used to program our AM station WTIC 1080, and since WOR was owned by our company, CBS, I called and secured an on-air audition for myself on a Friday and Saturday night.

For the first show, I planned a few bits on a couple of topics, and I then arrived at WOR about an hour before I had to go on. Ten minutes before air time, I made myself comfortable in the studio, tried to learn the lay of the land, and got myself ready.

The engineer came in. "Are you okay? Are you nervous?"

"No, why?"

"Because the girl that auditioned last night threw up before she had to go on the air."

Show time Friday night! The theme came up, the engineer threw the mic open and cued me, and I was off. It wasn't as easy as I thought it was going to be. I was flying by the seat of my pants with no safety net, no song to go to, and just me talking. The result, according to me, wasn't my best.

Show time Saturday night! This time, I booked some guests, and it went great. I was doing talk radio but with a more modern twist than I think WOR listeners were used to.

The sales manager came down from the office and handed me live commercial copy to read. I'd been doing commercials for years, so I took one look and knew exactly how I would approach it.

Gary behind Tina Few on 30 Rock.

Gary behind Gary Cole on 30 Rock.

During the show, the sales manager came into the studio. "Nobody has ever done live commercials as well as you do them. I'm going to personally recommend that you get the job!"

The program director was afraid that I would blow off the upper demographics—older listeners—so I wasn't hired. The reality was that they *should have* blown off the upper demographics and allowed me to bring in younger listeners, because that's what they really needed.

I was cast on *30 Rock* on "The Crabcatcher" episode. The scene was a bunch of Jimmy Buffett wannabes milling around in an

Gary on the set of Boardwalk Empire, *ready to shoot a scene.*

enclosed area right next to Rockefeller Center. Donned in shorts and a Hawaiian shirt, I joined all the other extras, getting ready to shoot. It was supposed to be a big party, just laughing and having a good time with our crazy hats and props. In the beginning, Tina Fey brushes by me and says, "Get out of the way." There were an awful lot of extras on the shoot, but I was determined to get some face time.

After the director said "cut," an extras wrangler positioned everyone in certain places for the next setup. "You stand here, and you two stand over here. You guys, just stay where you are, and don't move."

I didn't listen. I was determined to be seen, so I crept close to the scene they were shooting with Tina Fey and another actor and I stood behind Tina. After they shot that, they turned the camera around to get the other actor's reaction, and I snuck behind him. I kept doing that for the whole scene. Doing that created a nightmare for the poor guy editing the show, because it's physically impossible for me to be standing behind both Fey and the person she's talking to, but there I was plain as day. I can just imagine the editor saying, "Who the hell is this asshole? He's in every shot!"

At that point there was nothing they could do, because if they cut me out, they'd have to cut the principles out, and they weren't going to do that. What a pain in the ass I was, but every time I was on a set, I was always looking for the hook, the bit, the story I could tell on the air, that would substantiate me being away from the show. Probably the wrong thing to do, but I couldn't help it.

Also in 2012, I was also cast in a scene on the tv series, *Boardwalk Empire*. I played a political lobbyist in a scene where Steve Buscemi passes me in the hallway on his way to an important meeting. Like in all major television shows, there was a costume fitting, this one in New York at Steiner Studios in the Brooklyn Navy Yard, home base for the show. The day I was scheduled for my fitting, I blew a tire on the highway on the way in. I limped off the exit, and pulled into an empty parking space on the street. I believe I was somewhere in Queens, with very little time left to get to the studios. This was not good. I finally got Triple A to show up, and we put on that midget tire I had for a spare. I limped at 55 MPH to the studio.

The studio was a great place. Sound stages everywhere that were reminiscent of old Hollywood. I was instructed to go to this amazing, giant Quonset hut that housed all the show's costumes. I was stepping back into the 1920s. In one section, just hats, every hat you could think of. In another section, pants, shirts, and ties, all perfectly representing the period. Another area had every kind of shoes you could think of. The women's costume sections were equally as detailed with dresses, hats, shoes, jewelry, coats, fake furs, you name it.

After about an hour with a costume person, an outfit was selected, and now the finishing touch, the overcoat. They found one they liked, and when they were satisfied with the whole outfit, I was taken to the head of wardrobe to get the once over. He took one look at me and said, "Okay, good, but the overcoat is too big. I want it taken in here, and also here."

I thought, *They're going to go to the trouble of reworking the overcoat? I'll probably be seen on screen for two seconds. What attention to detail.* After they released me, I drove back to Connecticut.

The actual shoot took place on a different day in an old mansion up in Harlem. I decided to try something new to bring my listeners into the behind-the-scene world of *Boardwalk*. I acquired these "secret video glasses," ordinary-looking glasses that had a small camera in the bridge of the nose that recorded video and sound onto

Gary with Gladys Knight on the set of Seasons of Love.

Gary with actor Richard Portnow on Seasons of Love.

an SD card in the glasses' side. *Not only will they hear the story, but now they'll be able to see it!*

On breaks and before shooting, I walked around and recorded footage of what the house looked like inside, the set, and the old cars. Nobody had a clue what I was doing, and I thought, *What's the big deal?*

After I shot for the day and got home, I took the footage and edited up a nice little video that I put up on YouTube. I told the story on the air and directed people to the video. About two days after it was up, I got a call from the casting directors in New York telling me that the production company was pissed and they wanted the video taken down. Of course, I obliged, but I thought, *How stupid is that? Hell, I'm promoting the show!* I didn't give away any secrets, and I didn't do anything that tv news shows, like *Extra* or *Inside Edition*, would have done walking around with their cameras. I guess it didn't matter. I was just an extra, who pulled one off on them. I also guess it's the reason why that agency in New York never called me for any other project. Oops. On my card, it probably said, "Don't hire this idiot. He'll show up with a secret set of video glasses and spill the beans." Oh well. I got into trouble again just trying to bring the listener a different and cool perspective.

In 2014, my New York agent, Lisa Lax, called to say I landed a role in a lifetime Television movie, *Seasons of Love,* starring Richard Portnow and Gladys Knight. I played Johnny, the lead's friend.

Richard was veteran character actor, whose Internet Movie Data Base page was so long it seemed to never stop scrolling. Richard and I shared a dressing room, and I helped him run lines right before we went to the set. He was in one of my favorite films, as Dan The Man Levitan in *Good Morning Vietnam.* (1987).

I also thought it was slightly surreal to be hanging out with Gladys Knight. We all grew up listening to her soul group, Gladys Knight and The Pips, and now, there I was just joking around with the star that sang "Midnight Train to Georgia." She was very kind and down to earth.

A lot has happened to communication since I first cracked open a mic. I routinely auditioned for acting jobs online, and the internet is bursting with video content. I called myself an "internet dummy," but I have taught myself to use social media, because if I don't, I'm dead in the water. I've produced a ton of content on YouTube, including commercial parodies, novelty songs, and comedy routines. Some of the more highly-produced pieces were, "The Grinning Idiot," "The Gipper Knows," "Bernie Sanders doing ordinary Things," "Phoney Phone Crank Calls," and "The Crazyman Show." On other occasions, I have used my cell phone to seize the moment on the spot and then get it up online.

Since I lived in downtown Hartford, I had access to events going on at Riverfront. One weekend, the Latin Fest came through town, with great food, music, and fashion highlighting Latin culture ethnicity. I walked down there with my cell phone. The place was packed with people everywhere lining up at the various booths and buying t-shirts and food. Latin music was blaring everywhere, and live performers were taking the stage. I did what I always do: I shot what I thought was just another stupid video of Gary trying to be funny, which included me singing the "I love Lucy" theme to a table of pineapples. Well, as stupid as I am, it was the wrong country! I posted the video on the CBS website and my own Facebook page.

Well, you would have thought the world was coming to an end. Not too long after it was posted, media was tracking me down to see if I had any comment on what Luke Bronan, the Mayor of Hartford, was saying about me. Apparently, some people contacted his office and made complaints about the video. He saw it and said more or less that it was racist. He actually issued a statement targeting me. I got it. He was new in the office and wanted to show people he was a tough guy. I didn't have a racist bone in my body. I was the guy that had staged a children's party every year since 1985 for kids with every ethnic walk of life, but once I was labeled with that and people got it into their minds that it must be true, it was hard to defend myself. I now see how people misinterpreted what I was trying to do, but I just couldn't believe how the whole thing snowballed. You can't say or do anything without offending somebody, or some group going ballistic. The 1971 American tv series, *All in the Family*, would never be able to be aired today.

Latin organization heads wanted my head, and to make matters worse, they also lumped together other videos I did where I was reviewing food trucks in New Haven, and they said that those were also racist. The videos in New Haven had nothing to do with the one I did at the Latin Fest, but I was being accused of showing "a pattern" of racism. Funny, but comedy tv series like *Saturday Night Live* get away with murder, but because I was just a local radio schmuck, I became a viable target.

I immediately took the videos down, but it was too late. I always told young people that when you post stuff online, it's written in permanent ink. Too bad I didn't take my own advice. All hell broke loose. I told management that I should just go on the air and apologize, but they didn't want me to do that, for reasons that were beyond me, and I told them they were making a mistake. Their solution was to take me off the air for a week, and to have me record an apology that they would run on the air. I also had to do a live apology when I got back on the air. They were also bending to the demands of some groups that I be fired. Station management and I went through several little battles as to what I was going to say. Originally, they had this long, drawn out, pathetic apology that sounded like I was literally begging for my job. I told them, "I'm not going to do that, and if you want to fire me, go ahead." Instead, I wrote what *I would be comfortable saying*, and then they had to run it by the suits up at corporate. The whole thing was just fucking stupid and unreal.

A group consisting of local Latin organizations and politicians actually came to the station one afternoon to meet with management. I knew they would be there, so I came back to the station and popped my head in the meeting to let them grill me and to apologize in person. Apparently, that did the trick. Everybody's feathers were smoothed. Someone in that meeting actually said to me, "Would you come to next year's Latin fest and make an appearance? We'd love to have you." *What? A minute ago, you wanted my head, and now I'm your buddy?* Wow. People.

Management, and some listeners, often pointed out that they thought I was too negative on the air. What they didn't understand was that the negativity gave me an edge, and it was the edginess that made me funny, and that ultimately kept me #1 in the market more or less since 1981. Nobody gave a crap about happy, milquetoast morning guys. I believed that people want to hear me say the things that they were thinking but would never have the nerve to say. That was why people listened. I considered myself an entertainer. All I did, all I ever wanted to do, was make people laugh. Of course, I couldn't tell if radio listeners were laughing or not. All I knew was that I'd been there since 1981. If I wasn't getting the job done, I'd have been long gone.

I was always an idea guy. I had tons of ideas for books and tv shows, and then a stage musical called *Lounge Act*. The goal was to do something about them, not just dream of making them a reality. I had been walking around with this idea in my head for years and finally decided to take the steps to get it out of my head and develop it.

*Lounge Act i*s the story of Bobby D, a lounge singer in Las Vegas in 1962. Bobby has big dreams. All he wants to do is make it to "The big room" and open for Frank Sinatra. I envisioned the characters, the songs, and the look of the stage. I wanted people to see the show and actually feel like they're *in* the lounge back in 1962.

An actor friend of mine, Bob Dio, put me in touch with Alan Amaislen, a marvelous writer, who helped me take the idea out of my head and put it down on paper. As of this writing, we had a finished book and we were looking for music. I thought the piece was marvelous, and the subject matter had never been done before.

I was often asked why I didn't do standup comedy routines. The answer was that I was terrified of it. I just pictured myself up there with material that I had written, but then my mind would go blank or I'd discover that the material sucked. I knew my own strengths. Standup comedy wasn't one of them.

I rediscovered a Super 8 sound movie of me on stage at The Pirates Den in Tucson, Arizona, a nightclub that looked like a ship from the outside. I watched myself in fascination as I first took the stage as The Crazyman, and then taking the mask and trench coat off to show my real self. I had no material. It seemed like ad lib my entire time up there, zinging the audience with one liners and pulling them up on stage with me for silly games. The audience was laughing at every terrible joke I did, which only reinforced my resolve to not do standup comedy again.

Chapter 27

M & L Revisited?

I always had this fantasy idea that someday I might reopen Moskowitz and Lupowitz restaurant as a tribute to my grandfather. I know that's probably not going to happen, because I know nothing about opening and operating a restaurant of that kind, but the idea had been floating around in my head for quite some time. At the very least, I'm working on a book that will contain great photos of the movers and shakers, sports figures, and stage and screen stars that visited.

I was on Facebook one day, and I don't know exactly how I made contact with Ziggy Gruber. He might have made a comment on one of the Moskowitz and Lupowitz pictures I had posted. I found out that Ziggy operated a successful deli in Houston named Kenny and Ziggy's New York Delicatessen. The conversation drifted to Moskowitz and Lupowitz and how I grew up with the restaurant. Ziggy told me he loved Romanian food, and he sometimes did themed events with that type of food. I even sent him a copy of one of the Moskowitz and Lupowitz menus, and we talked about the prices, and this and that. The next day, following up on my idea to someday do something with the name, I performed a domain search for moskowitzandlupowitz.com and learned that it was taken. *WHAT? What do you mean it's taken?* I thought. *Who the hell would want that?*

I called the domain host and told them who I was—a customer with many other registered domain names—and I explained that it was the name of my grandfather's restaurant and part of our family history, and I asked for the name of who owned that domain name. They said they couldn't because it was registered privately. The representative said, "Well, I'm not supposed to do this, but I will tell you that the person who has the URL has the last name of Gruber!"

I hung up stunned. It *had* to be the same guy.

I went back to Facebook and Ziggy's page and asked, "Ziggy, did you register moskowitzandlupowitz.com?"

'Yes, and I also registered the trademark on the name."

I saw red. I said, "Ziggy, that's part of my family's history. I'm respectively asking you to abandon the trademark and the domain name."

"No. I trademarked that name and numerous other names of New York eateries. What are you planning to do with it?"

"What business is that of yours? I'm asking you to let it go."

"You're a DJ. What do you care about the name?"

"I have plans to reopen a restaurant using the name."

"You looking for an operating partner?"

"What? Why in hell would I get into business with someone who's holding my grandfather's restaurant name hostage?"

"Well, if you did go into partnership, I *might* be inclined to release it."

"The fact that we've been talking about the restaurant all this time—and you didn't bother telling me what you did—is shocking."

It didn't matter. He was unwilling to budge on the entire issue.

The next morning, I went to see my trademark attorney, Marina Cunningham. She had helped me trademark We Are The Children. I explained the entire story to her, and asked, "Is there anything I can do? This was my grandfather's legacy."

She handed the name to her assistant and said, "Please look this up."

Her assistant came back two minutes later and said, "There's nothing on it. Nobody has the trademark"

"Yes he does!" I said. "He told me he trademarked it."

Marina said, "Yes, he trademarked it . . . ten years ago, and he never did a thing with it, so it expired."

Apparently, when you're granted a trademark, you have about three years to use it or it goes away. As of this writing, I'm waiting for my trademark on Moskowitz and Lupowitz to come to me—where it belongs. Stay tuned to see what I do with it.

You've heard the catchphrase "death cleaning," when all your relatives come in after you kick the bucket and go through all your stuff, throwing out all everything you thought was super important

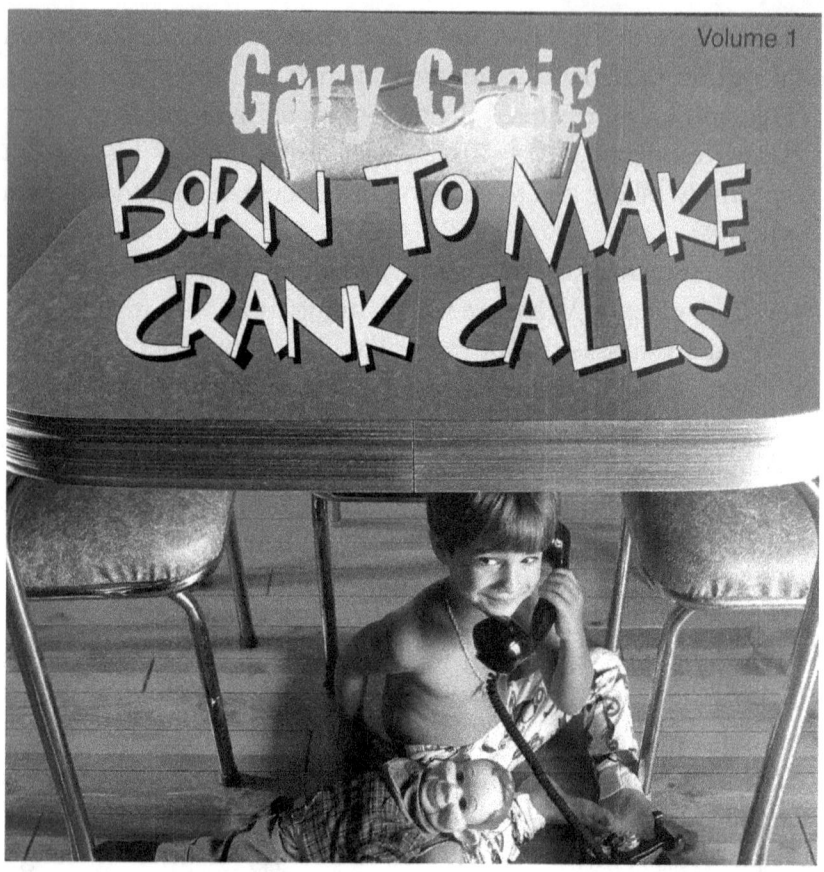

Phoney Phone Crank Call Vol. 1 CD cover.

and hoarded. *Oh, I can't get rid of that! I might need it someday.* Then, it sits there for twenty years. Not that I was planning on checking out, but I started to throw things out in order to save my family the task of going through it. I heard professional organizers say that if you hadn't used it in six months, chances are you're not going to use it at all. I started empting my office of old VHS tape, the hundreds of Phoney Phone crank call CDs that I had pressed all six volumes, now relegated to sitting there like a dead animal waiting for a final resting place. There was the "Craigwear" baseball caps—my failed attempt to start a fashion trend. There were t-shirts, mugs, Craig and Company coffee, and who could have forgotten the first and original item that just died on the vine, "Gary Craig's Dirty Little Joke Book." By that time, there were only a few of those floating around and they might be considered a collector's item. *What the hell was I thinking saving all that stuff?*

On Friday, December 22, 2016, after having spent the whole month and then some promoting the We Are The Children Christmas party on the air, everything was set. All the volunteers were signed up and ready to go. The band was about to load in all their equipment. Bruce Maneeley was getting the food ready for the kids as he had done every year. Jesse Branche was working on his amazing, magical Christmas village to greet the children as they arrived. He had done this every year for too many years to even count. The inflatable slides, the rides, and the electronic games truck were arriving and getting set up. The cavernous room at the Hartford Expo center was getting decorated with balloons, plush snow balls, and a giant sled filled with toys to greet Santa. Two machines were being hoisted up above the stage that at any given time during the day would produce *real* snow for kids to experience. I had been the host of this event since I started it in 1985. My family was always supportive and understanding over the years, especially when I couldn't wake up with them on Christmas morning and just spend the day.

This was my last day on the air before Christmas. After the last song that morning, I opened the mic and said, "I just want to thank all of you for once again for helping me to pull off the biggest party in America on Christmas Day, the We Are The Children party. You know, I've been on the air in this radio market since 1981, and I did a little calculation. Since I arrived in June 1981, I've done roughly 8,760 shows. That's a lot of entertainment. I've had a blast, and I couldn't ask for two better talents to share the spotlight with me than Christine Lee and John Elliott. But sometime this June, I will be stepping down as host of Craig and Company. This year will also be the last We Are The Children party. It's been a hell of a run. I will miss all of you. I do not know where the road is going to take me next, but I will always be there with you on social media, trying to enlighten you and entertain you as I always have. Merry Christmas to everyone, and let's make this the best holiday season ever."

Then, I shut the mic. There was an awkward silence in the room, like someone on life support who's flatlining. I knew the end was eventually coming, but it was still shocking when it arrived. But wait, it didn't happen yet. Didn't somebody once say, "Just when I thought I was out . . . they pull me back in"? I don't know what force took ahold of my hand and made me sign for another year, but that's what seems to have happened.

Epilogue

Or, Time to Go?

Gary with Hannah, Aaron, and Rachel.

What's next? Who knows? But the story isn't over.

I have wondered, *What can I do, when the only thing I really know is radio?* I wish I had an answer to that question, because I was staring it in the face with no idea what the next chapter of my life would bring.

I also question what the exact future of radio might be. Competition with so many other entertainment forms are vying for the audience's attention. Traditional tv, Netflix, Podcasts, Satellite radio, the entire Internet, and millions of people just tuning out of life itself by walking around all day with ear buds plugged in, locked into their own playlists, all compete with each other. The only thing that radio managers and program directors keep harping about is that radio is local, and that when something happens in a community, local radio can be a conduit for listeners to get information. Satellite radio can't do that, but I don't know if locality is enough to sustain commercial radio through the upcoming years. Time will tell.

In 2016, my current contract was coming to an end. Management wanted to know what "I wanted to do."

I had been eyeing stepping down from the show for some time, but I was never ready to really pull the trigger. Part of the problem was that we had property in Portland Oregon with a hefty mortgage. Our original plan, when I was no longer on the air, was to spend half a year in Portland, and half a year in Florida, where we had a place on the beach, what's called a "Work/Live" unit. The residence was upstairs, and downstairs on the street was a space that could have been turned into a store or whatever commercial application we wanted to make out of it. I was going to open an art studio in my post-radio life and teach people how to paint. For a series of reasons, the Portland idea fizzled, yet we were still saddled with the mortgage. Even if I wanted to step down, I couldn't. I had to keep working for at least another year so I could continue to pay the mortgage and keep the property.

Management gave me a choice: I could retire six months early and still get my salary, or we could talk about continuing. CBS was just about to be bought out by another giant radio conglomerate, Entercom, and I was sure that the offer for me to take an early retirement wasn't because they wanted to do something nice. They didn't want my salary on their fucking books for the new company. (I hadn't just rolled into town on a turnip truck!)

I had to consider what would be the financial strain if I took the early retirement and at the end of the six months we still had that property? I surprised them by saying I would do another year. Their reaction to that was to tell me, "We'd love to have you continue, of course, but we have to cut your salary in half." Half!

After making the company millions of dollars, and giving them half of my life—thirty-six years—this was the thanks I got. I believed that they were actually disappointed that I wanted to stay. I saw it in Steve Salhany's face. I was sure that he got a directive from the suits in corporate to get me to bail out early. I understood that it was just business, but that didn't make it hurt any less. What the fuck was I supposed to do? I was painted into a corner. Of course, when the new company took over, all bets are off. Who the hell knew what was going to happen?

Radio wasn't what it used to be. Someone asked me, "Why don't radio personalities make appearances anymore like the way they used to?" I think the answer was that management had no creativity and no vision. When I arrived on the scene, I actually said on the air, "If you need someone to host whatever it is that you're doing, I'm your guy. Just call me, and I'll say yes!" I realized that I had to do that. I had to ingratiate myself into the community. I hosted everything. We came up with amazing stunts, gave away cars, staged massive live performances in the theatre right before a movie premiere, rode live elephants through town to herald the circus arrival, and on and on. If it was fun and crazy, we did it.

At some radio stations, nobody gave a shit, and there didn't seem to be money to do anything. "It's not in the budget" was the stock answer given when someone was trying to orchestrate something. Don't get me wrong, most radio stations where I worked were always supportive, and if something I asked for was within their power, I got it, but as time went by, upper management "bean counters" ran the stations, and they didn't understand how radio really worked; they just looked at the bottom line and the salaries of on-air talent and said, "He's making what? Oh, we can replace him with someone that will cost us 75% less."

What they didn't understand was that the kid they might get to replace him has never done anything, has never experienced enough in his life to relate to anyone, and has no talent. They're just going to get a parrot, who reads liners and has no chops to entertain. Broadcast schools, although great at teaching the basics, were not turning out radio stars. Guys like me, Howard Stern, and a handful of others around the country were part of a club the likes of which you will never see again. I think I did what I did better than anyone else.

I also think that, aside from what I offered, I was #1 so long because everyone else around me sucked. When I first got into radio, I loved listening to other radio personalities. I was able to learn something from. I listened and said, "God this guy is great!" Or, "Shit I've never thought of doing it that way—that's brilliant!"

I hadn't learned a thing from anybody in a long time. Most people in radio around the country were not going to make a long living at it. To us, radio wasn't a job; it was our life. They weren't going to find someone that fit into that category again.

I have also wondered if there was something wrong with me. I play these stupid-ass games with myself. My co-workers thought I was bordering on obsessive-compulsive, because, for instance, I play this How Many Steps Game? When I get out of a car, I look at where I'm going to walk to and I estimate how many steps it's going to take . . . just to see if I'm right. *Let's see, the mall's front entrance—I say 121 steps. Let's see.* Or, while driving in the car, I might ponder, *If I get through this green light up ahead before it turns red, then such and such is going to happen,* and what I guess is going to happen usually does. Then, there's this other thing, where I try to precisely turn off my car radio so that I don't sloppily cut into a word or a line of a song. If I'm listening to a commercial, I have to try to turn the radio off at the end of a sentence cleanly, or if it's a song, it has to be at least at the end of one word and not in the middle of another. If I don't do it right, I have to turn the radio back on and try it again. Also, when I turn off the tv, I try to time it so it goes off at the end of a word.

Sometimes when I'm in a supermarket, I make car or truck motor sounds as I'm pushing my shopping cart. Sometimes I pretend that the cart is a boat ride at Universal Studios in Orlando.

Out of any window in my apartment, I can see Constitution Plaza and cars coming into downtown and leaving at the entrance of 91 and 84. Nearly every night after I get to bed, I get up at two o'clock in the morning to take a leak. When I walk back in the bedroom, I can't go back to bed until I see at least one car going by.

Is there something wrong with me?

What lies ahead? I know that when my eyes open every morning, I will be looking at the ocean. That's not bad, but I can't just sit around all day and do nothing. I've told myself stories about how I'll now have the time to really pursue acting, though I know I'm not going to become a star. Not in the cards. Maybe I'll paint every day.

Life has to be more than that, but what? I would like to see *Lounge Act* on stage . . . any stage. I, of course, will have mixed emotions stepping away from radio, but I think I've stayed too long at the fair as it is. But hey, I was just told that the ratings came in and *Craig and Company,* once again, is #1. It's nice to know that I can still do that.

Oh, and one more thing . . . my editor, David Menefee, told me that there's much too much profanity in this book. I told him, "Hey, if they can't take a fuck, joke em!"

The End

www.ingramcontent.com/pod-product-compliance
Lightning Source LLC
Chambersburg PA
CBHW050330170426
43200CB00009BA/1531